TORTURE AND ILL-

Israel's Interrogation of Palestinians from the Occupied Territories

**Human Rights Watch/Middle East
(formerly Middle East Watch)**

**Human Rights Watch
New York • Washington • Los Angeles • London**

Copyright © June 1994 by Human Rights Watch.
All rights reserved.
Printed in the United States of America.

Library of Congress Card Catalog Number: 94-76875
ISBN 1-56432-136-3

Human Rights Watch/Middle East (formerly Middle East Watch)
Human Rights Watch/Middle East was established in 1989 to monitor and promote the observance of internationally recognized human rights in the Middle East and North Africa. Christopher George is the executive director; Eric Goldstein is the research director; Aziz Abu Hamad and Virginia N. Sherry are associate directors; Suzanne Howard is the associate. Joost Hiltermann is director and Shorsh Resool is researcher for the Kurds Project. Gary Sick is the chair of the advisory committee and Lisa Anderson and Bruce Rabb are vice chairs.

HUMAN RIGHTS WATCH

Human Rights Watch conducts regular, systematic investigations of human rights abuses in some seventy countries around the world. It addresses the human rights practices of governments of all political stripes, of all geopolitical alignments, and of all ethnic and religious persuasions. In internal wars it documents violations by both governments and rebel groups. Human Rights Watch defends freedom of thought and expression, due process and equal protection of the law; it documents and denounces murders, disappearances, torture, arbitrary imprisonment, exile, censorship and other abuses of internationally recognized human rights.

Human Rights Watch began in 1978 with the founding of its Helsinki division. Today, it includes five divisions covering Africa, the Americas, Asia, the Middle East, as well as the signatories of the Helsinki accords. It also includes five collaborative projects on arms, children's rights, free expression, prison conditions, and women's rights. It maintains offices in New York, Washington, Los Angeles, London, Brussels, Moscow, Belgrade, Zagreb and Hong Kong. Human Rights Watch is an independent, nongovernmental organization, supported by contributions from private individuals and foundations. It accepts no government funds, directly or indirectly.

The staff includes Kenneth Roth, executive director; Cynthia Brown, program director; Holly J. Burkhalter, advocacy director; Allyson Collins, research associate; Richard Dicker, associate counsel; Jamie Fellner, foundation relations director; Barbara Guglielmo, controller; Robert Kimzey, publications director; Gara LaMarche, associate director; Liselotte Leicht, Brussels office director; Michal Longfelder, development director; Ellen Lutz, California director; Juan Méndez, general counsel; Susan Osnos, communications director; Jemera Rone, counsel; Rachel Weintraub, special events director; and Derrick Wong, finance and administration director.

The regional directors of Human Rights Watch are Abdullahi An-Na'im, Africa; Cindy Arnson and Anne Manuel (acting directors), Americas; Sidney Jones, Asia; Jeri Laber, Helsinki; and Christopher George, Middle East. The project directors are Kenneth Anderson, Arms Project; Lois Whitman, Children's Rights Project; Gara LaMarche, Free Expression Project; Joanna Weschler, Prison Project; and Dorothy Q. Thomas, Women's Rights Project.

The board includes Robert L. Bernstein, chair; Adrian W. DeWind, vice chair; Roland Algrant, Lisa Anderson, Peter D. Bell, Alice L. Brown, William Carmichael, Dorothy Cullman, Irene Diamond, Jonathan Fanton, Alan Finberg, Jack Greenberg, Alice H. Henkin, Stephen L. Kass, Marina Pinto Kaufman, Alexander MacGregor, Peter Osnos, Kathleen Peratis, Bruce Rabb, Orville Schell, Gary G. Sick, Malcolm Smith, Maureen White, and Rosalind C. Whitehead.

Addresses for Human Rights Watch

485 Fifth Avenue
New York, NY 10017-6104
Tel: (212) 972-8400
Fax: (212) 972-0905
email: hrwatchnyc@igc.apc.org

1522 K Street, N.W., #910
Washington, DC 20005
Tel: (202) 371-6592
Fax: (202) 371-0124
email: hrwatchdc@igc.apc.org

10951 West Pico Blvd., #203
Los Angeles, CA 90064
Tel: (310) 475-3070
Fax: (310) 475-5613
email: hrwatchla@igc.apc.org

33 Islington High Street
N1 9LH London, UK
Tel: (071) 713-1995
Fax: (071) 713-1800
email: hrwatchuk@gn.apc.org

CONTENTS

ACKNOWLEDGMENTS ix

SUMMARY AND RECOMMENDATIONS x
    Recommendations to the Government of Israel xii
    Recommendations to the U.S. Government xv
    Recommendations to Member States of the European
        Union xviii

1: INTRODUCTION 1
    Systematic and Government-approved Abuse 6
    Techniques of Abuse 8
    The Sample Used in This Report 11
    Torture and International Law 11
    The Interrogation Agencies 13
    Torture and Ill-treatment since September 1993 18

2: THE SAMPLE USED IN THIS REPORT 24
    Methods of Contacting Interrogation Subjects 26
    Profiles of Detainees Interviewed for this Report 30
        GSS Interrogations 30
        IDF Interrogations 36
        Testimonies Collected by Lawyers from Persons
            Still in Detention 43

3: ISRAEL'S INTERROGATION PRACTICES 46
    1967-1987: Denial 46
    The "Bureaucratization of Torture" 47
    The Early Years of the Intifada: 1988-1991 53
    Trends Since 1991: Standardization 55
    A Court Challenge to the Classified
            GSS Interrogation Guidelines 58
    Abuses by IDF Interrogators: A Neglected Problem 63

4: MONITORING ABUSE	66
International Committee of the Red Cross (Geneva)	66
B'Tselem: The Israeli Information Center for Human Rights in the Occupied Territories (Jerusalem)	68
Al-Haq (Ramallah, West Bank)	69
The Palestine Human Rights Information Center (Jerusalem)	71
Amnesty International (London)	71
5: THE LEGAL FRAMEWORK	73
Torture in International Law	73
Recognizing and Defining Torture	
Psychological Versus Physical Methods	77
"Low-visibility Torture"	78
Northern Ireland and the "Five Techniques"	79
Torture and Mistreatment in Israeli Law	83
6: THE ARREST EXPERIENCE	88
Failure to Inform	89
Beating and Ill-treatment en route to Interrogation Facilities	89
In Holding Facilities	91
7: ISRAELI INTERROGATION CENTERS: A CLOSED WORLD	94
8: THE MILITARY COURTS IN THE OCCUPIED TERRITORIES	99
Legal Procedures Governing Arrest and Interrogation in the Occupied Territories	101
The Right to be Brought Promptly before a Judge	103
The Right to Adequate and Timely Access to Lawyers	106
9: METHODS OF INTERROGATION	108
During versus Between Questioning Sessions	109

| Contents | vii |

10: ABUSIVE BODY POSITIONING 111
    "Waiting" 112
    Abusive Body Positioning — GSS Interrogations 114
    Abusive Body Positioning — IDF Interrogations 135

11: SUBJECTION TO TEMPERATURE EXTREMES 147
    Mechanically Induced Temperature Changes 147
    Exposure to Adverse Weather 152

12: PSYCHOLOGICAL ABUSE AND SLEEP DEPRIVATION 155
    Sleep Deprivation 163
    Isolation 174
    Subjection to Loud, Continual Noise 175
    Toilet Deprivation and Humiliation 177
    Deprivation of Personal Hygiene 180
    Space Deprivation 181

13: BEATING AND VIOLENT SHAKING 187
    GSS Interrogations 187
    IDF Interrogations 190

14: THE USE OF THREATS 199

15: THE ROLE OF PALESTINIAN COLLABORATORS IN
    INTERROGATIONS 205

16: THE COMPLICITY OF MEDICAL PERSONNEL IN
    TORTURE AND ILL-TREATMENT 209

17: POLICE INTERROGATIONS 233

18: THE ADMISSIBILITY OF COERCED CONFESSIONS 241
    The Role of Corroborating Evidence 245
    Contesting Confessions 246
    Obstacles Facing Palestinians in Mini-Trials 251
    Pressures to Plea-Bargain 261

19: DEATHS UNDER INTERROGATION 264
     Mustafa Akawi 265
     Ayman Sa'id Nassar 269
     Mustafa Barakat 271
     Hazem Eid 273

20: ISRAEL'S RECORD IN PUNISHING ABUSERS 275
     Investigative Bodies 281

APPENDIX A: THE INTERROGATORS 284

APPENDIX B: SOLDIERS INTERVIEWED FOR THIS
     REPORT 286

APPENDIX C: TESTIMONY OF AHMED AL-BATSH 287

APPENDIX D: TESTIMONY OF MUHAMMAD ANIS ABU
     HIKMEH 296

APPENDIX E: TESTIMONY OF SGT. TAL RAVIV 301

APPENDIX F: TESTIMONY OF SGT. A.M. 305

APPENDIX G: DECLASSIFIED GSS INTERROGATION LOG ... 312

ACKNOWLEDGMENTS

The principal writer and researcher of this report is James Ron, a consultant to Human Rights Watch/Middle East. Eric Goldstein, research director of Human Rights Watch/Middle East, researched and wrote several sections, and was the principal editor. Cynthia Brown, program director of Human Rights Watch, was the final editor. Consultant Walid Batrawi gave valuable help and guidance in the field. Fatemeh Ziai, the Orville Schell Fellow with Human Rights Watch, provided research on international law. Human Rights Watch/Middle East Associate Suzanne Howard and Human Rights Watch Associate Bettye Payne were responsible for the production, and Elizabeth Wilcox and Bryce Giddens helped with copy editing. The illustrations in this report were prepared by JFRA Design of Ramallah.

Of the many human rights attorneys who provided guidance on Israeli law and the military courts, five deserve special mention: Eliahu Avram and Tamar Pelleg-Sryck of the Association for Civil Rights in Israel, Shlomo Lecker, Ali Naouq, and Lea Tsemel. Lisa Hajjar and Melissa Phillips read drafts and gave extensive and valuable suggestions.

This report would not have been possible without the assistance of several human rights organizations, although responsibility for the findings rest solely with Human Rights Watch. Emma Naughton, of Birzeit University's Human Rights Project, shared data and helped to arrange meetings with ex-detainees. Al-Haq, the Ramallah-based affiliate of the International Commission of Jurists, and B'Tselem, the Israeli Information Center for Human Rights in the Occupied Territories, furnished data, assistance in the field, and advice.

Other groups that helped include the Palestinian Lawyers for Human Rights (Khan Yunis), the Association of Israeli-Palestinian Physicians for Human Rights (Tel Aviv), the Mandela Institute for Political Prisoners (Ramallah), and the House of Right and Law (Gaza City).

While disappointed that our requests to visit interrogation wings of IDF and GSS detention facilities were refused or ignored, Human Rights Watch appreciates the time that Israeli authorities took to meet with us and to reply to our frequent requests for information. These include officials in the IDF Spokesman's Office and Judge Advocate-General's Corps.

Finally, Human Rights Watch would like to thank the former Palestinian detainees who took the time to recount their experiences in detail, and the Israeli soldiers who shared their experiences working in detention facilities.

SUMMARY AND RECOMMENDATIONS

Israel's two main interrogation agencies in the occupied territories engage in a systematic pattern of ill-treatment and torture — according to internationally recognized definitions of the terms — when trying to extract from Palestinian security suspects confessions or information about third parties. This pattern has continued in 1994, despite the peace process now underway.

Israel's ill-treatment of Palestinians under interrogation is notable for the enormous number of persons who have experienced it. Well over 100,000 Palestinians have been detained since the start of the intifada in December 1987. Of those arrested, reliable sources indicate that some 4,000 to 6,000 are subjected to interrogation each year. The figures appear to have declined only slightly during the first quarter of 1994.

The overriding strategy of Israel's interrogation agencies in getting uncooperative detainees to talk is to subject them to a coordinated, rigid and increasingly painful regime of physical constraints and psychological pressures over days and very often for three or four weeks, during which time the detainees are, almost without exception, denied visits by their lawyers and families. These measures seriously taint the voluntariness of the confessions that they help to bring about, and therefore, compromise the fundamental fairness of the military courts that try Palestinians in the occupied territories.

The methods used in nearly all interrogations are prolonged sleep deprivation; prolonged sight deprivation using blindfolds or tight-fitting hoods; forced, prolonged maintenance of body positions that grow increasingly painful; and verbal threats and insults.

These methods are almost always combined with some of the following abuses: confinement in tiny, closet-like spaces; exposure to temperature extremes, such as in deliberately overcooled rooms; prolonged toilet and hygiene deprivation; and degrading treatment, such as forcing detainees to eat and use the toilet at the same time. In a large number of cases, detainees are also moderately or severely beaten by their interrogators.

Israeli interrogations consistently use methods in combination with one another, over long periods of time. Thus, a detainee in the custody of the General Security Service (GSS) may spend weeks during which, except for brief respites, he shuttles from a tiny chair to which he is painfully shackled; to a stifling, tiny cubicle in which he can barely move; to questioning sessions in which he is beaten or violently manhandled; and then back to the chair.

The intensive, sustained, and combined use of these methods inflicts the *severe* mental or physical suffering that is central to internationally accepted definitions of torture.

Israel's political leadership cannot claim ignorance that ill-treatment is the norm in interrogation centers. The number of victims is too large, and the abuses are too systematic. Official acquiescence is indicated also by the extreme infrequency with which abuses are punished, and the fact that the classified guidelines for GSS interrogators actually permit, under certain circumstances, the use of "moderate" physical pressure to obtain information. Since 1988, there has been only one case in which GSS interrogators were jailed for abusing a detainee under interrogation.

There are further obstacles to accountability for abuse:

- Many prison doctors and paramedics, in violation of the ethics of their profession, tend to serve the interests of the interrogation agency more than they serve the health interests of the detainee. Rather than ensuring that their patients are not subjected to illegal or health-endangering ill-treatment, these medical personnel tend to intervene in the interrogation process only in order to avert permanent injuries or deaths; and

- Palestinian defendants seeking to use the available legal procedure to challenge the voluntariness, and thus, the admissibility, of their confessions, face delays, pressures and obstacles that prejudice this important right.

The abuses documented in this report took place between 1992 and 1994. Comparing this period to interrogations during earlier years, as they were documented by other human rights organizations, some trends emerge:

- The GSS now resorts less frequently to beatings while relying more extensively on sustained psychological pressures and physical pressures, such as shackling detainees in contorted body positions, which fall short of direct violence but cause severe suffering nonetheless; and

- IDF interrogations have become more standardized: beating is still the norm, but instances of extreme violence are less common.

Despite these trends, the interrogation practices of both agencies continue to constitute a pattern of torture.

RECOMMENDATIONS TO THE GOVERNMENT OF ISRAEL

Human Rights Watch calls on the government of Israel to end the practice of torture and ill-treatment of detainees under interrogation, by adhering to and enforcing the provisions of the United Nations Convention against Torture and Other Forms of Cruel, Inhuman or Degrading Treatment or Punishment (Convention against Torture). Israel acceded to the Convention in 1991. Under Article 2, Israel is obliged to take "effective legislative, administrative, judicial or other measures to prevent acts of torture." To fulfill that obligation, Prime Minister Yitzhak Rabin and his government should:

- Enact domestic enabling legislation that makes the Convention against Torture enforceable in Israeli courts;

- Publicly state that the provisions of the Convention apply to the conduct of all state agents in the occupied territories;

- Make public all existing guidelines relating to the use of pressure during interrogation, including the secret appendix to the Landau Commission report and subsequent modifications of it, so that their compliance with international standards and Israeli domestic law can be assessed;

- Revoke those clauses of the GSS interrogation guidelines that permit the use of physical force despite its prohibition in Israel's Penal Code; and

- Review and revise the regulations and practices surrounding investigative detention so as to strengthen safeguards against abuse. The measures taken should include:

Summary and Recommendations

Providing the suspect with information at time of arrest: Regulations should be implemented requiring that any individual being taken into custody be informed of the reasons for arrest and the location to which he or she is being taken. At the request of the arrested person, his or her family should be provided promptly with this information.

Faster judicial review of detention: To protect against arbitrary detention, detainees in the occupied territories, like detainees in Israel, should be brought before a judge within forty-eight hours, instead of the current maximum of eight or eighteen days, depending on the nature of the case. The judge must assess the lawfulness and necessity of the detention, as well as the treatment received by the detainee, and authorize any continuation of detention.

Faster access to defense counsel: To ensure that their rights are protected throughout the investigative and judicial process, detainees must be provided with prompt access to a lawyer. Deprivation of this right should be exceptional rather than the norm; and in all cases the detainee's lawyer should be notified immediately that the detainee has been denied this right, so that the lawyer can challenge its denial before the courts. Defense lawyers should be given adequate notice of the dates of their clients' extension-of-detention hearing, and should have the opportunity to confer with the client before the hearing, and to represent the client at the hearing.

End anonymity of interrogation staff: To enable detainees to identify alleged abusers, all interrogators, medical and other staff coming into contact with detainees under interrogation should wear badges bearing their name and/or identification number.

Give content to the right to challenge confessions: Steps should be taken to ensure that defendants who wish to show in court that their confession was not given voluntarily are not penalized for exercising this right by prolonged pre-trial detention or a punitive sentence. Prosecutors should be forbidden from suggesting that a stiffer sentence will be sought against defendants who persist in challenging their confessions. Judges should investigate rigorously any evidence of torture or ill-treatment of defendants that comes to their attention, regardless of whether a complaint is made.

Investigate abuses promptly, impartially and publicly: Allegations of abuse should be investigated promptly and thoroughly, and details of the methodology and findings of such investigations should be made public. Any official found responsible must be brought to justice, and the punishment in each case should be disclosed.

Open interrogation wings to outside monitors: All wings of detention and incarceration facilities and prisons should be subject to periodic visits by non-governmental bodies, including human-rights organizations.

Require prison physicians to report evidence of abuse: End the complicity of doctors and paramedics in torture and ill-treatment by passing legislation requiring physicians to report to the proper authorities any suspicion that an injury or condition they have diagnosed may have been caused by the action of a public servant. Medical personnel should be informed of the interrogation methods in use in their facility, so that (1) they can be held to their professional ethical obligation not to participate in a process of certifying the fitness of detainees to undergo methods that constitute torture or ill-treatment; and (2) they can intervene effectively when the health of the detainee warrants restrictions on interrogation.

Finally, Human Rights Watch applauds the strong condemnation by the Israel Medical Association in 1993 of the medical "fitness-for-interrogation" form that had apparently been in use at Tulkarm prison. We urge the IMA to continue to investigate allegations concerning physicians at interrogation centers who are implicated in torture and ill-treatment, and to initiate disciplinary proceedings against any doctors found guilty of such involvement.

Summary and Recommendations xv

RECOMMENDATIONS TO THE U.S. GOVERNMENT

As Israel and the Palestine Liberation Organization take steps toward implementing self-rule for Palestinians in the occupied territories, the need to improve respect for human rights in the region is greater than ever. Progress beyond the interim agreement depends in part on persuading Palestinians living in the occupied lands that the new arrangements are bringing improvements in their lives, including in the realm of human rights.

Even if the withdrawal of Israeli troops from the Gaza Strip and Jericho proceeds as planned, Israel will continue to exercise direct rule over the majority of Palestinians who live outside these areas, and, will retain responsibility throughout the territories "for overall security of Israelis for the purpose of safeguarding their internal security and public order," according to the Declaration of Principles signed on September 13, 1993.

As an active supporter of the Israeli-PLO peace process, the U.S. should use its influence with both parties to promote respect for human rights as the negotiating process moves forward. In its dealings with the government of Israel, the PLO and Palestinian interim authorities, Washington must stress that a tangible reduction in human rights violations can build much-needed confidence in the process.

Israel's systematic torture and ill-treatment of Palestinians under interrogation is an issue that the U.S. administration should urgently confront, not only because torture has not disappeared with the signing of the Declaration of Principles, but also because it calls into question the very legality of American military and economic aid to Israel, which, at over $3 billion per year, makes Israel the largest recipient by far of U.S. bilateral assistance.

U.S. law prohibits the government from providing military or economic aid to any government that engages in systematic torture. Section 502(B) of the Foreign Assistance Act covers security aid, and a parallel provision in Section 116 covers economic aid. Section 502(B) states:

> Except under circumstances specified in this section, no security assistance may be provided to any country the government of which engages in a consistent pattern of gross violations of internationally recognized human rights. Security assistance may not be provided to the

police, domestic intelligence, or similar law enforcement forces of a country, and licenses may not be issued under the Export Administration Act of 1979 for the export of crime control and detection instruments and equipment to a country, the government of which engages in a consistent pattern of gross violations of internationally recognized human rights....The term "gross violations of internationally recognized human rights" includes torture or cruel, inhuman, or degrading treatment or punishment, prolonged detention without charges and trial, causing the disappearance of persons by the abduction and clandestine detention of those persons, and other flagrant denial of the right to life, liberty or the security of person.

Section 502(B) permits aid to flow to an abusive government only if the president certifies in writing to Congress "that extraordinary circumstances exist warranting provision of such assistance and issuance of such licenses."

Human Rights Watch urges the U.S. administration to address Israel's systematic use of torture against Palestinians under interrogation through both enhanced public reporting and enhanced advocacy. We urge the administration to:

- State publicly that Israeli practices during the interrogation of Palestinians amount to systematic torture, and that one of the two state bodies most responsible for the torture of Palestinians under interrogation is the Israel Defense Forces, which is the main beneficiary of $1.8 billion in U.S. security aid to Israel annually;

- Inform the government of Israel that future aid levels will depend on palpable progress toward curbing these abuses; and

- Request from the government of Israel a progress report on the steps taken to curtail such practices, including specific information about the measures taken against abusive personnel.

If the pattern of torture continues, the U.S. should either suspend aid or explain publicly the extraordinary circumstances that necessitate its continuation, as required by U.S. law.

Summary and Recommendations

A public U.S. intervention on torture is needed particularly because of the way that the government of Israel has sought to frame the debate. In contrast to abusive governments that flatly deny any pattern of coercion, Israel acknowledges permitting psychological and physical coercion but claims that these measures are strictly monitored so as never to rise to the level of ill-treatment or torture. This claim calls out for a public affirmation by the U.S. that Israel's well-documented interrogation practices do amount to impermissible torture and ill-treatment, just as the International Committee of the Red Cross has denounced them as violations of the Fourth Geneva Convention.

The State Department failed this challenge in the most recent *Country Reports on Human Rights Practices*, even while thoroughly cataloguing the prevalent forms of coercion used on detainees under interrogation.[1] By omitting the extent to which these methods are used in common with one another, and over what lengths of time, the State Department allows Israeli claims to stand that the methods of coercion do not reach a level that can be considered inhumane.

Human Rights Watch therefore urges the Department of State, in future editions of the *Country Reports*, to state in its own voice whether the methods it lists as being used by interrogators:

- amount to ill-treatment or torture in light of their duration, combined usage, and intensity;

- are practiced in a systematic fashion; and

- are employed with impunity, indicating approval or acquiescence at a high level.

---

[1] "According to credible reports, hooding, forced standing or tying up in contorted positions, prolonged exposure to extreme temperatures, blows and beatings, confinement in a small space, sleep and food deprivation, threats against the detainee's family, and threats of death were common practice in interrogation facilities." U.S. Department of State, *Country Reports on Human Rights Practices for 1993* (Washington: U.S. Government Printing Office, 1994), p. 1204.

RECOMMENDATIONS TO MEMBER STATES OF THE EUROPEAN UNION

The European Union has pledged to support the Middle East peace process in a number of ways. It is doubling development aid in the West Bank and Gaza Strip and has accelerated negotiations on a free-trade agreement long sought by Israel that would expand the pact signed in 1975. The new agreement would give Israel highly preferential trade status among countries outside the EU, enabling it to export services more freely, compete for EU public procurement projects, and to increase cooperation in research and development projects.

Signing of the new trade agreement would culminate the recent warming trend in European-Israeli relations. Relations were strained at times during recent years by European disapproval over Israel's stance on peace initiatives and human rights abuses in the occupied territories.[2]

The EU's heightened engagement in the region should include a continued commitment to raise human rights issues with the responsible parties. In its trade negotiations with Israel, the EU should stress that improved relations depend on protecting the rights of Palestinians living in the occupied territories.

Such linkage is explicit in EU trade agreements with other countries. For example, a cooperation agreement signed with India in December 1993 states in Article One: "Respect for human rights and democratic principles is the basis for the cooperation between the Contracting parties and for the provisions of this Agreement, and it constitutes an essential element of the Agreement."

Human Rights Watch urges the European member states, acting individually and in concert, to stress to the government of Israel that good political and economic relations will depend on steps taken to eliminate the practice of torture in the occupied territories.

---

[2] For example, in January 1990, the European Parliament recommended that member states impose science-related sanctions on Israel until it permitted the re-opening of Palestinian universities, all of which had been shut around the start of the intifada.

1
INTRODUCTION

This report documents a pattern of ill-treatment and torture by Israeli interrogators questioning Palestinian detainees from the occupied West Bank and Gaza Strip. The report, which is based on thirty-six lengthy interviews that Human Rights Watch (HRW) conducted with male security suspects[1] who were interrogated between June 1992 and March 1994, charges that these practices have continued on a systematic basis since Yitzhak Rabin became prime minister — and even since September 1993, when the current government co-signed with the Palestine Liberation Organization a Declaration of Principles on negotiating Israeli-Palestinian peace. The testimony of Palestinians who underwent interrogations was corroborated by interviews with soldiers who served in IDF detention camps, court testimony by security force agents, medical reports and other information.

Despite some differences in the methodologies of the two agencies, interrogators of both the General Security Service (GSS, also known as the Shin Bet or Shabak) and the Israel Defense Force (IDF) use techniques that amount to torture — according to internationally recognized definitions of the term — when trying to pressure security suspects to give and sign statements, or to provide information about third parties. These methods continue at present, despite some changes in the techniques employed in recent years (see Chapter Three).

The overriding strategy of Israel's interrogation agencies in getting uncooperative detainees to talk is to subject them to a coordinated, rigid and increasingly painful regime of physical constraints and psychological

---

[1] Palestinian women have also been subjected to routine abuse while under interrogation. However, the number of women interrogated during the intifada is only a tiny fraction of the total number interrogated. HRW did not have the resources to include a reasonably sized sample of women detainees in this study of interrogation methods. Teresa Thornhill, in her *Making Women Talk: The Interrogation of Palestinian Women Security Detainees by the Israeli General Security Services* (London: Lawyers for Palestinian Human Rights, 1992), argued persuasively that women detainees are routinely subjected to sleep deprivation, hooding, confinement in closet-like cells, slaps, kicks, hygiene deprivation, and sexual and other threats.

pressures over days and very often for three or four weeks, during which time the detainees are, almost without exception, denied visits by their lawyers and families. Not only do these methods constitute methods of torture and ill-treatment prohibited under international law; they also seriously taint the voluntariness of the confessions that they help to bring about, and with it the fundamental fairness of the military courts that judge Palestinians in the occupied territories (excluding Jerusalem).[2]

In fact, the extraction of confessions under duress, and the acceptance into evidence of such confessions by the military courts, form the backbone of Israel's military justice system. The end product of that system is one of the world's highest per capita rates of imprisonment.[3] Nearly all military court trials end in convictions — according to official statistics, of the 83,321 Palestinians tried in military courts in the West Bank and Gaza Strip between 1988 and 1993, only 2,731, or 3.2 percent, were acquitted.[4]

While not every Palestinian detainee confesses, the signed statements obtained through interrogations usually constitute the main piece of evidence against defendants. Because a defendant's signed statement is almost sufficient to convict him or her under the applicable laws of evidence, interrogators have strong incentives to obtain such a

---

[2] Shortly after the occupation began in 1967, Israeli authorities established military courts empowered to try Palestinians for offenses that were deemed related to security or the public order.

[3] The number of West Bank and Gaza Palestinians incarcerated by the Israeli authorities has fluctuated over the last three years between roughly 10,000 and 15,000 Palestinians. At the beginning of 1994, the figure was closer to the lower figure, which would give a per capita rate of roughly 550 per 100,000 inhabitants. This rate surpasses those of the two countries with the highest per capita rates, among the countries for which data are available: the United States, with slightly over 500 per 100,000, and South Africa, with 393 per 100,000. (Human Rights Watch, *Prison Conditions in South Africa* (New York: Human Rights Watch, February 1994), p. ix.) In contrast to the prisoner population in these two countries, most incarcerated Palestinians are held for security-related offenses or accusations, rather than for common criminal offenses.

[4] Letter to HRW from Lieutenant Colonel Moshe Fogel, Head, Information Branch, IDF Spokesman's Unit, February 24, 1994. The letter stated that in 1993, 15,676 Palestinians were tried in military courts, of whom 320 were acquitted.

Introduction

statement. And whether or not detainees incriminate themselves, they are frequently pressured to speak about others, who can then be convicted on the basis of third-party confessions (see Chapter Eighteen).

Abuses that occur during interrogation and during the trial cannot be seen in isolation from one another: they are interdependent. For example, pressures to plea bargain and inordinate delays in trial scheduling deter detainees from mounting court challenges to their confessions. This allows interrogators to escape what might otherwise be significant scrutiny of their methods.

Israel's ill-treatment of Palestinians under interrogation is distinguished not only by its conveyor-belt quality but also by the huge number of persons who experience it. Over 100,000 Palestinians had been detained since the start of the intifada in December 1987, the IDF told us in July 1993.[5] The Israeli human rights organization B'Tselem charged that roughly 5,000 Palestinians per year had been subjected during interrogation to some combination of the methods of torture or ill-treatment documented in its 1991 study on interrogations.[6] Information from reliable sources indicates that during 1993 the volume of interrogations remained close to this level.

Throughout 1993 some four hundred to six hundred Palestinians were under interrogation on any given day, according to reliable estimates. Since the majority of interrogations last one month or less, we can infer that the number of Palestinians who passed through interrogation during 1993 was over 4,000 and perhaps even substantially higher. To our

---

[5] IDF spokeswoman Captain Avital Margalit, in a July 10, 1993 telephone interview.

[6] B'Tselem, *The Interrogation of Palestinians during the Intifada: Follow-Up to March 1991 B'Tselem Report* (Jerusalem: B'Tselem, March 1992), p. 10. These methods included severe beatings on all parts of the body with fists, sticks and other instruments; verbal insults and abuse; threats to harm the detainee or his family members; sleep and food deprivation; hooding; painful confinement for long periods in deliberately painful positions; the use of collaborators to extract information either by violence or threats of violence; forced physical exercise; and cold showers and enforced sitting on a wet floor for prolonged periods. (p. 7)

knowledge, the government of Israel has never provided figures on the number of Palestinians interrogated.[7]

Nearly all Palestinians undergoing interrogation are put through some combination of the same basic methods, although the duration varies from case to case. Thus, the number of Palestinians tortured or severely ill-treated while under interrogation during the intifada is in the tens of thousands — a number that becomes especially significant when it is remembered that the universe of adult and adolescent male Palestinians in the West Bank and Gaza Strip is under three-quarters of one million.

The Israeli government maintains that there is no pattern of torture by its interrogators in the occupied territories. Abuses are exceptional, it states, and each time there is evidence of a "deviation from the permissible," it is investigated, and if wrongdoing is found, the perpetrators are disciplined or charged (see Chapter Twenty).

The official position is more nuanced than that of most abusive governments which simply deny that their interrogators ever lay a hand on detainees. While authorities state that IDF interrogators are strictly forbidden to use any form of physical force against persons under interrogation,[8] the GSS is permitted to use "exceptional" measures against

---

[7] The IDF responded to a February 13, 1994 request from HRW for data on IDF interrogations by advising us to contact the Ministry of Justice. Our query to that ministry, submitted on March 20, 1994, has not been answered.

[8] Senior officer in the Judge Advocate-General's corps, in interview with HRW in Tel Aviv, November 18, 1993 (the officer spoke in an official capacity, but on condition of anonymity). See also the statement of the IDF spokesman reprinted in B'Tselem, *The "New Procedure" in GSS Interrogation: The Case of 'Abd a-Nasser 'Ubeid* (Jerusalem: B'Tselem, 1993), p. 22:

> The IDF prohibits any use of force by soldiers in detention and questioning centers, including the use of "moderate physical force" by military investigators. Whenever a complaint is presented, or alternatively when there arises evidence concerning conduct unbecoming of an investigator, the matter is transferred to the military police for investigation without delay.

Note: the phrase "moderate physical force" is an allusion to the physical pressures that the GSS is authorized to exert on detainees undergoing interrogation when

Introduction

certain categories of detainees. These methods, delineated in guidelines that remain classified (see Chapter Three), include forms of what authorities characterize as "moderate physical pressure" to obtain information or statements. According to the government, the use of physical force, which would otherwise violate Israeli law, is carefully monitored to ensure that it does not violate the Convention against Torture and Other Cruel, Inhuman or Degrading Treatment or Punishment (hereinafter the Convention against Torture), ratified by Israel in 1991. In a recent statement, for example, a Justice Ministry official alluded to a prohibition that is "binding" on the GSS "on the use of physical torture or abusing the detainee or degrading him in a manner that strips him of his humanity."[9]

Israeli authorities have long stressed that the GSS restricts the use of "exceptional" methods to cases in which the offenses are serious, and the interrogator weighs "the degree of the anticipated danger according to the suspicions arising from the activity being investigated."[10]

As this report demonstrates, however, methods of torture and severe ill-treatment constitute more the rule than the exception. Contrary to the image that the Israeli government seeks to project, abusive methods are routinely practiced even on suspects who are not accused of involvement in plotting or participating in attacks involving firearms or explosives. Often, they are accused of membership in an illegal organization, and eventually charged with that offense alone. Quite often, the focus of the questioning is on others and not on the detainee himself.[11] Of the thirty-six ex-detainees interviewed for this report, only

---

psychological means do not achieve their purpose.

[9] Response by Shai Nitzan, Senior Deputy to the State Attorney, dated November 16, 1993, to B'Tselem, *The "New Procedure" in GSS Interrogation*. Nitzan's response is reprinted as an appendix to the B'Tselem report, on p. 19.

[10] Ibid., p. 18.

[11] The government-appointed Landau Commission (see text, below) reported in 1987:

> The GSS has always attached the utmost importance to collecting information for preventing and thwarting Hostile

four said they were eventually tried and sentenced; two were released on bail pending a trial, six were placed in administrative detention, and twenty-three said they were released without charge. (The disposition of one case was not known).

Of course, whether the victim of abuse is an accused murderer or an innocent bystander is irrelevant under international law. Conventions that Israel has ratified unequivocally forbid torture and other forms of cruel, inhuman or degrading treatment, regardless of the accusations against the suspect.

SYSTEMATIC AND GOVERNMENT-APPROVED ABUSE

Few of the abuses documented in this report are isolated occurrences. They are practiced with a considerable degree of consistency system-wide, and with virtual impunity for the practitioners. The abuses are clearly being carried out with the knowledge of the government — although officials deny that the methods constitute torture.

A disturbing phenomenon that is documented in this report is the involvement of Israeli medical personnel in the abusive interrogation process. While HRW has no evidence to suggest that doctors or medics have participated directly and actively in abuses, they have routinely checked and monitored the health of Palestinian detainees during interrogation, while remaining silent on the evidence of abuses confronting them. Their complicity sparked controversy in 1993, when an Israeli newspaper published a "fitness-for-interrogation" form that physicians at

---

> Terrorist Activity. Obtaining evidence for the trial of those interrogated did not have top priority in the work of the interrogators....
>
> Of the tens of thousands of interrogations carried out by the GSS during the period in question [1971–1987], some 50 percent were brought to trial on an annual basis.

State of Israel, *Commission of Inquiry into the Methods of Investigation of the General Security Service Regarding Hostile Terrorist Activity, Report*, Part One (Jerusalem: Government Press Office, October 1987) [hereinafter the Landau report], paragraphs 2.17 and 2.20.

Tulkarm prison had apparently been completing. The form asked doctors to verify the detainee's fitness for "a prolonged stay in an isolation cell," "chaining," "wearing a head/eye covering," and "prolonged standing." The head of the Israel Medical Association said such certification by physicians would constitute "participation in torture" and "a clear violation of medical ethics" (see Chapter Sixteen).

While laws exist to punish interrogators who use force or ill-treat detainees, there are few known instances in which interrogators have been convicted or significantly punished for abuse. The problem is two-fold. There is first of all a lack of political will to punish abusive interrogators (see Chapter Twenty). There is only one known case in which GSS agents received criminal sentences for mistreating a detainee in their charge; authorities have claimed that in an unspecified number of other cases, GSS and prison medical personnel have been disciplined. The IDF has also stated that allegations against its interrogators have been investigated, without disclosing how many were found guilty of wrongdoing and, if so, how and for what offenses they were punished.

The other facet of the problem is that some forms of abuse are evidently permitted by the GSS's interrogation guidelines. Since those guidelines are classified, it is not possible to know how much weight to give to the two factors in explaining why most abuse goes unpunished: how much is due to a failure to investigate and mete out appropriate punishment for deviations, and how much is due to abusive acts that are permitted by the regulations.

The most infamous aspect of what has been publicly divulged of the GSS guidelines is the authorization of unspecified means of "moderate physical pressure" to obtain information and statements. This phrase came in the 1987 report of the Landau Commission, which was appointed by the government to investigate the interrogation methods of the GSS. The specific methods it recommended were contained in a classified appendix to the Commission's report, and have been reviewed and modified by inter-ministerial committees since their adoption by the Israeli cabinet in 1987.

Although the specific guidelines have never been revealed, government approval of the techniques of hooding, position abuse,[12]

---

[12] For the sake of brevity, we use "position abuse" or "abusive body positioning" to denote the forcing of detainees to maintain painful and usually unnatural body positions for prolonged periods. It may involve requiring them to stand erect without moving for hours on end, or shackling them to tiny chairs

sleep deprivation and confinement in closet-like spaces is made abundantly clear by the system-wide employment of specialized equipment (such as tiny chairs, mechanically refrigerated stalls, and shackle attachments built into walls), and by the fact that interrogators admit in open court, readily and without fear of sanction, to practicing these techniques. As this report argues, a calibrated system of what could be characterized as "low-intensity torture" operates under government supervision.

When testifying in court, GSS agents have not acknowledged using beatings or threats. Yet even if the government has not learned through GSS court testimony and other channels that the security services regularly beat and threaten suspects, it has undoubtedly been made aware of these and other abuses through regular, private representations by the International Committee of the Red Cross (ICRC). The Geneva-based humanitarian organization, whose delegates are permitted by Israeli authorities to interview Palestinians after their fourteenth day of detention, regularly reports its findings of abuse to officials of the IDF and the Israeli government. Frustrated by the persistence of the mistreatment it documented, the ICRC departed in 1992 from its policy of communicating its concerns confidentially to the abusive government, and issued a public denunciation of Israeli interrogation methods (see Chapter Four).

TECHNIQUES OF ABUSE

While the abuses described in this report are generally employed in such a way as to cause no lasting, visible physical harm, they occasionally cause long-term injury and even death. Since 1992, four Palestinians have died while under interrogation; in some of these cases, ill-treatment or torture, combined with medical negligence, appear to have contributed substantially to the death (see Chapter Nineteen). In other cases, Palestinians have emerged from interrogation with lasting psychological and/or emotional damage. The case of a thirty-four-year old healthy man who emerged from interrogation in an enduring catatonic state is recounted in Chapter Twelve.

---

and/or to pipes or rings embedded in walls at awkward heights; or confining them in spaces so cramped they can barely move their limbs. These positions grow increasingly painful with time.

Introduction

At all stages of GSS interrogations, the methods of torture and ill-treatment tend to follow a well-defined set of steps and guidelines. Interrogation measures are selected to inflict extreme physical pain and mental anguish without causing lasting or traceable physical injury. This approach frustrates attempts to document torture and hold its practitioners accountable. Accountability is hampered also by the hooding of detainees, the interrogators' use of false names, and the lack of third-party witnesses who could confirm allegations by victims of abuse.

The IDF uses techniques of position abuse and sensory deprivation similar to those used by the GSS, albeit in a less systematized fashion. Army interrogators employ brute physical force, including severe beatings, more routinely than does the GSS. Interrogators at both agencies routinely threaten detainees, for example, that they will kill them or demolish the homes of their families.

Position Abuse
The GSS, and to a lesser extent the IDF, force detainees into painful and unnatural body positions for prolonged periods. The methods include forced standing; shackling detainees to pipes or rings embedded in walls at awkward heights, or to tiny chairs that are often angled downward or upward to maximize discomfort; or confining them in spaces so cramped that they cannot move their limbs, sit comfortably, or sleep soundly. Thus constricted for days at a time, with only brief respites, detainees suffer circulatory problems, backaches, abrasions, severe cramps, loss of sensation in the limbs, and other forms of mounting pain and discomfort.

Sensory Deprivation and Psychological Pressures
Interrogators and guards induce exhaustion, disorientation, and dread in detainees by placing them in strict isolation (through such methods as hooding and preventing communication with other detainees), broadcasting loud and jarring music round the clock, restricting access to the toilet, causing humiliation (such as by forcing detainees to eat in toilet stalls or to relieve themselves in their clothing), and exposing them to extreme cold or suffocating heat. The tight, shroud-like, canvas or felt hoods that are placed over their heads in GSS wings are often foul-smelling, and induce feelings of suffocation in some detainees.

Beatings and Physical Force

Beatings are far more routine in IDF interrogations than in GSS interrogations. Sixteen of the nineteen IDF detainees we interviewed reported having been assaulted in the interrogation room. Beatings and kicks were directed at the throat, testicles, and stomach. Some were repeatedly choked; some had their heads slammed against the wall.

GSS interrogators appear to beat detainees less often than they did in the past, and less often than do their IDF counterparts. The GSS relies more on its regime of position abuse and sensory deprivation to wear down detainees. However, beatings continue to occur during GSS interrogations — nine of the seventeen GSS detainees we interviewed reported being subjected to kicks, punches, or violent shaking during questioning. The shaking is better described as whiplashing: it involves grabbing and repeatedly shaking detainees during questioning, either by their shoulders or their collar. This can cause severe neck and back pains, and induce a choking sensation.

The abuse that detainees routinely undergo is compounded by depriving them of certain basic rights: the right to be promptly charged and brought before a judge (guaranteed by the International Covenant on Civil and Political Rights [ICCPR], Article 9) and the right to prompt access to a lawyer (guaranteed by the ICCPR, Article 14(3)(b), the U.N. Body of Principles for the Protection of All Persons under Any Form of Detention or Imprisonment, and the Fourth Geneva Convention, Article 72). In contrast to Israel, where detainees must be brought before a judge within forty-eight hours of their arrest, detainees in the occupied territories can be held without charge for eight or eighteen days, depending on the nature of the case, before they must be brought before a judge. They are, in practice, usually prevented from consulting with lawyers for the first two or three weeks of their detention, and often see a lawyer only after they have confessed. Contact with family members and other acquaintances is also routinely denied during interrogation. These practices both compound the pressures experienced by detainees and make it more difficult for abuse to be noted by their lawyers and the military judges before whom they are brought for extension-of-detention hearings.

Introduction

THE SAMPLE USED IN THIS REPORT

The findings of this report are based on detailed interviews that HRW researchers conducted face to face with thirty-six Palestinian ex-detainees who were interrogated between June 1992 and March 1994. The report also draws on cases of Palestinians who were still in detention and thus unavailable for interviews by HRW, but who provided information via their lawyers.

HRW's interview subjects were selected on the basis of recommendations by defense lawyers and human rights organizations, who indicated that the individuals in question had been under military or GSS interrogation. Statistics about the interview subjects and their experiences are provided in Chapter Two. We cannot assert that the sample represents the average level of abuse, the average period that legal counsel is denied, or represents an exact average of any other phenomena encountered by Palestinians during their interrogations. The experiences described here may be more or less severe than what most Palestinians endure under interrogation. What the sample of thirty-six strongly indicates, however, is that severe abuse, including torture, is widespread.

The sample is diverse in a number of ways. The subjects were interrogated by either the GSS or the IDF (police interrogations are described in a separate chapter that draws on separate interviews). Their interrogations took place in nine facilities, located both inside Israel and the occupied territories, where Palestinians from the occupied territories are commonly interrogated concerning security-related offenses. They were accused of activities on behalf of a variety of organizations, both Islamist and secular nationalist. In some cases, the interrogators apparently suspected them of serious crimes, including murder; in others, they were suspected of nonviolent offenses. For some, the apparent priority of the interrogators was to obtain information about third parties.

TORTURE AND INTERNATIONAL LAW

Some of the techniques discussed in this report, such as beating and prolonged position abuse, constitute methods of torture even when considered in isolation from other techniques. Other methods could be characterized as ill-treatment, and become torture when used in combination with other methods, as argued in Chapter Five. But Israeli interrogators do not commonly use these techniques one at a time; they consistently use them in combination with one another.

In international law, the distinction between torture and ill-treatment in its various forms is inconsequential: both are categorically prohibited. Israel is a signatory to the key human-rights covenants that address torture and ill-treatment, the ICCPR (Article 7), and the Convention against Torture. Israel is therefore legally bound by these prohibitions.

The government of Israel, as mentioned above, admits that the GSS employs "moderate" physical and psychological pressure during interrogations, but claims that the agency guidelines explicitly prohibit torture and degrading treatment.[13] A petition challenging this claim was filed before Israel's Supreme Court, but in 1993 the Court declined to hear the claim, on the grounds that the petitioner's case lacked the requisite degree of case-based concreteness (see Chapter Three).

While denying that the approved methods constitute torture or ill-treatment, Israeli officials point out that a courtroom remedy is available to any Palestinian detainee who wishes to challenge the voluntariness of his or her confession. In that procedure, known as a "mini-trial" or "trial-within-the-trial," the burden of proof is ostensibly on the prosecution to demonstrate that the defendant's confession was given voluntarily.

The relevant Israeli law is, on its face, quite satisfactory. It prohibits the introduction into evidence of tainted confessions and provides prison terms for public servants found to have used or directed the use of force against a person for the purpose of extracting information or a confession. While laudable in theory, the mini-trial procedure in practice does not offer defendants a meaningful avenue for challenging their confessions, for reasons that are explored in Chapter Eighteen. Defense lawyers interviewed by HRW knew of no case in the West Bank or Gaza military courts in which the judge ruled in favor of a Palestinian defendant who had challenged the voluntariness of his confession.

---

[13] "We wish to emphasize that the position of the State of Israel has been, and remains, that the [GSS] authorization procedure does not conflict with the 1984 Convention against Torture or with other prohibitions in international law." (Response by Shai Nitzan, Senior Deputy to the State Attorney, dated November 16, 1993, to B'Tselem, *The "New Procedure" in GSS Interrogation*. Nitzan's response is reprinted as an appendix to the B'Tselem report, on p. 19.)

Introduction

THE INTERROGATION AGENCIES

Israeli interrogations of Palestinian security detainees take place in ten GSS and three IDF interrogation facilities located throughout the occupied territories and, in the case of the GSS, in Israel itself. A small minority of security suspects are interrogated by the police at police stations located throughout the occupied territories.

The general division of labor between GSS and IDF interrogators is that the GSS typically questions Palestinians suspected of being involved in or having knowledge of relatively severe offenses, while the IDF interrogates persons suspected of relatively minor offenses. This triage was confirmed by a senior officer in the IDF Judge Advocate-General's corps, who told HRW in a November 18, 1993 interview, "In general, the GSS decides who does the interrogation. A case goes to the IDF if it's a less complicated, [less] serious case." Most of those interrogated by the police are youths below the age of eighteen and persons suspected of criminal offenses that are not politically motivated.

GSS and the IDF interrogation facilities constitute a closed world. Occasionally, visits have been conducted by Israeli officials, members of parliament, and judges. However, with extremely few exceptions, independent monitors or organizations have not been permitted to inspect IDF or GSS interrogation centers, even when those individuals or groups have been invited to tour the general sections of prisons.[14] The International Committee of the Red Cross (ICRC) is not allowed into interrogation wings, although its delegates regularly meet with prisoners undergoing interrogation in visiting rooms *outside* the interrogation wings.

The GSS is a secretive agency responsible only to the Office of the Prime Minister; other branches of the government exercise only limited oversight. The identity of its officials and agents is classified, as are its operating procedures, budget and the location of its bureaus.[15]

---

[14] The rare exceptions to this policy are described in Chapter Seven.

[15] The Landau report states:

> Since the GSS was made subordinate to the Prime Minister in 1963, a constitutional custom prevails according to which the Prime Minister bears direct responsibility for GSS activities, within the framework of the joint responsibility of the entire

In the occupied territories, the GSS collects information primarily through its interrogation of detainees, its extensive network of agents and Palestinian informants, and its cooperation with other branches of the security services. Information and directives from the GSS weigh heavily in decisions on imposing extrajudicial sanctions, such as who is to be arrested, administratively detained, deported, or prevented from leaving the occupied territories. The GSS plays a major role not only in deciding on security-related sanctions, but also in decision-making on mundane aspects of daily life that bear little or no apparent relation to Israeli security considerations, such as whether a particular Palestinian is to receive a driver's license, authorization to travel to Jordan to obtain medical treatment, or permission for a spouse to obtain permanent residence in the occupied territories. According to Palestinian testimony, GSS often barters its approval of such requests for the applicant's agreement to provide information of interest to the agency.

While Israel's Jewish citizenry tends to revere the GSS as effective in combatting Palestinian violence directed at Israeli citizens and property, the agency's reputation among the 1.8 million Palestinians living in the occupied territories is that of a secret police agency that exercises wide-ranging and non-accountable control over their daily lives, often by violent and/or coercive means.

> Government before the Knesset...Regarding the Administered Territories (Judea, Samaria, and the Gaza District), governmental powers are vested, of course, in the military commander....He issued an Order Concerning GSS Personnel Operating in the West Bank Region (No. 121), 1967...according to which the GSS personnel were vested with the powers given to soldiers, and a 1972 amendment to this order in 1972 [sic] states that a GSS man's superiors shall be "an authority which it is obligatory to obey." In practice the activity of the GSS in the territories is coordinated with Territorial Commands of the IDF, the headquarters in Judea and Samaria and the Gaza District, with the heads of the Civil Administration, and with the Coordinator of Activities in the Territories, and at the political level the coordination must take place between the Defense Minister, who is responsible for the Military Government in the territories, and the Prime Minister, who is responsible for the GSS. (paragraph 3.2)

GSS Interrogations

Suspects taken to GSS interrogation wings are typically suspected of relatively serious offenses: they include occupying middle- to senior-level posts in one of the several Palestinian organizations outlawed by the Israeli authorities; communication with other activists inside and outside of the territories; logistical support for armed militants; violent attacks against suspected Palestinian collaborators and/or Israeli soldiers or civilians, weapons training or transport, and preparation of explosives.

Arrests for the purpose of interrogation are often carried out between 11:00 P.M. and 3:00 A.M. by large groups of soldiers accompanied by plainclothes GSS agents. Typically, soldiers force open the doors of suspects' homes and overturn possessions and furniture, ostensibly to search for weapons or incriminating evidence. The arresting authorities rarely reveal the reasons for the arrest to the detainee or his family, or where the suspect is being taken.

When en route to the initial site of detention and in transit from one detention center to another, many of the interrogation subjects interviewed for this report said they were beaten, cursed or otherwise abused by soldiers guarding them in the vehicle. These abuses, as opposed to the position abuse and sensory deprivation methods inside the detention centers, do not appear to reflect official policy. However, their frequency indicates official tolerance.

Within one to two days of their arrest, persons taken to GSS interrogation wings are placed in a universe of discomfort, pain, humiliation and threats, from which there is no exit until the interrogation ends or the detainee provides information to the interrogators' satisfaction.

With the exception of questioning sessions, abusive body positioning in GSS wings continues round the clock with only brief breaks provided two or three times a day. It is nearly impossible to sleep for more than minutes at a time while hooded, chained to a position-abuse station, and subjected to loud and unpleasant music. Prisoners who appear to doze off risk being slapped or shouted awake by patrolling guards.

GSS interrogation subjects are questioned several times a day for periods generally ranging from one to four hours. In the interrogation room, all ex-detainees in our sample were exposed to a wide variety of psychological abuses, including threats of indefinite detention, being driven insane, death, maiming, or of harm or sexual abuse to themselves or family members.

As mentioned above and described in detail in Chapter Thirteen, GSS interrogators appear to beat detainees less often than they did in the past, and less often than do their IDF counterparts. However, beating continues in what appears to be a substantial minority of cases. In addition, many detainees who were not otherwise beaten reported being shaken violently and repeatedly by their shoulders or collars when questioned. Although it typically leaves few marks, the violent shaking induces pain and fear.

During breaks, detainees typically have no more than five minutes to eat and use the toilet. At some interrogation centers, they are forced to do both of these activities simultaneously in the same dark, rank toilet stall. Most of the GSS interrogation subjects interviewed for this report said they were permitted to sleep soundly only once a week, during a day-and-a-half respite that usually coincided with the Jewish sabbath. Some detainees reported that during the week, they were occasionally unshackled and allowed to lie down for an hour or more, after which they were returned to position abuse.

IDF Interrogations

Palestinians brought to one of the three IDF interrogation centers in the occupied territories are typically suspected of less serious offenses than those brought in for interrogation by the GSS. These include throwing stones and Molotov cocktails at Israeli troops or civilians, painting political graffiti on walls, and low-level membership in outlawed organizations.

IDF interrogations are in many ways similar to those conducted by GSS agents. They involve prolonged position abuse, sensory deprivation, threats, and prolonged detention without charge or access to lawyers or family members.

Nevertheless, there are important differences in the interrogation practices of the two agencies. In contrast to GSS interrogators, IDF interrogators have no authorization to deviate from Israeli law regarding proper means of interrogation. They are bound by the legal prohibition against using physical force or threats. Paradoxically, IDF interrogators beat detainees more regularly than do their GSS counterparts.

Abusive body positioning in IDF interrogation wings is generally less sophisticated, severe and protracted than in GSS facilities, where special instruments such as bars built into the walls and tiny chairs are used to intensify the discomfort. The three most common forms of IDF position abuse are prolonged standing, enforced sitting, and confinement in small,

Introduction 17

enclosed spaces. While standing or sitting on concrete blocks, interrogation subjects' hands are painfully and tightly cuffed behind their backs, their eyes are blindfolded, and they are ordered to remain in a fixed position for up to ten or twelve hours at a time.

As in the GSS, IDF abusive body positioning is accompanied by prolonged sleep, sight and toilet deprivation, and, in some cases, exposure to extremely cold or hot external temperatures.

IDF detainees generally spend their nights in cells, in contrast to GSS detainees. Their cells tend to be cramped and dirty, and, in many cases, guards deliberately interrupt their sleep every half hour or so. Still, sleep deprivation in the IDF wings is less severe than in the GSS.

***

This report is divided into four basic sections:

- Part One introduces the subject of ill-treatment and torture during Israeli interrogations. It describes the sample and methodology of this report, and surveys pertinent developments prior to our period of study, the work of other organizations on the issue, and relevant international law.

- Part Two places the interrogation phase in the wider criminal-judicial context. It describes the conduct of arrests, the environment of the interrogation wings, and, briefly, the military courts that try Palestinians in the occupied territories.

- Part Three contains the bulk of our findings about how interrogations are conducted. We describe in turn each method that we found to be common, stressing throughout how systematically they are used in combination with one another. Part Three also analyzes the complicity of prison doctors and paramedics in torture and ill-treatment, and touches on interrogations by the Israeli police, an issue that we did not study in depth.

- Part Four looks at what degree of accountability exists for abuses that take place during GSS and IDF interrogations. It first analyzes the remedies suspects have in court when they seek to repudiate their confessions as having been coerced. Next, we consider how the system has responded to deaths in detention. Finally, we assess the credibility of official claims that abuses that occur during interrogations are promptly investigated and appropriately punished.

TORTURE AND ILL-TREATMENT SINCE SEPTEMBER 1993

The peace process under way between Israel and the PLO has raised hopes that human rights abuses would diminish in the new political order. But at the centers of interrogation, all that seems to have changed since September 1993 is the target population. The inmates of interrogation centers now seem to include fewer supporters of PLO Chairman Yasir Arafat than in the past, and a higher proportion of suspected members of Hamas, Islamic Jihad, and nationalist factions opposed to Arafat's negotiations with Israel.

But the methods of the IDF and GSS seem little changed: their interrogation units are bureaucracies with entrenched and time-tested ways of doing their work. As long as the political establishment expects them to obtain information and confessions through interrogations, and as long as neither the political establishment nor the courts force changes in their conduct, there is little likelihood that either body will go about its business differently.

In preparing this report, HRW made two field missions to the West Bank and Gaza Strip since the Declaration of Principles was signed in September 1993. We conducted lengthy interviews with ten Palestinians who had been interrogated by the IDF or GSS between October 1993 and March 1994, and discussed recent interrogation trends with human rights lawyers and organizations.

The peace process, we found, has yet to trickle into the interrogation rooms: if a detainee is brought in for an earnest interrogation, he is likely to be subjected to some combination of several of the following abuses: sleep deprivation, verbal insults, prolonged position abuse, hooding or blindfolding, enclosure in closet-like spaces, subjection to temperature extremes and to distressing and continuous noise. He is also likely to be beaten, especially if the interrogators are from the IDF.

Introduction 19

The prospect of ill-treatment does not hinge on whether the detainee is suspected of a violent offense. Our sample, in fact, underrepresents persons suspected of grave offenses, who might be expected to face even harsher interrogation methods. Nine of the ten ex-detainees we interviewed had been released without charge after their interrogation, and the tenth had been released on bail.

Two interrogations conducted in late 1993 illustrate the ongoing problem:

> On November 10, Bassem Tamimi of Ramallah was rushed to Hadassah hospital in Jerusalem, where a CAT scan revealed a cerebral hemorrhage. The hemorrhage was due to a very recent trauma, according to a member of the medical staff who spoke with human rights lawyer Tamar Pelleg-Sryck. Tamimi had been brought to the hospital from Ramallah prison, where he was under interrogation by the GSS. He had been arrested the day before in a round-up of several suspected members of a rogue Fatah unit that had abducted and killed Jewish settler Chaim Mizrahi on October 29.[16] Tamimi described what happened to him after his arrest and arrival at the GSS wing at Ramallah prison:

> > They hooded me, and then took me straight to an interrogation office. They took my hood off. It was about six in the evening. In the interrogation room, there was a small chair. An interrogator tied my hands to the back of the chair, and left me there with the hood on.

> Tamimi said he remained on the chair all night, except for a trip to the toilet. In the morning an interrogator code-named "Abu Ghazal" came in and began questioning him about various matters. Then the subject turned to the killing of Mizrahi:

> > From that minute, he started to beat me, and all the questions were only about the Mizrahi killing. He grabbed my chin and began to flip my head back and forth, very powerfully. He did that continuously. Then he started

---

[16] PLO chief Yasir Arafat condemned the killing as a renegade action carried out "without the knowledge of the leadership." (Clyde Haberman, "Arafat Condemns Settler's Slaying," *The New York Times*, November 14, 1993)

shaking it right and left, twisting my neck from side to side.

Then he made me stand up. He grabbed me by the shoulders, and began to push me back and forth violently. He would come up close to me, hold my shirt, and then thrust his hands out very quickly, and then pull me back up to him. When he did that, my head flapped back and forth very quickly. He did this many times....

At one point, I was kneeling on the ground, my legs tied together and my hands cuffed behind my back. "Abu Ghazal" sat on one of those revolving office chairs, the kind that go up and down when you turn them. He screwed the seat of his chair down very low until it trapped my knees between the seat and the floor. Then he grabbed my chin and yanked it back and forth. When he did that, I fell backwards very quickly. He then pulled me up, and did it again. Sometimes, when I was on the ground, he would grab my collar and shake me like he did when I was standing.

When he was doing the pushing with the seat, I felt as if my brain was rolling around loose in my head. I thought my head was going to explode, it hurt so much....

At first, he was asking me only about the Mizrahi case. Then, he started asking me questions about a "wanted" person caught in my house a year ago. He also said that someone else had said that there were weapons hidden in my house. Then he said, "I won't ask you about that other stuff. I want you only to talk about the killing of Chaim Mizrahi. If you do not talk, you will be killed. You have two choices: to talk or to die. Don't bet that because you were interrogated before you can withstand this....Your case is very serious. You either confess or you die."

He started shaking me again, but even more violently. He kept asking about Mizrahi. Then he pulled me up so that

> I was standing, knees bent, with my back to the wall. If I tried to sink down to the ground, he pulled me up to my feet. If I stood up straight, he smacked the top of my head with his hand, forcing me back down. I stood that way, knees bent, for about half an hour. He then put me back on the ground, screwed the chair down again, and trapped my knees, and began the pushing and shaking again. He was sitting at one point on my knees, and I was feeling very sick and dizzy. Then, all of a sudden, I fainted. I woke up five days later in the hospital with the injury.

Tamimi said he did not know whether the cerebral hemorrhage he suffered was caused by a blow, or hitting his head on the chair or floor as he fainted. The diagnosis, however, suggests a higher-velocity impact than a simple fall. Tamimi underwent surgery and spent four weeks recovering, most of it in a Prison Service hospital, and was then released without charge.

Tamimi's lawyer, Jawad Boulos, submitted formal complaints to the Justice Ministry and the Israeli police, demanding to know the results of any investigation into the case. (The Israeli press had reported in November that an investigation had been opened.[17]) As of March 16, Boulos told HRW, he had received no reply from the authorities.

***

N.S., a nineteen-year-old university student from Ramallah, was interrogated for thirty days in November and December by IDF interrogators at al-Far'a detention center. N.S. was charged with membership in Hamas, and writing and distributing leaflets and posters for that organization. He was released on bail.

The abuses at al-Far'a he described at resemble those recounted by detainees held there in earlier periods:

> *Shabeh* [enforced sitting or standing while blindfolded and handcuffed] consisted mostly of standing from nine in the morning until eight at night, in the courtyard. Some days,

---

[17] Israel Radio in Hebrew, November 12, 1993, as reported in Foreign Broadcast Information Service, November 15, 1993.

I stood all the time, with no food, or no visit to the toilet. This happened four or five times. Sometimes they would put me instead on a stone seat in the yard.

Sometimes, I was put in a leaky, damp "closet" [a closet-sized room]...for eight or ten hours, other times for three or four hours. In the "closet," you sit all the time. You can't move. The guards come around and bang on the door. Often, people relieved themselves in the "closet" because they weren't allowed to go to the toilet, and there was no container in there. Many people did that, and the closets stank very badly.

At night, you lie in the cells like animals. The mattresses and blankets are filthy, and they stink. There is no sun or air. The cell is full of water, because it leaks and there is rain. The blankets were soaked, the mattresses too. There was no toilet. There was a container to go in, but it was very difficult to go in there.

All the time, I was wearing the same clothes that they first gave me when I came to the prison. They were very thin clothes, and it was very cold when standing in *shabeh*, or in the closet. The closet was especially cold.

In the interrogation room, the interrogators slapped me and kicked me between the legs while I was sitting on the chair. My prison number was 2048, so once an interrogator tried to make me squat 2,048 times. This is impossible, of course, so after a while, I fell on the ground. Then he kicked me in the legs and testicles.

When in interrogation you feel destroyed psychologically. For example, when they give you the same cup to drink from and to wash your behind with after defecating. It's disgusting. This is the atmosphere there all the time.

Testimonies such as those of Bassem Tamimi and N.S. indicate that the peace process, by itself, has done little to eradicate a pattern of torture and ill-treatment. The places where they were interrogated, Ramallah prison and al-Far'a military detention center, continue to induct scores of Palestinians for interrogation each month. Even if the withdrawal of Israeli troops from the Gaza Strip and Jericho area proceeds as planned, Israeli security forces will continue to exercise direct rule over the majority of Palestinians who live outside these areas; and throughout the occupied territories, Israel will retain responsibility "for overall security of Israelis for the purpose of safeguarding their internal security and public order," according to the Declaration of Principles. In this context, systematically abusive interrogations are likely to continue unless strong pressure is brought to bear to end them.

2
THE SAMPLE USED IN THIS REPORT

In preparing this report, HRW conducted lengthy interviews with thirty-six ex-detainees who were interrogated by the IDF or the GSS between June 1992 and March 1994. In addition to our own interviews, this report draws on five interviews conducted by defense lawyers with Palestinians still in prison. We included the latter cases in order to diversify the sample.

While not a cross-section or random sample of the population that undergoes interrogation, our diverse sample demonstrates that Israel's principal interrogation agencies routinely mistreat Palestinians in their custody in ways that constitute torture. The Palestinians interviewed by HRW for this report are varied with regard to several key criteria:

- age: ranging from seventeen to forty-seven, with most in their early twenties;

- area of residence: twenty are from the northern West Bank, five are from the southern West Bank and eleven are from the Gaza Strip;

- suspected political orientation: detainees said their interrogators accused them of membership in a variety of illegal organizations, including Hamas, Islamic Jihad, Fatah (a mainstream movement within the PLO), the Popular Front for the Liberation of Palestine (a leftist faction of the PLO), and the Arab Liberation Front, all of them illegal organizations at the time;

- duration of interrogation: between two and seventy-five days, with most in the range of two to four weeks;

- place of interrogation: of the GSS detainees, six were interrogated at Ramallah, five at Hebron, three at Tulkarm, and one each at

The Sample Used in This Report 25

Gaza, Ashkelon and Petach Tikva[1]; of the IDF detainees, eight were interrogated at al-Far'a, six at the Beach facility and five at Dhahiriya[2];

- severity of accusations or charges: detainees said they were accused of offenses ranging from homicide to writing nationalist graffiti; others said the questioning focused on the activities of third parties;

- legal disposition of the case:
  twenty-three said they were released without charge;
  six were placed in administrative detention;
  four were tried and sentenced;
  two were released on bail pending their trial; and
  the disposition of one case is not known.

By interviewing only Palestinians who had been interrogated since mid-1992, HRW was unable to include in its sample any Palestinians who had been convicted and sentenced to actual prison terms longer than eight months. (Detainees sentenced to long prison terms would have been in prison at the time of HRW's fieldwork, and thus unavailable for

---

[1] The GSS is known to interrogate Palestinians at nine facilities, five of which are in the West Bank and four are in Israel. The West Bank facilities are located at Jenin prison, Nablus prison, Ramallah prison, Tulkarm prison, and Hebron prison. In Israel, there are GSS interrogation centers at the police station in Petach Tikva, the Kishon police station in Haifa, the Russian Compound police station in Jerusalem, and in Ashkelon prison. The only GSS facility in the Gaza Strip, located at Gaza prison in Gaza City, is reported to have closed in early 1994. See map in this report.

[2] These are the three IDF interrogation centers in operation during the period under study. Al-Far'a is located in the northern West Bank, Dhahiriya in the southern West Bank, and the Beach facility (nicknamed Ansar II by Palestinians) near Gaza City in the Gaza Strip. Two other IDF interrogation centers, located at the Ofer detention facility near Ramallah (known to Palestinians by the name of the nearby village of Beitunia) and Khan Yunis prison (nicknamed Ansar IV by Palestinians) in the southern Gaza Strip, were closed a few years ago. In early 1994, the Beach facility was also closed as a major interrogation center.

interviews.) Our data therefore are insufficient to prove our impression that persons suspected of relatively serious offenses experience harsher treatment under interrogation. What our sample does show is that even those Palestinians who are suspected of relatively minor offenses, and/or are released without charge, routinely undergo severe forms of mistreatment.

METHODS OF CONTACTING INTERROGATION SUBJECTS

With the help of Israeli and Palestinian defense lawyers and human rights organizations, HRW made contact with ex-detainees who were willing to be interviewed about their interrogation. We pursued all promising leads, and did not attempt to pre-select interview subjects on the basis of their reported political affiliation, activities, or severity of interrogation experience.

Most of the interviews were conducted in Arabic. Several were in Hebrew and one was in English. For some of the Arabic interviews, an interpreter hired by HRW was used. Each interview was conducted separately, with none of the other interview subjects present. They took place in private homes, lawyers' offices, or in school buildings. Whenever possible, the interviewer and the ex-detainee sat by themselves in the room, except when an interpreter was present.

During the interviews, ex-detainees were asked to provide the nicknames and appearance of their interrogators, which we checked against the descriptions provided by others interrogated at the same facility (for the nicknames of interrogators, see the Appendix). All of the former detainees were asked to demonstrate the body positions they had been forced to maintain and the blows they had received. Many agreed to reenact segments of the interrogation, playing the role of the interrogator while the HRW field-worker or translator took the role of the interrogation subject.

The Sample Used in This Report

ABUSES UNDER INTERROGATION: A STATISTICAL PROFILE

The following data are drawn from the testimony provided by the ex-detainees. In a few places, as indicated, the data do not include the entire GSS or IDF sample. This is due to two factors: ex-detainees sometimes did not recall all details of their interrogation; and second, not all ex-detainees were asked the identical questions, since the pertinence of some questions became evident only during the course of conducting the interviews.

Duration of Interrogation

For this statistic, the duration of the interrogation phase was counted from the arrival of the detainee in the interrogation wing until his release from the wing. For nearly all of the detainees we interviewed, this phase began shortly after arrest. However, a few detainees reported being first held without charge in cells or holding centers for several days.

The average length of interrogation for GSS detainees was twenty-nine days. The median was twenty-three days.

The average length of interrogation for IDF interrogation subjects twenty-one days. The median was eighteen days.

The average for all interrogation subjects was twenty-five days. The median was twenty-two days.

Beating and Violent Shaking (See Chapter Thirteen)

Of the seventeen GSS interrogation subjects, nine reported being beaten or violently shaken. Two of sixteen GSS subjects reported being beaten on the testicles (the seventeenth was not specifically asked about this).

Of the nineteen IDF interrogation subjects, sixteen reported being beaten. Thirteen said they were beaten on the testicles.

Six of eighteen IDF subjects said they were beaten en route from their place of arrest to the detention center. Five of fifteen GSS subjects said they were beaten en route. The other members of the sample were not questioned about this phase of custody.

(**Note:** The term "beating" in this report excludes light slaps, jabs, or punches, that may be degrading but are not intended primarily to inflict physical pain.)

Abusive Body Positioning (See Chapter Ten)
Ring/Pipe-shackling
Ten of the seventeen GSS interrogation subjects reported being shackled to pipes or rings embedded in the wall. The confinement ranged in duration from a few hours to, in one case, three days, with short breaks for questioning, eating, and using the toilet. Of the ten, seven were shackled while seated on "kindergarten chairs," and six while standing (three experienced both methods). Seven reported no wall-shackling. Only one of the IDF interrogation subjects reported experiencing wall-shackling.

Prolonged Standing
Fifteen of the nineteen IDF interrogation subjects said they were forced to stand in the standing areas (*shabeh*) or in "closets" for periods of at least three hours. The standing periods commonly exceeded ten hours, interrupted only by short toilet and eating breaks or questioning sessions.

Prolonged standing does not appear to be a standard practice of GSS interrogators, although six GSS detainees reported being forced to stand while shackled to the wall (see above).

Prolonged Sitting on "Kindergarten Chair"
Thirteen GSS subjects reported being forced to sit for prolonged periods on tiny chairs. The other four said they were confined for prolonged periods on ordinary chairs. The IDF does not commonly use prolonged seating as a form of abuse.

Deliberate Subjection to Temperature Extremes (See Chapter Eleven)
Five GSS detainees reported being confined in deliberately overcooled rooms ("refrigerators"). Two others were exposed to cold weather without adequate clothing, and one was placed in a hot and poorly ventilated cubicle, under circumstances that strongly suggested that the discomfort was being deliberately caused.

Hooding/Blindfolding (See Chapter Twelve)
All seventeen GSS interrogation subjects reported that they were hooded for prolonged periods between questioning sessions. All nineteen IDF subjects reported being blindfolded for prolonged periods between questioning sessions.

Sleep Deprivation (See Chapter Twelve)

Sixteen GSS detainees reported being deprived of sleep for prolonged periods, through confinement day and night in uncomfortable standing or sitting positions and denial of opportunities to lie down. IDF detainees, in contrast, said they spent virtually every night in cells, where they could lie down. However, of the sixteen IDF subjects who commented on the nights they spent in cells, nine said their sleep was interrupted constantly in what appeared to be a pattern of deliberate harassment by soldiers.

Deliberate Subjection to Loud and Continuous Noise (See Chapter Twelve)

All seventeen GSS detainees reported that the interrogation wings were continuously bombarded with loud and grating music. The music was broadcast in a manner that left no doubt that its purpose was to distress the detainees.

Length of Time between Arrest and First Meeting with Lawyer (See Chapter Eight)

Of the eleven GSS detainees who were permitted to meet their lawyer during interrogation, the average length of time before the first meeting was twenty days, and the median length of time was twenty-one days.

The other six GSS subjects were interrogated and released without meeting their lawyer. Of these, one was held for less than one week, one was held for between one and two weeks, two were held for between two and three weeks, and two were held for between three and four weeks.

Among the seventeen IDF detainees who were able to provide this information, the breakdown was as follows: of the ten who were permitted to meet their lawyer during interrogation, the average length of time before the first meeting was nineteen days, and the median length of time was 18.5 days. Seven IDF subjects were released before being permitted to confer with their lawyers. Of these, one was held for less than one week, two were held for between one and two weeks, three were held for between two and three weeks, and one was held for between three and four weeks.

PROFILES OF DETAINEES INTERVIEWED FOR THIS REPORT

Below are data about the thirty-six ex-detainees interviewed by HRW for this report. They are divided according to whether they were interrogated by the GSS or the IDF. Within each category, the cases are in reverse chronological order according to the time of their interrogation.

At the end of the list are data about five additional Palestinians whose testimony was studied in the preparation of this report.[3] (Their cases, however, are not included in the statistical profile above.) At the time of the HRW fieldwork, these five men were still in detention and therefore not accessible to HRW researchers; their testimony was collected by defense lawyers, who shared it with HRW.

For each of its thirty-six cases, HRW interviewed the ex-detainee at length and was convinced of his credibility about the interrogation experience. Some ex-detainees, however, were vague or elusive when discussing the charges and accusations against them. HRW did not independently verify the nature of those charges and accusations; they are provided below as given by the ex-detainees themselves.

All of the persons listed below except one gave HRW their full names. Most, however, asked that their names not be used in the report. To respect their requested anonymity, these ex-detainees are referred to by their initials or partial names, and some identifying details are omitted.

GSS Interrogations
Name: Bassem Tamimi
Age: 26
Occupation: Unemployed
Area of residence: Ramallah, West Bank
Period of interrogation: November 9-10, 1993
Duration of interrogation: One day, then hospitalized
Place of interrogation: Ramallah prison
Accusations made during interrogation: Linked to killing of a Jewish settler
Formal charges: None
Date of interview: March 16, 1994
Place of interview: Ramallah, West Bank

---

[3] One of these cases involves a later detention of a person who is among the sample of thirty-six interviewed by HRW.

The Sample Used in This Report

Name: A. Z.
Age: 23
Occupation: University student in history and political science
Area of residence: Qalandiya refugee camp, West Bank
Approximate period of interrogation: October-November 1993
Duration of interrogation: 18 days
Place of interrogation: Ramallah prison.
Accusations made during interrogation: Campus leader of Hamas
Formal charges: None, but given a three-month administrative detention order
Date of interview: March 15, 1994
Place of interview: Ramallah, West Bank

Name: M. Z.
Age: 21
Occupation: Painter
Area of residence: Gaza City, Gaza Strip
Approximate period of interrogation: October 1993
Duration of interrogation: 20 days
Place of interrogation: Ashkelon prison
Accusations made during interrogation: knowledge of location of fugitives
Formal charges: None
Date of interview: November 23, 1993
Place of interview: Journalist's office in Gaza City

Name: Ali Ayed Ali Radaydeh
Age: 23
Occupation: Manual laborer
Area of residence: Village of Abadiyeh, Bethlehem district
Approximate period of interrogation: January–February 1993
Duration of interrogation: 18 days
Place of interrogation: Hebron prison
Accusations made during interrogation: Possessing information about the killing of a Jewish settler
Formal charges: None
Date of interview: March 1, 1993
Place of interview: Home in Abadiyeh village

Name: *Nasser Radaydeh*
Age: 20
Occupation: Construction worker
Area of residence: Abadiyeh village, Bethlehem district, West Bank
Approximate period of interrogation: January–February 1993
Duration of interrogation: 23 days
Place of interrogation: Hebron prison
Accusations made during interrogation: Possessing information about the killing of a Jewish settler
Formal charges: None
Date of interview: February 19, 1993
Place of interview: Home in Abadiyeh village

Name: *Sh. Z.*
Age: 22
Occupation: Student at a West Bank university
Area of residence: Ramallah, West Bank
Approximate period of interrogation: December 1992
Duration of interrogation: 15 days
Place of interrogation: Ramallah prison
Accusations made during interrogation: Armed attack on Israeli settler
Formal charges: Unknown; tried in military court and sentenced to sixty-four days in prison, six months' suspended sentence, and a 2,500 shekel fine (U.S. $800). Prison sentence corresponded to time already served
Date of interview: March 31, 1993
Place of interview: University campus in the West Bank

Name: *M. R.*
Age: 29
Occupation: Unemployed
Area of residence: Khan Yunis refugee camp, Gaza Strip
Approximate period of interrogation: December 1992
Duration of interrogation: 8 days
Place of interrogation: Gaza prison
Accusations made during interrogation: Organizational activities abroad for an illegal Palestinian organization
Formal charges: None
Date of interview: March 20, 1993
Place of interview: Lawyer's office in Khan Yunis

The Sample Used in This Report

Name: Ahmed Husni al-Batsh
Age: 47
Occupation: Former high school teacher; now an aide to Faisal al-Husseini, director of the Arab Studies Society
Area of residence: Dir Naballah, Ramallah district, West Bank
Approximate period of interrogation: September–November 1992
Duration of interrogation: 75 days
Place of interrogation: Ramallah prison
Accusations made during interrogation: Senior member in, and activities on behalf of an illegal organization (Fatah)
Formal charges: None
Date of interviews: February 19 and 26, 1993
Place of interview: Home in Dir Naballah

Name: Ribhi Suleiman Qatamesh
Age: 45
Occupation: Lawyer, researcher at social studies institute
Area of residence: Ramallah, West Bank
Approximate period of interrogation: October 1992
Duration of interrogation: 23 days
Place of interrogation: Hebron prison
Accusations made during interrogation: Knowledge of location of weapons cache
Formal charges: None
Date of interview: March 7, 1993
Place of interview: Lawyer's office in Ramallah

Name: Hassan Zebeideh
Age: 34
Occupation: Grocer
Area of residence: Anabta village, Tulkarm district, West Bank
Approximate period of interrogation: September–October 1992
Duration of interrogation: 33 days
Place of interrogation: Tulkarm prison
Accusations made during interrogation: Membership in Hamas
Formal charges: None
Date of interview: May 14, 1993
Place of interview: Home in Anabta

***Name:** Rashid Hilal*
Age: 33
Occupation: Journalist, Palestine Press Service
Area of residence: Ramallah, West Bank
Approximate period of interrogation: September–October 1992
Duration of interrogation: 42 days
Place of interrogation: Petach Tikva police station
Accusations made during interrogation: Aiding members of the Popular Front for the Liberation of Palestine
Formal charges: None
Date of interview: March 6, 1993
Place of interview: Palestine Press Service office, Ramallah

***Name:** Ad. M.*
Age: 20
Occupation: Engineering student at a West Bank university
Area of residence: Tulkarm, West Bank
Approximate period of interrogation: Autumn 1992
Duration of interrogation: 47 days
Place of interrogation: Tulkarm prison
Accusations made during interrogation: Receiving military training abroad, membership in Islamic Jihad, planning armed operations
Formal charges: None
Date of interview: March 18, 1993
Place of interview: University campus in the West Bank

***Name:** S. R.*
Age: 25
Occupation: Student at a West Bank university
Area of residence: Ramallah, West Bank
Approximate period of interrogation: Early autumn 1992
Duration of interrogation: 38 days
Place of interrogation: Ramallah prison

Accusations made during interrogation: Membership in an illegal organization (Hamas), "intifada activities"[4]
Formal charges: Same; tried and sentenced to 7.5 months in prison (time already served)
Date of interview: April 3, 1993
Place of interview: Home in Ramallah

Name: B. Ah.
Age: 23
Occupation: Unemployed
Area of residence: Bethlehem area, West Bank
Approximate period of interrogation: Late summer 1992
Duration of interrogation: 22 days
Place of interrogation: Hebron prison
Accusations made during interrogation: Armed operations, recruiting others into an illegal organization
Formal charges: None
Date of interview: March 29, 1993
Place of interview: Home near Bethlehem

Name: U. Gh.
Age: 23
Occupation: Computer programming student
Area of residence: Ramallah, West Bank
Approximate period of interrogation: Late summer 1992
Duration of interrogation: 24 days
Place of interrogation: Tulkarm prison
Accusations made during interrogation: Membership in Hamas, stone-throwing
Formal charges: None
Date of interview: February 15, 1993
Place of interview: Home in Ramallah

---

[4] "Intifada activities" as a description of accusations or charges can refer to offenses such as throwing stones or Molotov cocktails, participating in demonstrations, or writing political graffiti. It generally does not include offenses relating to the use of firearms or explosives.

Name: H. M.
Age: 33
Occupation: Night guard
Area of residence: Ramallah area, West Bank
Approximate period of interrogation: Late summer 1992
Duration of interrogation: 39 days
Place of interrogation: Ramallah prison
Accusations made during interrogation: Senior membership in Fatah
Formal charges: None, but given a six-month administrative detention order
Date of interview: January 20, 1993
Place of interview: Lawyer's office in Ramallah

Name: Abd A.
Age: 26
Occupation: Student at a university in the West Bank
Area of residence: Bethlehem area, West Bank
Approximate period of interrogation: Summer 1992
Duration of interrogation: 50 days
Place of interrogation: Hebron prison
Accusations made during interrogation: Membership in the Popular Front for the Liberation of Palestine, interrogating suspected Palestinian collaborators, involvement in armed activity
Formal charges: None, but given a six-month administrative detention order
Date of interview: March 16, 1993
Place of interview: University campus in the West Bank

IDF Interrogations
Name: Sh. S.
Age: 21
Occupation: University student, West Bank
Area of residence: Khan Yunis refugee camp, Gaza Strip
Approximate period of interrogation: February-March 1994
Duration of interrogation: 18 days
Place of interrogation: Al-Far'a
Accusations made during interrogation: Aiding fugitives, membership in Hamas

The Sample Used in This Report

Formal charges: None
Date of interview: March 16, 1994
Place of interview: Ramallah, West Bank

Name: Abd R.
Age: 19
Occupation: Student at a university in the West Bank
Area of residence: Khan Yunis refugee camp, Gaza Strip
Approximate period of interrogation: February-March 1994
Duration of interrogation: 8 days
Place of interrogation: Al-Far'a
Accusations made during interrogation: Not known
Formal charges: None
Date of interview: March 15, 1994
Place of interview: University campus in the West Bank

Name: N. S.
Age: 19
Occupation: Student at a university in the West Bank
Area of residence: Ramallah, West Bank
Approximate period of interrogation: Late November–late December 1993
Duration of interrogation: 30 days
Place of interrogation: Al-Far'a
Accusations made during interrogation: Membership in Hamas. Student activities on behalf of Hamas, including writing and printing leaflets and distributing posters
Formal charges: Same; released on bail of 2,000 shekels (U.S. $640) and, at time of HRW interview, awaiting trial
Date of interview: March 16, 1994
Place of interview: Ramallah

Name: A. A.
Age: 25
Occupation: Unemployed
Area of residence: Aida refugee camp, Bethlehem district, West Bank
Approximate period of interrogation: November 1993
Duration of interrogation: About 17 days
Place of interrogation: al-Far'a
Accusations made during interrogation: Membership in Hamas

Formal charges: None
Date of interview: November 22, 1993
Place of interview: Home in Aida refugee camp

Name: S. Mas.
Age: 23
Occupation: Studied computer engineering
Area of residence: Gaza City, Gaza Strip
Approximate period of interrogation: October 1993
Duration of interrogation: 12 days
Place of interrogation: Beach facility
Accusations made during interrogation: participating in setting off an explosive device
Formal charges: None
Date of interview: November 23, 1993
Place of interview: Journalist's office in Gaza City

Name: A. abu M.
Age: 23
Occupation: Agricultural worker
Area of residence: Al-Bureij refugee camp, Gaza Strip
Approximate period of interrogation: October 1993
Duration of interrogation: About 18 days
Place of interrogation: Beach facility
Accusations made during interrogation: Membership in an illegal organization
Formal charges: None
Date of interview: November 23, 1993
Place of interview: Journalist's office in Gaza City

Name: M. N.
Age: 18
Occupation: Student at a university in the West Bank
Area of residence: Jabalya refugee camp, Gaza Strip
Approximate period of interrogation: October 1993
Duration of interrogation: Slightly over two weeks
Place of interrogation: Beach facility
Accusations made during interrogation: Membership in Islamic Jihad
Formal charges: None

The Sample Used in This Report

Date of interview: November 17, 1993
Place of interview: University campus in West Bank

Name: H. H.
Age: 20
Occupation: Student at a university in the West Bank
Area of residence: Ramallah area, West Bank
Approximate period of interrogation: Spring 1993
Duration of interrogation: 9 days
Place of interrogation: Dhahiriya
Accusations made during interrogation: Membership in an illegal organization, throwing stones at Israeli troops, erecting roadblocks
Formal charges: None
Date of interview: March 31, 1993
Place of interview: University campus in the West Bank

Name: Muhammad R.
Age: 31
Occupation: Unemployed teacher
Area of residence: Village in Jenin area, West Bank
Approximate period of interrogation: Early 1993
Duration of interrogation: 45 days
Place of interrogation: Al-Far'a
Accusations made during interrogation: Leader of Fatah's youth wing in the village
Formal charges: Same; released on bail and awaiting trial at time of HRW interview
Date of interview: April 1, 1993
Place of interview: Lawyer's office in Jenin

Name: I. M.
Age: 17
Occupation: Unemployed
Area of residence: Dir el-Balah refugee camp, Gaza Strip
Approximate period of interrogation: January 1993
Duration of interrogation: 16 days
Place of interrogation: Beach facility
Accusations made during interrogation: Aiding fugitives
Formal charges: None

Date of interview: February 20, 1993
Place of interview: Home in Dir el-Balah camp

Name: Ali A.
Age: 25
Occupation: Unemployed
Area of residence: Ramallah, West Bank
Approximate period of interrogation: December 1992-January 1993
Duration of interrogation: 3 days
Place of interrogation: Al-Far'a
Accusations made during interrogation: Membership in Hamas, stone throwing, burning tires
Formal charges: None, but placed in administrative detention for one month
Date of interview: February 20, 1993
Place of interview: Home in Ramallah

Name: I. K.
Age: 20
Occupation: Unemployed, day laborer
Area of residence: Khan Yunis refugee camp, Gaza Strip
Approximate period of interrogation: December 1992–January 1993
Duration of interrogation: 29 days
Place of interrogation: Beach facility
Accusations made during interrogation: Membership in an outlawed organization (the Arab Liberation Front), stone throwing, throwing of Molotov cocktails
Formal charges: None
Date of interview: February 13, 1993
Place of interview: Lawyer's office in Khan Yunis

Name: H. D.
Age: 18
Occupation: Unemployed
Area of residence: Ramallah area, West Bank
Approximate period of interrogation: Winter 1992–1993
Duration of interrogation: 40 days
Place of interrogation: Dhahiriya

Accusations made during interrogation: Throwing stones at Israeli troops, organizing local youths for intifada activities
Formal charges: Throwing stones, painting nationalist graffiti, distributing nationalist leaflets, blocking traffic; convicted in military court trial and sentenced to two-and-a-half months in prison and a fine of 3,000 shekels (U.S. $960). Prison sentence corresponded to time already served.
Place of Interview: Ramallah

Name: Y. D.
Age: 20
Occupation: Unemployed
Area of residence: Ramallah, West Bank
Approximate period of interrogation: December 1992
Duration of interrogation: 17 days
Place of interrogation: Dhahiriya
Accusations made during interrogation: Membership in an illegal organization, throwing stones and Molotov cocktails, interrogation of suspected Palestinian collaborators
Formal charges: None
Date of interview: February 23, 1993
Place of interview: Home in Ramallah

Name: Muhammad Anis abu Hikmeh
Age: 21
Occupation: Student at a university in the West Bank
Area of residence: Al-Bireh, West Bank
Approximate period of interrogation: November–December 1992
Duration of interrogation: 22 days
Place of interrogation: Dhahiriya
Accusations made during interrogation: Membership in an illegal organization, leadership of activists at the local level, interrogation of suspected Palestinian collaborators
Formal charges: None, but placed in administrative detention for three months
Date of interview: March 25, 1993
Place of interview: Home in al-Bireh

Name: Yasir Abdullah Salman Mughari
Age: 22

Occupation: Unemployed
Area of residence: Nuseirat refugee camp, Gaza Strip
Approximate period of interrogation: November–December 1992
Duration of interrogation: 22 days
Place of interrogation: Beach facility
Accusations made during interrogation: Membership in the Popular Front for the Liberation of Palestine, "intifada activities"
Formal charges: Unknown; released on bail pending trial; disposition of case unknown
Date of interview: February 26, 1993
Place of interview: Nuseirat refugee camp

Name: O. T.
Age: 23
Occupation: Political science student at a West Bank university
Area of residence: Jenin area, West Bank
Approximate period of interrogation: September–October 1992
Duration of interrogation: 25 days
Place of interrogation: Al-Far'a
Accusations made during interrogation: Membership in Fatah, throwing stones at Israeli troops
Formal charges: Membership in an illegal organization; convicted in military court and sentenced to two months and eight days. Prison sentence corresponded to time already served
Date of interview: April 1, 1993
Place of interview: Lawyer's office in Jenin

Name: A. (Refused to supply name to HRW)
Age: 21
Occupation: Unemployed
Area of residence: Jenin, West Bank
Approximate period of interrogation: August 1992
Duration of interrogation: 18 days
Place of interrogation: Al-Far'a
Accusations made during interrogation: Membership in an illegal organization, "intifada activities"
Formal charges: None, but placed in administrative detention for six months
Date of interview: April 1, 1993

The Sample Used in This Report 43

Place of interview: Lawyer's office in Jenin

Name: Ah. al-M.
Age: 23
Occupation: Unemployed
Area of residence: Bethlehem, West Bank
Approximate period of interrogation: Early summer 1992
Duration of interrogation: 50 days
Place of interrogation: Dhahiriya
Accusations made during interrogation: Membership in the Popular Front for the Liberation of Palestine, throwing Molotov cocktails at Israeli troops, interrogating suspected Palestinian collaborators
Formal charges: None
Date of interview: March 30, 1993
Place of interview: Home in Bethlehem area

Testimonies Collected by Lawyers from Persons Still in Detention
Name: U. Gh.
Age: 23
Occupation: clerk
Area of residence: Ramallah, West Bank
Approximate period of interrogation: Early autumn 1993
Duration of interrogation: Over two months
Place of interrogation: Ramallah prison
Accusations made during interrogation: Membership in Hamas and incitement by giving slogans to a writer
Formal charges: Not known, was in pre-trial detention at time of interview
Date of interview: Interview by Attorney Ahmed Sayyad on October 25, 1993
Place of interview: Ramallah prison

Name: Nader Raji Mikhail Qumsiyeh
Age: 25
Occupation: Unknown
Area of residence: Beit Sahour, West Bank
Approximate period of interrogation: May 6-11, 1993
Duration of interrogation: 6 days
Place of interrogation: Dhahiriya

Accusations made during interrogation: Membership in an illegal organization, "intifada activities"
Formal charges: None, but placed in administrative detention for four months, reduced to two and-a-half months on appeal
Date of interview: Interview by Attorney Tamar Pelleg-Sryck on June 7, 1993
Place of interview: Ketziot detention center

Name: Ribhi Shukeir
Age: Approximately 35
Occupation: Unknown
Area of residence: A-Zawiya village, Tulkarm area, West Bank
Approximate period of interrogation: March–May 1993
Duration of interrogation: 52 days
Place of interrogation: Tulkarm prison
Accusations made during interrogation: Senior member of an illegal organization (Fatah), and participation in armed activities
Formal charges: None, but given a four-month administrative detention order, reduced on appeal to three months
Date of interview: Interview by Attorney Tamar Pelleg-Sryck, during interrogation
Place of interview: Tulkarm prison

Name: Muhammad Abd al-Mouata Muhammad Sa'd
Age: Unknown
Occupation: Unknown
Area of residence: Gaza Strip
Approximate period of interrogation: February 1993
Duration of interrogation: Unknown
Place of interrogation: Gaza prison, Ashkelon prison
Accusations made during interrogation: Killing suspected Palestinian collaborators, armed attacks on Israeli troops
Formal charges: Specific charges not known
Date of interview: Interview by Attorney Tamar Pelleg-Sryck on February 14, 1993
Place of interview: Ashkelon prison

Name: Na'im Ibrahim abu Seif
Age: Unknown

The Sample Used in This Report   45

Occupation: Unknown
Area of residence: Gaza Strip
Approximate period of interrogation: February 1993
Duration of interrogation: Unknown
Place of interrogation: Gaza prison, Ashkelon prison
Accusations made during interrogation: Killing of suspected Palestinian collaborators, carrying out armed attacks on Israeli forces
Formal charges: Unknown, awaiting trial
Date of interview: Interview by Attorney Tamar Pelleg-Sryck on February 14, 1993
Place of interview: Ashkelon prison

3
ISRAEL'S INTERROGATION PRACTICES HISTORICAL OVERVIEW

A review of trends in Israeli interrogation practices in the occupied territories can be divided into two periods: from 1967 to 1987, the year the Landau Commission report was issued and endorsed by the government; and from 1987 to the present.

1967-1987: DENIAL

Between 1967 and November 1987, the overall position of Israeli governments was that interrogators did not employ coercive methods during interrogations. In public, officials flatly denied allegations, by the media, human rights organizations, and others, that ill-treatment or torture was common.

For example, in response to a ground-breaking exposé of Israeli interrogation methods published by the *Sunday Times* of London on June 19, 1977, the Israeli Embassy in London ridiculed the article's main charge that torture "is organized so methodically that it cannot be dismissed as a handful of 'rogue cops' exceeding orders." Referring to the *Times'* description of interrogations conducted at the Russian Compound police station in Jerusalem, the embassy wrote in the July 3, 1977 issue of the paper:

> A place such as the Jerusalem local police station is ominously termed "a detention and interrogation centre" in order to try and create a suitable *mise en scène* for the *Sunday Times* horror fiction. Yet this local police station is in the centre of town and, as every Jerusalem lawyer and journalist is aware, local police are perfectly willing to allow visitors....[A]ny Jerusalem resident who has lost a camera will also be visiting these "barracks."
>
> Israel police and security have every reason to refrain from use of force. Such use of force is a serious criminal offence, and where cases of police brutality have been

found in the past, police officers have been prosecuted, and it is Israel's policy to do so in the future.

Furthermore, as has been emphasized, any statement obtained by such methods is inadmissible.[1]

In the military courts in the occupied territories — where the bulk of Palestinians suspected of security offenses are tried — GSS agents routinely lied to military judges when rebutting allegations of torture by Palestinians, according to the Landau Commission report (see below for a discussion of the report's findings). In the overwhelming majority of cases, military judges accepted the security agents' version of events, and the coerced confessions were allowed to stand as evidence.

HRW did not closely examine pre-1987 interrogation methods. According to several interviews we conducted with Palestinians detained during that period, Israeli and Palestinian defense lawyers, and reports by other organizations, interrogators employed a range of violent and humiliating measures. The Landau report acknowledged cases of "criminal assault, blackmail, and threats" that did not necessarily deviate from the GSS guidelines (see below). Some of these measures continue until the present, while others have been discontinued or used less often.

THE "BUREAUCRATIZATION OF TORTURE"

A new phase in Israel's ill-treatment and torture of Palestinians under interrogation began after the publication of the Landau Commission report. This government-initiated inquiry into GSS interrogation practices demolished the official façade of denial that coercive methods were commonplace.

---

[1] The *Sunday Times* report, the Israeli Embassy's reply and the *Times'* reply to the Embassy were reprinted in the *Journal of Palestine Studies* 6 (Summer 1977), pp. 191-219.

Absolute denials, such as the one by the Embassy cited here, rang particularly hollow after the Landau Commission released its report in 1987. As for the Embassy's ridicule of the allegation that the Russian Compound police station contains a detention and interrogation center, it can only be dismissed as lying.

The Landau Commission, headed by former Supreme Court Justice Moshe Landau, was appointed in May 1987 in the wake of two scandals that shook the Israeli public's confidence in the agency. In the first case, GSS officials fabricated evidence to cover up a 1984 incident in which agents beat to death two Palestinians who had been taken into custody after hijacking a civilian bus (an incident known as the "Bus 300 Affair"). In the second incident, Lieutenant Izzat Nafsu, a member of Israel's Circassian (Turkic Muslim) minority, was released from prison after the Supreme Court ruled that he had been convicted of espionage on the basis of a false confession extracted under duress by GSS agents, who later lied in court when Nafsu challenged his confession.

Issued in November 1987 and endorsed by the Israeli cabinet, the Landau report stands as the preeminent official statement on the interrogation of Palestinians. Most of the report was made public, but its most sensitive findings and recommendations — such as what interrogation techniques the GSS had used from 1967 to 1987 and which methods should henceforth be permissible — remain classified to this day.

In endorsing the Landau report, the government of Israel for the first time acknowledged that GSS agents had for years used coercive methods that were illegal under Israeli law but consistent with the agency's internal guidelines. The report states:

> In regard to the acts of physical pressure or psychological pressure that they [GSS interrogators] employed: in retrospect, there were cases of criminal assault, blackmail, and threats. However, it appears to us that so long as these practices did not deviate from the guidelines that existed in the service at the time of the interrogation (and generally speaking, they did not deviate from the guidelines), the interrogator who employed such measures can justly claim, on the basis of paragraph 24 (1) (a) of the Penal Code, that he was obeying the orders of his superiors, and that these orders were not clearly illegal, and that he had reason to believe that he was acting in order to extract necessary information on the terrorist activity of an organization which the suspect was suspected of belonging to.[2]

---

[2] Paragraph 4.20.

Israel's Interrogation Practices

The Landau report revealed that since 1971, GSS interrogators had systematically lied to the military courts. When Palestinian defendants sought to invalidate confessions on the grounds that they had not been given freely, GSS agents testified that the confessions had been obtained through non-coercive methods only:

> [I]nterrogators found themselves facing a severe dilemma.... Like all other witnesses testifying in Court, they were bound by the law to tell the whole truth and nothing but the truth....[Yet] truthful testimony required disclosing and uncovering what went on in the interrogation premises during interrogation, including an exposure of interrogation methods and, in consequence, the impossibility of employing these methods in the future, once they have been made known to the adversary. The methods in question are numerous and diverse, including means of pressure applied against suspects.
>
> The second [classified] part of this Report refers to the various types of pressure employed by interrogators against persons investigated. For our purposes here, suffice it to say that the pressure exerted — even if permitted at that time [by GSS guidelines] — was such as could be expected to appear to the court as violating the principle of the person's free will, and thus causing the rejection of the confession.
>
> Hence, as he stood on the witness stand, the GSS interrogator considered telling the truth as doubly dangerous, since it would involve ap1779Xdisclosure interrogation methods and the application of physical pressure, and the rejection of the confession by the Court and the consequent acquittal of the accused. From the point of view of the GSS, each of these results was grave and undesirable — while GSS personnel were convinced, on the basis of reliable information, that the accused was indeed guilty as charged.[3]

---

[3] Ibid., paragraphs 2.25-2.26.

The result was that "interrogators chose from the very beginning to conceal from the Court the exertion of any physical pressure whatsoever," and perjury "became an unchallenged norm which was to be the rule for sixteen years."[4]

The Landau Commission dismissed the charge made by some GSS personnel that some military judges were parties to the cover-up. "We can only note our sorrow that such an allegation was made in the first place," the Commission wrote, while acknowledging that not a single judge was summoned to testify during their inquiry.[5] The Commission also dismissed claims that successive prime ministers knew of the conspiracy to conceal evidence of GSS abuse.[6]

THE LANDAU COMMISSION'S RECOMMENDATIONS

The Commission proposed abandoning the hypocrisy of an interrogation system in which illegal methods were used and systematically covered up. Instead, the government should acknowledge that some measure of coercion is permissible, and then codify and carefully monitor the allowable techniques.[7] Those techniques, the commission stated:

> should principally take the form of non-violent psychological pressure through a vigorous and extensive interrogation, with the use of stratagems, including acts of deception. However, when these do not attain their purpose, the exertion of a moderate measure of physical pressure cannot be avoided. GSS interrogators should be guided by setting clear boundaries in this matter, in order

---

[4] Ibid., paragraphs 2.29–2.30.

[5] Ibid., paragraph 2.45.

[6] Ibid., paragraph 2.46.

[7] Ibid., paragraphs 4.7–4.8.

to prevent the use of inordinate physical pressure arbitrarily administered by the interrogator.[8]

In the classified appendix of the report, the commission recommended a variety of methods that it claimed were consistent with these guidelines and with international legal prohibitions of torture and ill-treatment. To the extent that, in the public section of the report, the commission found some methods to be problematic from this perspective, they were the physical methods. It showed little recognition that psychological means might also be problematic.

In testimony since 1987 before military courts, GSS agents have acknowledged using psychological and nonviolent physical methods of pressure, including hooding, prolonged sleep deprivation and shackling to a small chair (see Chapter Eighteen). The readiness with which they admit to these techniques, without fear of prosecution, strongly suggests that these methods are sanctioned in the classified GSS guidelines. It also shows that military courts will not automatically discard confessions simply because these methods were used on the defendant to induce his statement. By contrast, interrogators have never, to our knowledge, testified during the trial of a Palestinian to having beaten the defendant during interrogation. (This does not, however, prove that beatings are forbidden by the guidelines.)

---

[8] Ibid., paragraph 4.7.

"The Landau Commission, in my opinion, made a cardinal mistake in trying to distinguish between physical pressure and psychological pressure....The distinction between psychological pressure and physical pressure is certainly not valid from a legal point of view for the matter of evidence laws. The question is whether or not the confession is made willingly and freely, and as far as this goes, it is totally irrelevant whether the pressure was psychological or physical....

"[The members of the Commission] tried, in my opinion, to con the public, in other words to create the impression that if you use psychological pressure — that is, if you don't beat people, if you don't use physical means — then the damage is not so bad.

"It has been known all over the world for a long time that this is not true. Most of the regimes which employ dubious methods of interrogation hardly ever use physical force. They know very well that you can apply psychological pressure which, sooner or later...will achieve the desired result, so that you can present the client to his lawyer clean and physically sound. It is enough...to apply the combined method of sleep deprivation and sensory deprivation to a person. Most people can be broken down from this combination and nothing else. If you do not let a person sleep, see daylight, see and talk to people, if you almost totally isolate him and simultaneously interrogate him, many people will break down under this situation."

— Israeli psychiatrist Joachim Stein, speaking at a symposium on the Landau Commission report, held in Jerusalem on July 12, 1990. A transcript of the symposium was printed as *Moderate Physical Pressure: Interrogation Methods in Israel*, by the Public Committee Against Torture in Israel (Jerusalem, n.d.).

Israel's Interrogation Practices

THE EARLY YEARS OF THE INTIFADA: 1988–1991

One month after publication of the Landau Commission report, the Palestinian uprising broke out. In an effort to quell the unrest, the Israeli military rounded up thousands of Palestinians each month, cramming detention centers and prompting the hasty construction of new facilities.

Reports by human rights groups indicate that during the early years of the intifada, GSS and IDF personnel commonly resorted to crudely violent methods of interrogation. For example, B'Tselem's 1991 report on interrogations states that forty of the forty-one-member sample said that interrogators beat them severely using fists, sticks, and other implements. Fifteen reported being beaten so badly that they lost consciousness.[9]

HRW interviewed an IDF reserve soldier who spent his annual thirty-day reserve duty in 1989 as a military policeman at al-Far'a military detention center in the West Bank. To the best of HRW's knowledge, Sergeant A. M. — he asked that his full name not be used — is the first Israeli present *within* an interrogation room to relate his experiences for the record to outsiders. His testimony paints a picture of brutal violence at al-Far'a's interrogation wing in 1989. HRW's interview with Sergeant A. M. appears in the appendix to this report; excerpts are provided here.

On his first day at al-Far'a, Sergeant A. M. was recruited by IDF interrogators to participate in the interrogation of Palestinian detainees. Although his job was nominally to "guard" the interrogator while he questioned suspects, Sergeant A. M.'s actual duty was to beat some eight to ten Palestinians per day with his fists, his boots and a club:

Sergeant A. M.: I stood inside the room with the interrogator and the detainee. The interrogator sat facing me, the detainee with his back to me. And they would talk, in Arabic. I don't understand Arabic. And then, when the interrogator didn't get the answer he wanted, he made a sign, and I hit the detainee.

HRW: What did you hit him with?

---

[9] B'Tselem, *The Interrogation of Palestinians during the Intifada: Ill-Treatment, "Moderate Physical Pressure" or Torture?* (Jerusalem: B'Tselem, March 1991), p. 71. See also al-Haq, *A Nation Under Siege* (Ramallah: al-Haq, 1990), pp. 172-173.

Sergeant A. M.: With a club, my hand, foot, anything. Just hit him, we "blew him up," beating like I can't describe. Just beating and beating.

HRW: Were there any orders about how to beat?

Sergeant A. M.: No, nothing. They would just say, "Try not to kill him." That's all. We hit them everywhere — head, face, mouth, arms, balls.

HRW: Describe an interrogation.

Sergeant A. M.: Well, the detainee comes in, he is handcuffed behind his back, and blindfolded. The interrogator sits in front of him, at the beginning behind a desk. The detainee sits on a chair, for as long as he is able. Then the questions start. I didn't understand, you see, it was in Arabic. But if the answer was not good, he gave me a sign....You just knew what he wanted. It was clear. He didn't need to say anything, he just looked at me. And then I would hit. Wherever I wanted. There were no rules. We kept on beating, and if he fell down on the ground, the interrogator would tell him to get back up. If he couldn't, we hit him on the floor. Just hit him everywhere.

HRW: What was their situation after they left the rooms?

Sergeant A. M.: In 99.9 percent of the cases, they couldn't leave on their own. They had to call for a couple of detainees from the yard, who came and carried them back to the cells, or to the yard. They simply couldn't walk on their own.

Other soldiers have provided accounts to the press of conditions in other IDF interrogation wings. One reservist, for example, told two Israeli reporters that during his service at the Beach facility in 1990:

> [A military policeman] went to bring prisoners from the compounds....[When] they would interrogate them, here and there you'd hear the "thump" and the "whack" of the blows that they were receiving, and then they'd come out and stand there, crying and shivering....

> The screaming I heard on Saturday morning...and those were screams which until today, when I sleep at night, I hear them inside my ears all the time....They were horrible screams, really.[10]

TRENDS SINCE 1991: STANDARDIZATION

Beginning approximately in 1991-1992, there were gradual changes in both GSS and IDF interrogation practices, according to ex-detainees, defense lawyers and other sources. The trend was toward increasing standardization of methods within each agency, toward calibrated combinations of psychological and physical measures, combined with a more restricted policy toward beating.

While reducing, without eliminating, physical violence, the GSS relied increasingly on prolonged position abuse, sleep deprivation, isolation, hooding, threats, toilet deprivation, enclosure in small spaces, and loud, grating music — all or most of these applied in concert with one another.[11]

Ex-detainees stressed that both GSS and IDF interrogators since 1991-1992 seemed intent on inflicting severe pain without breaking bones or causing irreversible injuries. The beating techniques were virtually identical in all three IDF centers, concentrating on the upper body and the testicles, but avoiding the face and limbs.

Rashid Hilal, a journalist who was interrogated several times over the past ten years, observed:

> The Israelis have tried to convince people that beating is the worst torture of all, and that since they do this less now, things are better. This is not necessarily true. Now, they use a variety of methods to weaken a person, to bring him to a position where he mentally and physically

---

[10] Roly Rosen and Ilana Hammerman, "Yossi's Testimony," in *Poets Won't Write Poems* (Tel Aviv: Am Oved Publishers, 1990). English translation in B'Tselem, *The Interrogation of Palestinians during the Intifada*, pp. 125 and 127.

[11] See B'Tselem, *The Interrogation of Palestinian during the Intifada, Follow-Up*, p. 43.

> collapses. They do this through isolation, hooding, *shabeh* [position abuse] and sleep deprivation.[12]

Ribhi Qatamesh, a lawyer who operates a research institute in Jerusalem, offered a similar analysis. Qatamesh said he had been interrogated six times during the last decade. Over the years, he said:

> The interrogation system got "better," that is, more efficient. In 1982, for example, I was interrogated and then brought back to a regular holding area. Now, there is a sealed "interrogation section," which you never leave until the interrogation ends. You stay in this world throughout.

Qatamesh said he first detected a shift during his 1991 interrogation:

> Before, they used outright violence: they would break your bones. This was what we call the German school of interrogations, which uses nothing but physical violence to force you to sign a confession. Then, after two to three days, you had signed. Now, they rely more on psychological methods that wear you down until you are broken. It just takes a little longer.[13]

Ibrahim Ali Ahmed al-Tarsha, a thirty-five-year old economist, was interrogated several times during the 1980s and early 1990s. He said:

> In the 1980s, beating was the main method. Today, beating is only one of the methods used....[W]hat they do now has psychological effects. Not to sleep for twenty-five days is terrible; you begin to talk to yourself, and if your head is hooded, and you are tied, it is terrible.[14]

---

[12] HRW interview, Ramallah, March 6, 1993.

[13] HRW interview, Ramallah, March 7, 1993.

[14] HRW interview, Ramallah, March 6, 1993.

Jenin-based journalist Naif Sweitat, who underwent several interrogations over the past decade and now often interviews ex-detainees interrogated at al-Far'a and at the GSS wing of Jenin prison, said that the techniques had evolved:

> Until one-and-a-half years ago, the violence during interrogations [at al-Far'a and Jenin] was very heavy. Now, as a result of the international organizations, the use of direct beating and violence has gone down. Beating is now used more selectively; it is being used primarily against the military activists.[15]

Palestinian and Israeli lawyers who represent Palestinians accused of security offenses also noted this general trend. Hebron-based Abd al-Ghani Aweiwe has had many clients who were interrogated at the IDF detention center at Dhahiriya and the GSS interrogation center at Hebron prison. He said that suspected "small fish" — typically younger men or youths suspected of low-level membership in outlawed organizations, participation in demonstrations, and throwing stones — go to Dhahiriya, while suspects in more serious offenses go to Hebron. The two facilities use different methods:

> In Dhahiriya, they use beatings. There, the violence is simply brutal and random, mostly beating on the testicles. In Hebron, the violence is sophisticated, they use no sleeping, the small chair, long, protracted periods of intensive shabeh, usually for four to five days at a time.

Beating at Hebron, Aweiwe said, is selective: "They study you in Hebron. If they need to beat you, they do. If they don't, they use other methods."[16]

Attorney Lea Tsemel, who has had clients who were held at most of the interrogation wings in the West Bank, agreed with Aweiwe's conclusions. She reported receiving fewer reports of severe beatings in recent years, and more reports of isolation, sleep deprivation and abusive body positioning. These changes were a mixed blessing, she said:

---

[15] HRW interview, Jenin, April 1, 1993.

[16] HRW interview, Hebron, March 22, 1993.

Each time we make some progress and get a certain technique abolished or reduced, they come up with something that is harder to see and more difficult to focus on in court. Now, the measures they use don't leave marks.[17]

A COURT CHALLENGE TO THE CLASSIFIED GSS INTERROGATION GUIDELINES

In June 1991, the Israeli Supreme Court was asked to rule on whether the Landau report's classified interrogation guidelines should be declared illegal on the grounds that they contravened Israeli law and effectively sanctioned torture. The Court was also asked to require that the guidelines be made public. The co-petitioners were a rights group called the Public Committee Against Torture in Israel (PCATI) and Murad Adnan Salahat, a Palestinian who said he had been tortured under interrogation.[18]

As the respondent to the petition, the State requested and received time to form a ministerial committee that would review the GSS guidelines. On April 25, 1993, the State submitted to the Court an affidavit outlining GSS interrogation policies. Portions of the affidavit's non-classified sections support HRW's findings regarding shifts in interrogation policies. The affidavit provided the following information:

- In September 1990, a booklet entitled *The Procedure for Extraordinary Authorizations during Interrogation* was distributed to GSS interrogators.[19] This booklet updated a previous set of

---

[17] Remarks delivered at a conference titled, "The International Struggle against Torture and the Case of Israel," sponsored by the Association of Israeli-Palestinian Physicians for Human Rights and the Public Committee against Torture in Israel, Tel Aviv, June 14, 1993.

[18] High Court of Justice, case 2581/91.

[19] Section 8 of affidavit submitted by respondent in Supreme Court case 2581/91, signed by State Attorney Dorit Beinish and dated April 25, 1993.

Israel's Interrogation Practices

> guidelines distributed to GSS interrogators in August 1988, which were based on the secret portion of the Landau report.

- The government of Prime Minister Yitzhak Shamir had created an inter-ministerial committee to review the 1990 booklet. The committee's deliberations were interrupted by the June 1992 parliamentary elections that led to the formation of a new government headed by Yitzhak Rabin.[20]

- Under the new government, review of GSS interrogation guidelines was assigned to a new committee composed of Prime Minister Rabin, who held the defense portfolio, Justice Minister David Libai, and Police Minister Moshe Shahal. In September 1992, this committee authorized a subcommittee to pursue the review. The affidavit states:

  > After an in-depth and substantive debate which took place over a number of meetings, the subcommittee recommended that changes be introduced into the procedure of permissions for GSS interrogators. These recommendations were approved by the ministerial committee on April 22, 1993.[21]

  > The various committees all accepted the principle that extraordinary measures are sometimes necessary. The principles underlying the new procedures were already established in the Landau Commission, but were modified over time as a result of the experiences of the interrogators.[22]

---

[20] Ibid., section 12.

[21] Ibid., section 12.

[22] Ibid., section 14.

- The affidavit offered a rationale for the selective use of unspecified "exceptional measures":

  > It has been emphasized that the seriousness of the interrogation method used must be directly proportional to the nature of the suspicion against the detainee, and to the foundation of that suspicion in evidentiary material or intelligence information held by the interrogator.
  >
  > It has therefore been determined that in general, the greater [the interrogator's] suspicion of a more grievous offense, and the greater the basis for that suspicion based on information, then the stronger is the basis for suspecting that the person being interrogated is withholding dangerous information that is crucial to obtain; and therefore there is justification for using methods in the interrogation for obtaining the information.
  >
  > Therefore, it has been stated in the new procedure, that the methods detailed in the procedure may be used only against persons suspected of grave offenses. These offenses do not include offenses related to "disturbances of order."

The affidavit gave no hint of the nature of the "exceptional measures," other than enumerating some practices that they did *not* include. At no point were interrogators allowed to "starve" interrogation suspects, prevent them from drinking, "abandon" them to heat or cold, or prevent them from going to the toilet.[23] Beating was not listed among the measures deemed impermissible.

---

[23] Ibid., section 16. Also reported on Radio Israel in Hebrew, April 25, 1993, as reported in Foreign Broadcast Information Service, April 26, 1993; and Dalia Schori, "GSS Head to HCJ: New Interrogation Policy Implemented," *Haaretz*, April 27, 1993.

- Use of "exceptional measures" was restricted by the following conditions:

   They are permitted only in certain categories of interrogations;

   They can only be employed at certain stages of the interrogation;

   Only interrogators of a certain rank may authorize their use;

   The detainee's health must be taken into consideration; and

   The "absolute necessity" of their use must be weighed in each case.[24]

The substance of the permissible "exceptional measures" remains classified. But in researching this report, HRW found the following means of pressure to be *un*exceptional, in fact routine, in GSS interrogation wings: prolonged hooding, sleep deprivation, abusive body positioning, humiliation (including both verbal remarks and obliging detainees to eat their meals while using the toilet stalls), partial toilet deprivation (see Chapter Twelve), and subjection to intentionally distressing and constant noise. Confinement in closet-sized spaces and exposure to intentionally overcooled rooms were somewhat less common but hardly rare enough to be considered "exceptional." About half of the GSS detainees interviewed for this report said that interrogators had either severely beaten or violently shaken them.

Supreme Court Rejects Petition on Interrogation Guidelines

In July 1993, three months after the State had provided the Court with the GSS affidavit, Avigdor Feldman, the attorney for the petitioner, submitted further materials to the Court detailing abusive GSS techniques.

Feldman's submission described testimony by GSS interrogators at Muhammad Adawi's trial (see Chapters Thirteen and Eighteen), the "fitness-for-interrogation" form apparently in use at the Tulkarm interrogation wing (see Chapter Sixteen), and court testimony by Police Superintendent Nidam on conditions in the GSS interrogation wing at the Russian Compound police jail in Jerusalem. Nidam had recounted how

---

[24] Ibid., sections 15–17.

detainees were forced to stand for long periods, bound and hooded, and were placed in a very small and bad-smelling enclosed space. He said the GSS wing had a wall outfitted with hooks, to which detainees could be chained, either while standing or sitting.[25]

On August 12, 1993, the Supreme Court announced its rejection of the petition. The Court held that it could decide only concrete disputes with known facts. The three-judge panel stated that the GSS guidelines had the status of internal directives whose legality the Court could not rule on except in connection with a specific case. The Court said, however, that the directives "cannot be regarded as equal to the law...and they must be abolished if they contravene the law."[26]

The petitioners filed a formal request to the Court to reconsider its rejection of the case. The Court's decision was pending as this report went to press.

***

According to Attorney Feldman, GSS torture during interrogation has gone through a process of "bureaucratization":

> [Torture methods] are given nicknames which are usually used in legitimate methods of investigation, bureaucratic forms and documents are used, and there are regulations, there is oversight, there are authorizations....The bureaucratization of torture is based upon these memos, the office-style jargon, the hierarchies of authority....[They also] eliminate responsibility by individuals for the torture.[27]

---

[25] Jerusalem District Court, case 576/91, November 17, 1992 session.

[26] Cited in B'Tselem, *The "New Procedure" in GSS Interrogation: The Case of 'Abd a-Nasser 'Ubeid*, p. 8. See also Evelyn Gordon, "Petition Against GSS Rejected," *Jerusalem Post*, August 13, 1993.

[27] Avigdor Feldman, "Welcome to the Modern Inquisition," *Haaretz* weekend supplement, July 16, 1993.

The process of "bureaucratization" is characterized by several salient features:

- **Authorization and oversight:** Strict guidelines and an authorization process supposedly governs the employment of "exceptional" methods.

- **Euphemisms:** The GSS uses terms such as "waiting" when referring to their practice of hooding detainees, shackling them in painful positions, and denying them sleep. These euphemisms refer to methods that may have legitimate origins.[28]

- **A willingness to acknowledge some methods of coercion:** GSS agents testifying in court readily admit to hooding and shackling detainees in painful positions for prolonged periods.

- **Involvement of medical personnel in the process:** Doctors at Tulkarm prison were apparently asked to complete forms attesting to detainees' fitness for abusive interrogation methods.

ABUSES BY IDF INTERROGATORS: A NEGLECTED PROBLEM

Public debate and activism in Israel over interrogation methods has focused on the GSS, as did the Landau Commission. The relative neglect of IDF interrogation practices is a grave mistake. The army has conducted a significant percentage of the tens of thousands of interrogations that have taken place since the start of the intifada. As this report documents, a detainee is far more likely to be beaten severely if his interrogators are IDF personnel than if they are from the GSS.

HRW's findings from 1992-1994 suggest that the IDF may have standardized and restrained its interrogation methods compared to earlier

---

[28] The practice of hooding is a good example. In the past, Israeli courts authorized interrogators to hood detainees while they waited their turn outside interrogation rooms. Hooding was permitted in order to prevent suspects from identifying one another. But this is a far cry from the current practice of using hoods in ways that often serve no preventive purpose, but rather seem intended to exacerbate feelings of isolation, anxiety, and discomfort (see Chapter Twelve).

years. Of our nineteen IDF interrogation subjects, sixteen reported being beaten, thirteen of them on the testicles. Although beating is systematic, several ex-detainees said they sensed that blows were calculated to inflict pain without leaving long-lasting physical traces. None of the thirteen sustained broken bones. Prolonged position abuse is routine, although restricted to the daytime; at night, detainees are placed in cells.

The apparent trend toward standardization of IDF interrogation methods may stem partly from an investigation commissioned by the IDF Chief-of-Staff in 1991 in response to the publication of a report by B'Tselem charging that severe abuse was systematic.[29]

According to the IDF spokesman, the officer in charge of the inquiry, Major General (Reserve) Rafael Vardi, visited military detention centers and spoke with Palestinian complainants and IDF interrogators.[30] His final report was classified, but an IDF statement summarized portions of it. According to the statement, Vardi recommended that the IDF:

> refine and elucidate IDF orders which forbid any use of violence, and rule out even the possibility of [using] threats against residents of Judea, Samaria and the Gaza Strip, following their arrest, and during the course of their interrogation. The responsibility to uphold the orders must be required of commanders at all levels, and to this end, the report suggests that persons be named who are responsible for this matter in the General Staff and the [regional] Commands.[31]

In contrast to the GSS, the IDF has steadfastly denied that physical pressure is ever permissible under the agency's interrogation guidelines. For example, at an IDF press conference in Jerusalem on July 7, 1993, then-Deputy Judge Advocate-General Colonel David Yahav stated:

---

[29] B'Tselem, *The Interrogation of Palestinians during the Intifada.*

[30] IDF press release, August 13, 1991, See also B'Tselem, *The Interrogation of Palestinians during the Intifada, Follow-Up,* pp. 18-20.

[31] Ibid.

Israel's Interrogation Practices

> The GSS is authorized, in some instances, according to the regulations, to use moderate physical pressure. IDF interrogators do not have this authorization. IDF interrogation methods are identical to those used by Israel police within Israel.

The evidence collected in this report demonstrates that, whatever the regulations may be, beatings continue to be so commonplace in IDF interrogation wings that they could not take place without the knowledge and acquiescence of senior officers. This report also documents psychological and nonviolent physical abuses that are routine in IDF interrogation centers. We believe that these methods, as employed by the IDF, violate the prohibition in international law of torture and various forms of ill-treatment (see Chapter Five).

4
MONITORING ABUSE
THE INTERNATIONAL RED CROSS
AND HUMAN RIGHTS ORGANIZATIONS

This chapter describes some of the major reports and statements on Israeli interrogation methods that have been issued over the last several years by human rights and humanitarian organizations.

Many organizations not listed below have also documented abuses under interrogation, including the Gaza Centre for Rights and Law, the Association of Israeli-Palestinian Physicians for Human Rights, the Public Committee against Torture in Israel, and the Alternative Information Center.

INTERNATIONAL COMMITTEE OF THE RED CROSS (GENEVA)

The International Committee of the Red Cross (ICRC) has maintained a sizeable presence in the Israeli-occupied territories since 1967. The group's mandate is to ensure respect for the Fourth Geneva Convention, which governs the treatment of civilians living in areas under military occupation.

The ICRC's delegates, all of whom are Swiss nationals, regularly interview Palestinians undergoing interrogation. The Israeli government permits delegates to meet with detainees privately in visiting rooms after the first fourteen days of their detention. Delegates who are physicians are able to examine detainees there and communicate recommendations to the authorities.

Israeli authorities have touted the ICRC's regular access to detainees under interrogation as a safeguard against abuse. For example, in its submission to the U.N. Committee against Torture, the government stated, "All complaints made by the ICRC regarding treatment of prisoners are fully investigated by the relevant Israeli authorities and the findings are made known to the ICRC."[1]

But the value of ICRC access as a safeguard against abuse is limited by the fact that the ICRC, in keeping with its worldwide *modus operandi*, does not go public with what it sees. Instead, the ICRC reports confidentially to the responsible authorities, noting areas of concern, urging investigations, and making recommendations. While the ICRC can monitor interrogation conditions more closely than any human rights organization, it does not ordinarily inform the public of its findings or attempt to mobilize public opinion.

In May 1992, however, the ICRC broke its silence about Israeli interrogation practices. As a rule, agency officials say, the ICRC departs from its policy of confidentiality only when the violations it observes are systematic and grave, and when the conditions have failed to improve despite the ICRC's repeated and confidential contacts with the relevant authorities.

Calling for an end to "the ill-treatment inflicted during interrogation on detainees from the occupied territories," the ICRC statement declared:

> [T]he ICRC has for many years conducted interviews in private with detainees under interrogation. It has reached the conclusion that to obtain information and confessions from the detainees, means of physical and psychological pressure are being used that constitute a violation of the [Fourth Geneva] Convention....
>
> The ICRC deeply regrets that the numerous and detailed reports it has regularly submitted to the Israeli authorities...have been to no avail. It has in particular urged the authorities to prohibit all forms of ill-treatment, including insults and threats, to forbid interrogation by co-detainees and the exertion of pressure to induce detainees to collaborate, to improve the material conditions of

---

[1] Initial Report of Israel to the U.N. Committee against Torture, CAT/C/16/Add.4, February 4, 1994, paragraph 40.

detention and to limit to the strict minimum the time detainees have to spend in interrogation sections.[2]

B'TSELEM
THE ISRAELI INFORMATION CENTER FOR HUMAN RIGHTS IN THE OCCUPIED TERRITORIES (JERUSALEM)

In March 1991, B'Tselem published a 151-page report examining Israeli interrogation methods, based on forty-one interviews with Palestinians who were interrogated by the GSS or IDF between 1988 and 1990. B'Tselem found that, almost without exception, the victims were subjected to a combination of:

> verbal abuse, humiliation and threat of injury; sleep and food deprivation, hooding for prolonged periods; enforced standing for long periods, sometimes in an enclosed space, hands bound behind the back and legs tied ("al-Shabah"); being bound in other painful ways...; prolonged periods of painful confinement in small, specially constructed cells (the "closet" or "refrigerator") and severe and prolonged beating on all parts of the body....
>
> By formal criteria, at least, these methods, particularly when used together...fall under most accepted definitions of "torture." Even if we object to using this word, these methods are self evidently forms of ill-treatment, abuse, or "cruel and inhuman treatment."[3]

In March 1992, B'Tselem published an eighty-five page sequel to its 1991 study, based on interviews with twenty-five ex-detainees interrogated since the previous study, as well as other sources.[4] B'Tselem has since published case studies on the death under interrogation of

---

[2] ICRC press release no. 1717, May 21, 1992.

[3] B'Tselem, *The Interrogation of Palestinians during the Intifada*, pp. 106-107.

[4] B'Tselem, *The Interrogation of Palestinians during the Intifada: Follow-Up.*

Mustafa Barakat, and on a 1993 interrogation in the context of the GSS's revised interrogation guidelines.[5]

AL-HAQ (RAMALLAH, WEST BANK)

Al-Haq, the West Bank affiliate of the International Commission of Jurists, has regularly documented Israeli torture in the occupied territories since the start of the intifada in 1987. It also issued a report in 1984 on torture at al-Far'a military detention center.[6]

In its 1989 annual report, al-Haq stated that during the first year of the uprising (1988), the authorities frequently used violence as an end in and of itself against detainees, and less as a method of extracting information. In the second year of the uprising, however, al-Haq hypothesized:

> It seems that the reconstruction and improvement of intelligence became a prerequisite, and the extraction of information from detainees a priority....The increased use of torture during the second year of the uprising would appear to indicate a change in official assessments of the uprising and of the role of interrogation and detention in suppressing it....[7]

The report then proceeded to detail Israeli torture methods, which included beating, hooding, prolonged abusive body positioning, food deprivation, hygienic deprivation, prolonged isolation, sleep deprivation, restriction of toilet facilities, space deprivation, partial suffocation,

---

[5] B'Tselem, *The Death of Mustafa Barakat in the Interrogation Wing of the Tulkarm Prison* (B'Tselem: Jerusalem, September 1992); and B'Tselem, *The New Procedure in GSS Interrogation: The Case of 'Abd a-Nasser 'Ubeid*.

[6] International Commission of Jurists and al-Haq/Law in the Service of Man, *Torture and Intimidation in the West Bank: The Case of al-Fara'a Prison* (Ramallah: Al-Haq, 1984).

[7] *A Nation Under Siege*, pp. 172-173.

subjection to threats against self and family, *falaqa* (beating applied to the soles of the feet with a stick or length of hose).[8]

In 1993, al-Haq published a booklet containing thirteen affidavits about torture and ill-treatment under interrogation.[9] These affidavits are part of an ambitious data-collection project focussing on detention experiences. It includes 474 interviews conducted in 1991 with former detainees, all of whom were detained since November 1987. Al-Haq presented some of its findings at the World Conference on Human Rights in Vienna in 1993. It stated that 85 percent of the 474 ex-detainees said they had been tortured or ill-treated during their detention. Of the 474, the organization said, 274 underwent interrogation by the GSS, the IDF, or the police. Of the 274 interrogation subjects:

98.7 percent were subjected to beating;

91.5 percent were subjected to position abuse;

44 percent were subjected to suffocation through closing the mouth and nose with a hood or hand;

6.8 percent were subjected to electric shock;

Al-Haq's survey also found that detainees were subjected, with varying frequency, to: food and/or sleep deprivation, restriction on the use of toilet facilities, pulling out of body hair, exposure to extremes of temperature, confinement in a cell too small to sit or lie in, and verbal threats, including threatened harm to the interrogation subject or to his or her family.[10]

---

[8] Ibid., pp. 173–179.

[9] *Al-Haq, Palestinian Victims of Torture Speak Out* (Ramallah: Al-Haq, 1993).

[10] Al-Haq, "Human Rights in the Occupied Palestinian Territories — Torture," information sheet distributed at the World Conference on Human Rights in Vienna, June 1993.

THE PALESTINE HUMAN RIGHTS INFORMATION CENTER (JERUSALEM)

The Palestine Human Rights Information Center (PHRIC) publishes monthly updates on human rights conditions in the occupied territories, which frequently include reports of torture and ill-treatment of Palestinian detainees by Israeli interrogators. PHRIC, like al-Haq, operates a large network of fieldworkers based in Palestinian communities.

In 1991, PHRIC published a report documenting eight allegations of electric shock torture at the Hebron military headquarters. All of the victims were young males suspected of relatively minor offenses.[11]

AMNESTY INTERNATIONAL (LONDON)

Amnesty International has issued numerous press releases and short reports regarding the torture and ill-treatment of Palestinians by the Israeli security forces. Its most detailed study of interrogations and military trials in the occupied territories stated:

> Amnesty International believes that the substantial evidence available indicates the existence of a clear pattern of systematic psychological and physical ill-treatment, constituting torture or other forms of cruel, inhuman or degrading treatment, which is being inflicted on detainees during the course of interrogation.
>
> Methods used on a systematic scale include hooding...sleep and food deprivation while held in solitary confinement...prolonged bondage in plastic or metal handcuffs, usually in painful positions...and being confined in very small and darkened cells...as well as in small cold cells called "refrigerators." Beatings all over the body, often severe...are also inflicted with relative frequency. Other methods include burning with cigarettes; prolonged

---

[11] Palestine Human Rights Information Center, *Israel's Use of Electric Shock Torture in the Interrogation of Palestinian Detainees* (Jerusalem: Palestine Human Rights Information Center, December 1991). See Chapter Seventeen of this report.

denial of access to toilets; verbal abuse and threats of various kinds; and forms of sexual harassment, particularly with regard to women.[12]

---

[12] Amnesty International, *The Military Justice System in the Occupied Territories* (London: Amnesty International, July 1991), p. 58.

5
THE LEGAL FRAMEWORK

This report concludes that the methods used by Israeli interrogators in the occupied territories amount to a pattern of torture, as the term is defined in international law. This conclusion is based on an evaluation of the extent to which the methods are used in combination with one another, and of the lengths of time during which detainees are subjected to them. While not every Palestinian security detainee under interrogation experiences mistreatment amounting to torture, it is clear that thousands of Palestinians have been tortured since the intifada began in late 1987.

TORTURE IN INTERNATIONAL LAW

The international community has demonstrated its commitment to an international legal standard prohibiting torture and cruel, inhuman or degrading treatment or punishment. A large body of international legal authority has evolved that unequivocally forbids the use of torture and other ill-treatment both during times of peace and of armed conflict. Thus, the prohibition of torture and other ill-treatment has come to be considered a principle of customary international law, to which all nations are bound under all circumstances.[1]

---

[1] The authoritative statement of U.S. law with regard to international law affirms that a state violates customary international law if:

> as a matter of state policy, it practices, encourages, or condones...torture or other cruel, inhuman, or degrading treatment or punishment....
>
> A government may be presumed to have encouraged or condoned acts prohibited by this section if such acts, especially by its officials, have been repeated or notorious and no steps have been taken to prevent them or to punish the perpetrators.

The American Law Institute, *Restatement of the Law: The Foreign Relations Law of the United States*, II § 702, May 14, 1986 (St. Paul: American Law Institute Publishers,

The prohibition is embodied in the United Nations Universal Declaration of Human Rights, which states in Article 5: "No one shall be subjected to torture or to cruel, inhuman or degrading treatment or punishment." That right is reaffirmed verbatim in Article 7 of the International Covenant on Civil and Political Rights (ICCPR). Pursuant to Article 4(2) of the ICCPR, a state party may not take measures derogating from its obligations under Article 7, even "[i]n time of public emergency which threatens the life of the nation."

In addition, provisions of humanitarian law treaties, such as Common Article 3 of the 1949 Geneva Conventions, prohibit the subjection of protected persons to, *inter alia*, "cruel treatment and torture," both in the context of international and non-international armed conflict. Torture is considered a "grave breach" of the Fourth Convention (Article 147).

Israel ratified the Geneva Conventions in 1951 but, in defiance of virtually the entire international community,[2] disputes the *de jure* applicability of the Fourth Geneva Convention to the occupied West Bank and Gaza Strip.[3] However, it has pledged to abide de facto by what it terms the Convention's "humanitarian provisions."[4] Although Israel has not specified which provisions it considers "humanitarian," no reasonable interpretation of the phrase could be put forward that omitted the Convention's unqualified ban of "cruel treatment and torture."

Treaties and declarations developed during the last two decades have helped to advance an internationally recognized definition of a

---

1987).

[2] In a 1981 resolution (No. 35/122A) specifically on the applicability of the Convention to the Israeli-occupied territories, the U. N. General Assembly voted 141 in favor to one (Israel) against, with one abstention (Guatemala). The United States has consistently maintained that the Fourth Geneva Convention applies *de jure* to the occupied territories (see, e.g., the Department of State, *Country Reports on Human Rights Practices for 1993* (Washington: Government Printing Office, 1994), p. 1202.

[3] For a recent statement of Israel's position, see Military Advocate-General's Unit, Israel Defense Forces, *Israel, the "Intifada" and the Rule of Law* (Tel Aviv: Israel Ministry of Defense Publications, 1993), pp. 21-23.

[4] See e.g., ibid., pp. 22-23.

The Legal Framework

torture, while continuing to prohibit *both* torture *and* cruel, inhuman or degrading treatment. The Declaration on the Protection of All Persons from Being Subjected to Torture and Other Cruel, Inhuman or Degrading Treatment or Punishment, adopted by the U.N. on December 9, 1975 (hereinafter the Declaration on Torture), stated in Article 2 that "[T]orture constitutes an *aggravated and deliberate* form of cruel, inhuman or degrading treatment or punishment," (emphasis added) while stressing in Article 3 that no state may permit or tolerate any of the above under any circumstances.

The 1984 U.N. Convention against Torture and Other Cruel, Inhuman or Degrading Treatment or Punishment (hereinafter the Convention against Torture) defines torture in Article 1 as:

> any act by which severe pain or suffering, whether physical or mental, is intentionally inflicted on a person for such purposes as obtaining from him or a third person information or a confession, punishing him for an act he or a third person has committed or is suspected of having committed, or intimidating or coercing him or a third person, or for any reason based on discrimination of any kind, when such pain or suffering is inflicted by or at the instigation of or with the consent or acquiescence of a public official or other person acting in an official capacity. It does not include pain or suffering arising only from, inherent in or incidental to lawful sanctions.[5]

Israel ratified both the ICCPR and the Convention against Torture in 1991. The government has stated that ratification did not apply to the occupied territories, on the grounds that this would contradict the government's official position that the political status of the territories remains to be determined.[6] But no official Israeli source has ever

---

[5] Such sanctions, the Declaration on Torture affirms (Article 1), must be consistent with the Standard Minimum Rules for the Treatment of Prisoners.

[6] Letter from Robi Sabel, legal advisor to the Ministry of Foreign Affairs, to B'Tselem, February 9, 1991. Israel's Supreme Court has not ruled on this question. Some jurists argue that by ratifying the ICCPR, the Convention against Torture and other human rights conventions, Israel has committed itself to

questioned the applicability of the ban against torture, nor has Israel imposed any change in local (Jordanian) law that would allow torture.

Regardless of any legal disputes regarding these treaties' applicability to the occupied territories, Israel is bound by those provisions that are considered customary international law, including the prohibition on torture and other forms of ill-treatment. The Supreme Court has held that customary law, defined as "[g]eneral practice [of states], which means a fixed mode of action, general and persisting...which has been accepted by the vast majority of those who function in the said area of law," is considered part of the domestic law, and binding unless overpowered by a statute.

The Landau Commission tacitly acknowledged the customary status of the prohibition on torture and other forms of ill-treatment. Its report, which was approved by the cabinet before Israel had ratified the ICCPR and Convention against Torture, stated that the Commission's recommendations were formulated "with the aim of abiding by the general prohibitions [that international conventions] posit" with respect to "torture or to cruel, inhuman or degrading treatment or punishment."[7]

Human rights instruments stress the need for effective means to prevent and to provide remedies for acts of torture. The Convention against Torture requires in Article 2 that "Each State Party shall take effective legislative, administrative, judicial or other measures to prevent acts of torture in any territory under its jurisdiction." The Convention also obliges states parties to review interrogation rules and practices to prevent torture (Article 10), to investigate impartially allegations of torture (Article 11), and to ensure that any statement found to have been obtained through torture shall not be used as evidence in judicial proceedings, except against the person accused of torture (Article 15).

The Fourth Geneva Convention also requires states to act forcefully to prevent acts of torture. Article 146 calls on High Contracting Parties to search for and bring to trial all persons alleged to have committed, or to have ordered to be committed, grave breaches of the Convention, including acts of torture or inhuman treatment.

---

implement them in the occupied territories. See, e.g., Eyal Benvenisti, "The Applicability of Human Rights Conventions to Israel and the Occupied Territories," *Israel Law Review* 26 (1992), pp. 24-35.

[7] Paragraph 3.21.

RECOGNIZING AND DEFINING TORTURE
PSYCHOLOGICAL VERSUS PHYSICAL METHODS

The Convention against Torture explicitly includes mental suffering in its definition of torture, but, like other international instruments, does little to resolve the difficulty in classifying specific methods as torture. The Convention refers to the severity of the pain or suffering inflicted as the criterion that distinguishes torture from other ill-treatment.

While some acts would be universally deemed torture, other, less brutally violent abuses are not so easily classified under international legal definitions of the concept. This is particularly true of psychological and non-impact methods, such as prolonged position abuse or sleep deprivation — the kinds of mistreatment that are among the most prevalent in Israeli interrogation centers. Whether these methods inflict the "severe pain or suffering" specified in the Convention against Torture's definition of torture would depend very much on such factors as how long they are inflicted, whether they are inflicted simultaneously with other methods, and the health of the victim.

The International Committee of the Red Cross usually avoids the term "torture" when referring to abuses against detainees they monitor. The reason given is that it is often impossible to establish the point at which ill-treatment becomes torture. Such a distinction, moreover, is immaterial in international law, since all of the key instruments unconditionally prohibit both.

Interrogators around the world share the goal of overcoming a detainee's resistance to providing information. Israeli interrogators, like many of their counterparts worldwide, employ both psychological and physical techniques, usually in combination with one another. Attempts to distinguish between the two is somewhat artificial, as the U.N. Special Rapporteur on Torture has stated:

> There are two main types of torture: physical and psychological or mental. In physical torture, pain is inflicted directly on the body; in the psychological or mental torture the aim is to injure the psyche. The two

types are interrelated and ultimately, both have physical and psychological effects.[8]

As experts have pointed out, the psychological context in which physical pain occurs can have far-reaching consequences on the way in which the victim experiences suffering or pain. Verbal threats or menacing, disorienting or psychologically debilitating environments can exacerbate the pain induced by "physical" mistreatment.[9]

"LOW-VISIBILITY TORTURE"

Less violent methods tend to leave less compelling physical evidence of abuse. This frustrates attempts at medical documentation, making it more difficult for victims to prove the abuse, to cast doubt on the reliability of the confession, and to contribute to the prosecution of the abusers.

The "severe pain or suffering" that psychological or non-impact physical methods cause may be harder to appreciate, when no single act or implement can be identified as the source of the severe pain, and there are no obvious physical scars or injuries.

It is difficult, for example, for an outsider to comprehend the debilitating effects of such methods as prolonged sleep deprivation, hooding, subjection to relentless loud noise, abusive body positioning or confinement in a closet-like cell. These methods are not as viscerally terrifying as a knife or a club. Yet such methods, if used in combination and unrelentingly over a certain period, can easily amount to a kind of "low-visibility torture" that both causes severe suffering and effectively compels most detainees to provide information or sign a statement.

---

[8] Question of the Human Rights of All Persons Subjected to Any Form of Detention or Imprisonment — Torture and Other Cruel, Inhuman or Degrading Treatment or Punishment — Report of the Special Rapporteur, Mr. P. Koojmans.

[9] See, for example, Ronald Melzack and Patrick D. Wall, *The Challenge of Pain* (New York: Basic Books, 1983), which argues on p. 37 that a state of anxiety can significantly enhance the level of pain experienced in a patient or victim.

The Legal Framework

Northern Ireland and the "Five Techniques"

The difficulty of evaluating and documenting the severity of suffering caused by nonviolent measures was highlighted by the case of British interrogation methods in Northern Ireland. These methods are of interest also because of the scrutiny they received from the European Commission of Human Rights and the European Court of Human Rights. These two bodies attempted to determine whether the methods in question constituted torture. Their conclusions were cited at length by the Landau Commission as part of the legal background for its recommended interrogation guidelines, and are worth recounting here.

In 1971, in response to communal violence and attacks on British troops and installations, the British army rounded up large numbers of suspected Irish Republican Army activists, fourteen of whom were sent for "interrogation in depth" and subjected to a combination of abuses since known as the "five techniques."

The five techniques, according to the European Court of Human Rights, consisted of:

> "(a) **wall-standing:** forcing the detainees to remain for periods of some hours in a 'stress position,' described...as being 'spread-eagled against the wall, with their fingers put high above the head against the wall, the legs spread apart and the feet back, causing them to stand on their toes with the weight of the body mainly on the fingers';
>
> (b) **hooding:** putting a black or navy coloured bag over the detainees' heads and, at least initially, keeping it there all the time except during interrogations;
>
> (c) **subjection to noise:** pending their interrogations, holding the detainees in a room where there was a continuous loud and hissing noise;
>
> (d) **deprivation of sleep:** pending their interrogations, depriving detainees of sleep;

(e) **deprivation of food and drink:** subjecting the detainees to a reduced diet during their stay at the centre and pending interrogations."[10]

All fourteen victims were subjected to these techniques for seven days, during which time they were interrogated in an unidentified military or police center. The Court found it impossible to determine the exact number of hours during which each detainee had been subjected to the five techniques, but it noted:

- detainees were forced to stand against the wall for periods of up to twenty-three and twenty-nine hours at a time;

- hooding took place "all the time," except during interrogations;

- the noise was "continuous"; and

- sleep deprivation occurred "pending their interrogations," but its duration could not be determined.

These non-impact techniques had been unanimously defined earlier by the European Commission of Human Rights as "torture," provided they were used cumulatively.[11] However, when the case was brought before the European Court of Human Rights, the majority of judges ruled that the five methods constituted "inhuman and degrading treatment," but not "torture." The Court held:

> The five techniques were applied in combination, with premeditation and for hours at a stretch; they caused, if not actual bodily injury, at least intense physical and mental suffering to the persons subjected thereto and also led to acute psychiatric disturbances during interrogation.

---

[10] *Ireland v. U.K.*, European Court of Human Rights, 1978, paragraph 96.

[11] European Commission of Human Rights, *Application No. 5310/71, Ireland against The United Kingdom of Great Britain and Northern Ireland, Report of the Commission,* January 25, 1976 ("Survey of the Commission's Opinion with Conclusions," part II.B), p. 490.

> They accordingly fell into the category of inhuman treatment....The techniques were also degrading since they were such as to arouse in their victims feelings of fear, anguish and inferiority capable of humiliating and debasing them and possibly breaking their physical or moral resistance....
>
> Although the five techniques, as applied in combination, undoubtedly amounted to inhuman and degrading treatment... they did not occasion suffering of the particular intensity and cruelty implied by the word torture as so understood.[12]

Even though the Court refrained from labelling the five techniques "torture," it condemned them as a violation of Article 3 of the European Convention on Human Rights. Article 3, like all international legal instruments barring torture, also prohibits inhuman and degrading treatment. The British government, for its part, voluntarily discontinued use of the five techniques well before either the Commission or the Court reviewed the issue, in the wake of its own commission of inquiry into interrogation practices in Northern Ireland.

The Court's ruling that the five techniques did not constitute torture was criticized by a variety of experts. Some of the judges who dissented from the majority opinion noted that the Court had focused in their deliberations on physical methods and physical pain, whereas the internationally accepted definition of torture includes mental suffering. Amnesty International criticized the Court's ruling, declaring that it considers "any technique that causes 'intense physical and mental suffering'

---

[12] *Ireland v. U.K.*, paragraph 168. The government of Israel, in its recent submission to the U.N. Committee against Torture, completely misinterpreted the ruling by claiming that the European Court, in declining to characterize them as torture, had "sanctioned the use of certain forms of pressure in the interrogation process, such as hooding (except during the actual questioning), sleep deprivation and reduction of food and drink supply." (Initial Report of Israel to the U.N. Committee against Torture, CAT/C/16/Add.4, February 4, 1994, paragraph 34.) The Court clearly condemned these methods, as employed in the case under review, as contravening the Convention against Torture's prohibition on inhuman and degrading treatment.

leading to 'acute psychiatric disturbances during interrogation' to constitute torture, wherever they [sic] are applied."[13]

In determining the significance of the Northern Ireland case for the analysis of Israeli interrogation methods, several factors need to be considered. First, as stated above, both torture and other forms of ill-treatment are unequivocally prohibited by international law. Second, the European Court of Human Rights is a regional body. Its reasoning and decisions are of interest for general interpretative purposes, but are binding only on states party to the European Convention. Even in the European context, the precedential value of this particular case, whose holding has been vigorously contested, remains to be seen.

Most importantly, as the Court itself stated, the determination of the degree of ill-treatment that will be considered torture depends "on all the circumstances of the case, such as the duration of the treatment, the physical health of the victim, etc...."[14] Thus, an action is considered "torture" on the basis of the facts of that specific case and the intensity of suffering brought about in the victims, and not on the basis of a generic formula.

The Landau Commission characterized Great Britain and Israel as liberal democracies faced with significant terrorist threats, which require government agents to use interrogation techniques that are morally or legally problematic.[15] The Commission noted approvingly the ruling of the European Court of Human Rights that the five techniques did not constitute torture, and then went on to claim that the classified interrogation guidelines it was recommending were "less severe" than those used by British interrogators in Northern Ireland.[16]

HRW, in this report, argues that the actual practice of IDF and GSS interrogators cannot easily be characterized as "less severe" than Great Britain's five techniques, as they were presented to the European Commission and Court of Human Rights.

---

[13] Amnesty International, *The Military Justice System in the Occupied Territories* (London: Amnesty International, July 1991), p. 64.

[14] (1978) 2 E.H.R.R. 25, p. 79 (Judgment, paragraph 162).

[15] Paragraphs 3.22-3.29

[16] Paragraph 4.13.

First, GSS interrogators currently practice some version of at least four of the five techniques: they hood detainees, deprive them of sleep, force them into abusive body positions, and subject them to loud and intentionally distressing noise. HRW did not find that GSS agents currently engage in a pattern of food or drink deprivation. However, the position abuse they practice is intensified by the use of implements such as tiny chairs and tight handcuffs. They also routinely combine these methods with other forms of abuse, such as toilet deprivation, confining detainees in closet-like cells, and exposing them to temperature extremes for hours at a time. Moreover, the GSS consistently threatens interrogation subjects, and also beats or violently shakes some of them.

With regard to the techniques used in *both* places, duration is key, since their effects are, above all, cumulative. Thus, the longer victims are subjected to these methods, the more abusive they become. The fourteen Irish detainees whose cases were scrutinized had been detained for seven days each. The average length of time that Palestinians are subjected to GSS interrogation methods is considerably longer.

The pattern of GSS abuse continues to the present day in the Israeli-occupied territories. In contrast, Great Britain abandoned its use of the five techniques even before the European Commission of Human Rights ruled that they constituted torture, and did not revive them after the European Court classified them as inhuman and degrading treatment rather than torture.

TORTURE AND MISTREATMENT IN ISRAELI LAW

The government of Israel claims that "While Israeli legislation does not specifically define torture, statutory provisions clearly cover all acts of torture as found in the definition in Article 1 of the Convention [against Torture]."[17] Offenders are subject to prosecution, and possible imprisonment, whether their actions take place inside Israel or in the occupied territories.

Israeli legislation is weaker with regard to ill-treatment than torture. There are no statutes that clearly cover nonviolent physical abuse (such as shackling of detainees in contorted positions, painfully binding

---

[17] Initial Report of Israel to the U.N. Committee against Torture, CAT/C/16/Add.4, February 4, 1994, paragraph 6.

hands) and psychological abuse other than threats (such as sleep deprivation, nonstop exposure to distressing noise). The absence of clear legal prohibitions, combined with the relatively permissive approach of Israeli courts toward the admissibility of confessions obtained under some measure of duress,[18] contributes to a legal environment in which these forms of abuse have become institutionalized.

Since Israel ratified the Convention against Torture in 1991, some rights advocates have lobbied the government to pass legislation that would incorporate it into domestic law. (Under current Israeli practice, international treaties require such enabling legislation—except where they express tenets of customary law — before they become part of Israeli law and can be directly invoked before the courts.[19]) But in June 1993 the cabinet sent proposed enabling legislation to the Justice Ministry for study,[20] and it has remained there since.

Existing Israeli civil and military law is uneven in its firmness toward state agents who abuse persons in custody. The law explicitly criminalizes threatening or deceiving a suspect, and using force against a suspect who is neither resisting physically nor attempting to escape. While these legal prohibitions may be binding on the IDF, it is not clear that they are binding on the GSS. Since late 1987, GSS interrogators have been authorized to use "nonviolent psychological pressure via a vigorous and lengthy interrogation," "acts of deception," and a "moderate measure of physical force" on detainees.[21] Exactly what these methods entail is not publicly known, since they are classified. However, the Landau Commission, by justifying the classified methods with reference to the

---

[18] "Israeli laws of admissibility are more permissive than those of countries like the United States or Great Britain." B'Tselem, *The Interrogation of Palestinians during the Intifada*, p. 18.

[19] Initial Report of Israel to the U.N. Committee against Torture, CAT/C/16/Add.4, February 4, 1994, paragraph 4.

[20] The Ministerial Law Committee of the Cabinet referred the proposed legislation to a committee headed by the Attorney General, according to an Israel Radio report of June 15, 1993. As reported by Foreign Broadcast Information Service, June 15, 1993.

[21] Landau report, paragraph 4.7.

necessity defense in Israeli law,[22] strongly implied that these were methods that might in other circumstances constitute criminal offenses.

The strongest prohibition in Israeli law against the use of physical force and threats is contained in Article 277 of the Penal Code, which provides:

> A public servant who does one of the following is liable to imprisonment for three years: (1) uses or directs the use of force or violence against a person for the purpose of extorting from him or from anyone in whom he is interested a confession of an offense or information relating to an offense; (2) threatens any person, or directs any person to be threatened, with injury to his person or property or to the person or property of anyone in whom he is interested for the purpose of extorting from him a confession of an offense or any information relating to an offense.

---

[22] The relevant article provides:

> A person shall not bear criminal responsibility for an act or an omission if he acted in the way that he did against an assailant in order to ward off an unlawful assault, which placed his own or another's life, liberty, person or property in danger of harm....
>
> [The act or omission in question must be] immediately necessary in order to prevent the danger of grievous harm to his or another's life, liberty, person or property, stemming from a given situation, provided he had no other way to prevent it and that the harm he caused was not disproportionate to the harm he wished to prevent.

Article 22 of the Penal Code, Amendment No. 37, 1992. For an analysis of the amended statute, see B'Tselem, *Activity of the Undercover Units in the Occupied Territories* (Jerusalem: B'Tselem, May 1992), pp. 23-25. For a critique of the necessity defense as a long-term basis for employing otherwise illegal interrogation methods, see Alan M. Dershowitz, "Is it Necessary To Apply 'Physical Pressure' to Terrorists — and To Lie about It?" *Israel Law Review* 23 (1989), pp. 192-200.

Both state employees and soldiers are included in the definition of "public servant," according to Article 2 of the Penal Code. Thus, it is applicable both to IDF and GSS interrogators. Moreover, as regards the IDF, Article 65 of the 1955 Military Justice Law (5715-1955) provides for up to three years' imprisonment for "[a] soldier who strikes or otherwise maltreats a person committed to his custody."

Also relevant are the articles of the Penal Code that address physical assaults (378 to 382),[23] and provide for punishments of up to three years' imprisonment if actual bodily harm is caused. Other sections of the Penal Code provide more severe penalties for assaults that cause injury, ranging from twenty years for intentionally causing serious injury (Article 329), seven years for serious injury without special intent, or fourteen years where committed by two or more assailants or with a weapon, and six years for minor injury committed by two or more assailants, or with a weapon (Articles 333-335).

The Penal Code also prohibits "blackmail by use of threats" (Article 428) and "blackmail by use of force" (Article 427). Under both articles, the maximum penalty is nine years imprisonment if the threat or force leads the person being blackmailed to commit the omission or the act, or seven years if it does not lead to the person committing the act.

The Penal Code contains no explicit prohibition of psychological abuse or nonviolent physical abuse. However, Article 322 states that a person in charge of another's well-being, due, *inter alia*, to the person's imprisonment or custody, must provide for that person's basic sustenance and health needs, and will be liable for the consequences to that person's life or health if the person does not fulfill that obligation. A ruling of Israel's High Court of Justice stated that responsibility for a prisoner's well-being rests "on all public authorities vested with this responsibility, and if they receive information regarding a risk which is likely to be realized, they

---

[23] Article 378 defines simple assault as "hitting a person, touching, pushing or applying force to his body by any other means, directly or indirectly...including applying heat, light, electricity, gas, smell or any other thing or substance, if applied to a degree which could cause damage or discomfort," all of this without consent.

are obliged to consider, in light of the available measures, what is necessary in order protect whomever requires protection."[24]

Article 322 may provide a vehicle for holding interrogators accountable for psychological and nonviolent physical abuse. It also seems to be a potential means of prosecuting physicians and paramedics who fail to order a halt to the interrogation of a detainee who shows possible signs of abuse or health problems (see Chapter Sixteen).

Regarding IDF interrogations, a wide range of abuses might arguably be covered by the general prohibition in Article 65 of the Military Justice Law against "maltreating" a person in custody, although HRW is not aware of any ruling or official clarification regarding whether any of the practices we found to be commonplace constitute "maltreatment" in terms of the statute. As amended in 1993, Article 65 provides that if the abuse was committed in "aggravating circumstances," the maximum penalty is seven years imprisonment.

Challenges by defendants to the voluntariness of their own confessions provide, at least in theory, another legal weapon against psychological and nonviolent physical abuses by interrogators. Israel's Evidence Ordinance (New Version 5731-1971, in Section 12) states that a defendant's confession is admissible only "when the prosecution has produced evidence as to the circumstances in which it was made and the court is satisfied that it was free and voluntary." However, precedents set by Israeli courts suggest that confessions obtained by means of pressure would not be ruled out automatically, provided that "extreme means" had not been used that contradict basic values or are degrading.[25]

Military courts in the occupied territories have heard admissions by GSS agents that defendants were subjected to prolonged shackling, hooding and sleep deprivation, without the courts disqualifying the defendants' confessions as having been coerced. For this and other reasons that are laid out in Chapter Eighteen, the option of challenging in court the voluntariness of a confession is of limited value as a safeguard against abuse.

---

[24] HCJ 324/86, *Hamed N. v. Commander of IDF Forces in the Judea and Samaria area et al.*, Piskei Din 40(3) 361.

[25] See B'Tselem, *The Interrogation of Palestinians during the Intifada*, pp. 17-18.

6
THE ARREST EXPERIENCE

Any Israeli soldier or policeman is authorized to arrest, without a warrant, a Palestinian for whom "there is reason to suspect" that he has committed a security offense. Arrested persons are to be taken to an official place of custody, where they can be held for up to ninety-six hours without a warrant. After that period, continued detention is allowed only on the orders of an officer or a military court. Suspects can be held for up to eight or eighteen days, depending on the case, before they must be brought before a judge or released.[1]

The traumatic nature of the interrogation experience begins with the arrest itself. About two-thirds of the persons interviewed for this report were arrested from their homes between 11 P.M. and 3 A.M. In virtually all of these cases, the arrest was carried out by a contingent of between ten and fifty soldiers or Border Police,[2] accompanied by two or more plainclothes agents. The plainclothesmen were often recognized by the arrested persons as local GSS operatives.

When the arrest was made at home, it was often carried out in a disruptive manner, regardless of the behavior of the household, the age of the suspect or the eventual accusations against him. In some cases soldiers broke open the front door before giving the family a chance to open it, shoved people to and fro, and searched the house in a violent and destructive way. Furniture was overturned or otherwise damaged, drawers were spilled onto the floor, and objects were knocked over and broken. Some detainees reported that male family members were forced to stand for long periods of time with their faces to the wall and with their hands on their heads while soldiers conducted the search. The arrested person was usually prevented from speaking with family members before being escorted away.

---

[1] Military Order 378 for the West Bank, Article 78. See also Chapter Eight of this report.

[2] The Border Police is a paramilitary force attached to the Israeli police. When operating in the occupied territories, Border Police units are under the direct authority of the regional IDF commander.

FAILURE TO INFORM

The International Covenant on Civil and Political Rights states in Article 9(2), "Anyone who is arrested shall be informed, at the time of arrest, of the reasons for his arrest and shall be promptly informed of any charges against him." There is no requirement in Israeli military legislation that authorities inform suspects at the time of arrest why they are being taken into custody. A senior officer in the Judge Advocate-General's Corps acknowledged to HRW that:

> As in Israel, it is the right thing to do, but it's complicated to implement it, owing partly to the language problem. But, as soon as possible after the arrest, the suspect should be informed. It's a basic thing: the suspect should be informed of the reasons for arrest.[3]

All of the ex-detainees we interviewed stated that the arresting authorities had not informed them why they were being arrested, where they were being taken, which agency would have custody over them, or what rights they had under the circumstances. Some ex-detainees said they feared at the time of their arrest that they were being deported to Lebanon. At most, suspects were told that were being taken away "just to answer a few questions," although most did not return for three weeks or longer.

BEATING AND ILL-TREATMENT EN ROUTE TO INTERROGATION FACILITIES

One-third of the ex-detainees we interviewed said they were beaten by soldiers en route to the place of detention. A larger subset reported being verbally insulted and humiliated, or jabbed with rifle butts by the soldiers or policemen in charge of them. The abuse occurred either in the transport vehicle or at a holding facility to which the detainees were first brought.

---

[3] The officer, meeting in an official capacity with HRW, spoke on condition that his name not be used. The interview took place in Tel Aviv on November 18, 1993.

After their arrest, most detainees were taken in military or Border Police jeeps to rooms or tents at local police stations or at military compounds. In the vehicle, they were handcuffed but not always blindfolded. Detainees remained at the holding facilities for periods ranging from a few hours to several days. During that time they were either questioned briefly or not at all. They were then transported by military vehicles to GSS or IDF interrogation centers.

In Vehicles

M. N., arrested October 6, 1993 at his home in Jabalya refugee camp, described what happened when he was placed in a jeep:

> My hands were handcuffed behind my back. There was one other detainee in the jeep. They drove us to Beit Hanoun to arrest another person, and then to the military compound in Jabalya camp. Along the way, I asked the soldiers why they were arresting me. They replied to me, "Only you know." They hit me on my head and neck with their hands and their helmets, some hard, others not.

Khaled Suleiman Muhammad Salah, aged seventeen, was arrested on July 7, 1992 from his home in the village of al-Khader near Bethlehem. He and three other youths were taken to the Bethlehem military headquarters, where they were interrogated by the police (see Chapter Seventeen).

> "Captain Nissan" and "Captain Shai" came with soldiers, at about eleven at night. They started breaking the closets, the windows, the doors. The children were crying and screaming; they were very frightened. The soldiers blindfolded me and tied my hands behind my back.

> They put me in the jeep, and once I was in the jeep, they started to hit me. They lay me down on my stomach and began to step on me with their boots. They also hit me with their fists and with clubs. I don't know how many were in the jeep. They kept hitting me throughout the ride, on the sides of my legs, in between my legs, on my arms, and on my head and shoulders.

The Arrest Experience

When detainees are transported in buses between facilities, they are sometimes made to sit, handcuffed, on the buses for a far longer than the travel time itself. Ali A., twenty-five, was arrested at approximately 11:30 P.M. from his home in Ramallah on December 14, 1992. After being held at Ramallah's Civil Administration headquarters for two days, he was transferred to al-Far'a by bus.

> We were put on an Egged bus.[4] We spent the night on the bus. There were about seventy of us on board. Our hands were tied, very tightly, but we were not blindfolded.

> We sat there until 2:00 the following afternoon. They wouldn't let us go to the toilet, or have any food. If you wanted to defecate, you did it on the bus. A lot of us did that.

In Holding Facilities

The most common locations for pre-interrogation abuse of detainees were the holding facilities. A. abu M., twenty-three years old, was arrested at his home in al-Bureij refugee camp in Gaza on October 19, 1993 and taken to the police station near the camp. He told HRW:

> They made us sit outside the station for about an hour. We still had handcuffs and blindfolds on. Then they brought us into a room, where policemen, in uniforms, removed our blindfolds. They said nothing to us. Then, for the next fifteen minutes, they hit us. One of them punched me with his fists, hard, in my stomach. I was in the corner — they rammed my head face-first into the corner. My eyes were swollen afterward.

Later the same day, A. abu M. was taken to the Beach facility for interrogation.

Ali Ayed Radaydeh, of Abadiyeh village, near Bethlehem, was arrested on January 25, 1993. Prior to being transported on February 7 to the GSS interrogation wing at Hebron prison, he was kept in the holding

---

[4] Egged is Israel's largest bus company. The military frequently hires Egged buses to transport soldiers and detainees.

facility in the Bethlehem military headquarters. Radaydeh told HRW that the Border Police guarding the detainees in Bethlehem beat them at night and during the weekends, when GSS agents and IDF officers were absent:

> They took us, one by one, into a small room adjoining the larger room we were in. The detainee would be alone in there with three Border Police. Another two stood guard outside the small room, and another three stood guard at the entrance to the larger room. They were all carrying wooden clubs and guns.
>
> When they took me into the small room, two of them held my arms while the third hit me in the stomach. Then the two who were holding me put me against the wall. The third took several steps back, came running, and gave me a karate kick in the stomach. They also used a stick to hit me on the legs and kidneys. They did this to me three times during my two weeks there. Each session lasted about ten minutes.

Yasir Abdullah Salman Mughari, twenty-two, was arrested on November 12, 1992 in the village of Zuweida, in the Gaza Strip. Before going for interrogation at the Beach facility, he was taken to a local police station, where he was beaten:

> The soldiers left us for about an hour, sitting there in the police station. Then the police came and separated us. One of them tried to handcuff me, and I laughed at him. He began to hit me. He hit me a few times and slammed my head against the wall. Then they tied my hands behind my back with plastic and iron cuffs, two kinds, and put a hood over my head. Then I stood there in the corridor.
>
> We stood there for about an hour and a half, our foreheads against the wall, hands tied behind our backs. When the soldiers passed by they hit us. After a while, we began to call out, because our wrists were hurting so

much. After about twenty minutes a policeman came and cut the handcuffs off.[5]

While we stood there, the soldiers would hit us, kick us. The blows came suddenly, you couldn't know when it would come. They would come along and just push your face against the wall. If your forehead was leaning up against the wall, they would suddenly grab your hair, pull your head back, and then slam it back into the wall.

---

[5] The IDF uses handcuffs that are made of wire coated with thick plastic and can be removed only by using a wire cutter.

7
ISRAELI INTERROGATION CENTERS A CLOSED WORLD

When placed under investigative arrest in connection with purported security offenses, Palestinians from the occupied territories face questioning by agents of one of three agencies: the GSS, the IDF, and the police. When researching this report, there were, to the best of HRW's knowledge, ten GSS interrogation centers located in the West Bank, the Gaza Strip, and inside the Green Line, and three IDF interrogation facilities located inside the territories. In the spring of 1994, both the GSS and the IDF interrogation facilities in the Gaza Strip were reportedly closed. Preliminary reports suggest that the interrogation of Gazan suspects by the GSS was transferred primarily to the GSS facility at Ashkelon prison.

The interrogation of Palestinians takes place in centers that are virtually sealed off from the outside world. First, detainees under interrogation are far more restricted than other types of prisoners in terms of their ability to contact persons on the outside. Second, outsiders are almost never permitted to set foot inside an interrogation wing — when those who are invited to visit the adjoining prisons or jails. These obstacles to outside scrutiny greatly diminish the potential for exposing and curtailing the abuse of detainees under interrogation.

With regard to the GSS, these obstacles compound those posed by the fact that its interrogation practices are governed by classified guidelines that may even contravene Israeli law (see Chapter Five). In contrast, IDF and police interrogators can be held accountable to published military orders, legal codes, and regulations from which no derogations are permissible. For example, IDF interrogators are bound by prohibitions in both Israel's penal code and military justice law against the use of physical force on a person in custody; GSS interrogators are not bound by military law.

Moreover, GSS personnel are subordinate not to the IDF regional commanders, but to their own superiors within the agency,[1] who report

---

[1] The Order Regarding Security Force Members Operating in the Area (West Bank Area) (No. 121) 1967 states, in Article 2A:

ultimately to the prime minister. GSS interrogation wings are run autonomously, with little or no oversight by the IDF, Israel Prison Service (IPS), or police commanders who administer the larger facilities that house the interrogation wings.

Israeli interrogation facilities have been visited by Israeli government officials and a few parliamentarians. However, they have remained off-limits to all independent parties, i.e. persons who are neither elected officials nor persons employed or designated by government agencies, the judiciary, or the security forces. This includes detainees' families, defense lawyers, journalists, and nongovernmental monitors and organizations.

To our knowledge, the only exceptions to this policy in recent years are the following:

- In 1989 the Association for Civil Rights in Israel (ACRI) filed a petition at the Supreme Court, sitting as the High Court of Justice,[2] over conditions of detention at Dhahiriya (HCJ 29/89, *Yasir Mikbal et al. vs. Military Commander, Judea and Samaria*). In April of that year, court justices, along with counsel for ACRI and the IDF, toured the detention facility, including the interrogation wing. No interrogations were being conducted at the time of their visit.

- In at least two cases of deaths in detention, independent pathologists appointed by the deceased's family visited GSS interrogation wings in the company of the state forensic pathologist, as part of their investigations into the cause of death. In both cases, the pathologist was able to question GSS personnel

---

Regarding [members] of the security service [i.e. the GSS], the superiors [from within the service] shall constitute the responsible authority which must be obeyed.

[2] In its capacity as the High Court of Justice, the Supreme Court rules on petitions to grant relief against the state or any administrative authority. It has original jurisdiction over virtually every power exercised by the branches of the government, including the IDF and the military government in the occupied territories.

who said they were in involved in interrogating the deceased. (See Chapter Nineteen, on Deaths under Interrogation.)

None of these visits occurred unannounced; the interrogation agencies had time, if they wished, to relocate detainees or alter the interrogation environment prior to the visit. Nevertheless, the access provided to independent pathologists was a commendable step in heightening public accountability for the conduct of interrogators. (One of the deaths investigated by an independent pathologist led to the only instance in recent years in which GSS agents were imprisoned for mistreating Palestinians under interrogation; see Chapter Twenty.)

The Israeli authorities permit delegates of the International Committee of the Red Cross (ICRC) to meet with all Palestinians undergoing interrogation, following the fourteenth day of their detention. But these visits take place in visiting rooms, not in the interrogation wings themselves. The delegates are escorted by Israeli security personnel to and from the room where they interview Palestinian detainees (for more on the ICRC's role, see Chapter Four).

HRW's requests to visit interrogation wings have been consistently refused or ignored by the government of Israel, even though the government has authorized visits by HRW to the general sections of IPS, IDF and police detention facilities. The office of the prime minister, to which the GSS reports, failed to respond to two requests from HRW, dated August 21, 1993 and February 14, 1994, to visit GSS interrogation facilities.[3]

The IDF, in a letter dated October 10, 1993, turned down a request by HRW to visit interrogation wings in its facilities. In a meeting with HRW on November 18, 1993, a senior officer in the Judge Advocate-General's Corps who spoke on the condition of anonymity, again refused HRW's request to visit interrogation wings, saying, "It's the long-standing policy." When pressed for a reason, the officer stated, "There have, in the

---

[3] On March 4, 1992, representatives of the Israeli rights group B'Tselem visited the general section of Tulkarm prison, but were not permitted to enter the GSS interrogation wing. Major Shlomo Gispan, head of the Department of Detainees at Military Police Headquarters, explained, "There is an ethical problem here — one doesn't enter the interrogation wing." (B'Tselem, *The Death in Detention of Mustafa Barakat*, p. 11.

past, been attempts to interfere with interrogations." The officer did not elaborate.

IDF reservists interviewed for this report stressed the compartmentalization of IDF interrogation wings from the rest of the detention centers in which they are located. Even unauthorized security-force personnel were not permitted to enter interrogation wings.

Tal Raviv, a reserve sergeant who served as a guard at al-Far'a in December 1992–January 1993, told HRW that unauthorized personnel were strictly prohibited from entering the interrogation wing. The closest he got to the wing was doing guard duty atop its roof, which allowed him to see into the courtyard and hear sounds from the interrogation rooms below.[4]

Reserve soldier Shimon M. told HRW that when he served as a guard at the Beach facility in 1990, he was strictly forbidden from entering the interrogation wing, although he could see parts of it from one watchtower.[5] Sergeant A. M., a reserve military policeman who served at al-Far'a's interrogation wing in 1989, recalled:

> The MPs [military policemen] could not come into the interrogation area. We would call out, Bring me so-and-so! and they would bring the detainee to the door of the wall surrounding the interrogation rooms, and then I brought them in.[6]

Avshalom Benny, a reserve paramedic at Dhahiriya in 1992, told the Association for Civil Rights in Israel (ACRI):

> The two wings [the general and interrogation wings] are strictly separated. There is a steel door between them with a bell, and a guard on the interrogation wing side. [Only] medics are permitted to pass from one side to the other. There is another entrance to the interrogation wing, from the side of the military base. Only soldiers who are

---

[4] HRW interview, Tel Aviv, June 16, 1993 (see Appendix to this report).

[5] HRW interview, Petach Tikva, July 15, 1993.

[6] HRW interview, central Israel, June 15, 1993.

attached to the interrogation wing and the medical team are allowed in through that entrance.[7]

---

[7] Benny's comments are contained in an affidavit given to the Association for Civil Rights in Israel on September 14, 1992, and translated from the Hebrew by HRW. The above passage is from section 12 of the affidavit.

8
THE MILITARY COURTS IN THE OCCUPIED TERRITORIES

Palestinian residents of the occupied territories who are charged with security offenses,[1] wherever they allegedly took place, are tried before Israeli military courts in the territories.[2] These courts were established by military orders shortly after Israel took control of these lands and established military rule over them. They are not the same courts in which soldiers are court-martialed.

The military court system is based on English common law, with an adversarial system of procedure. In general, the military courts follow the rules of evidence in effect in Israeli courts-martial, which apply the rules of evidence obtaining in criminal courts within Israel, with minor exceptions.[3] Recently, the military authorities brought the rules of evidence into closer conformity with those that operate in Israel, eliminating the discretion that military courts had under Military Order 378 (Article 9 of Section 2) to deviate from the laws of evidence "in special circumstances which must be recorded, if they deem it to be in the interests of justice to do so." (For more on the rules of evidence as they affect the admissibility of confessions, see Chapter Eighteen).

As many human rights organizations have shown, these courts follow practices and utilize procedures that essentially deprive many

---

[1] There is no official definition of what constitutes a security offense. However, it includes offenses of varying degrees of gravity. It includes "disturbances of the public order," such as writing political graffiti on walls and throwing stones; and membership in, or violent or nonviolent activities on behalf of, outlawed organizations.

[2] International humanitarian law permits the occupying power to establish military courts in occupied territories for the trial of security offenses. However, provisions of the Geneva Convention seek to ensure that those courts are "properly constituted, non-political" bodies that provide the defendant with certain minimum rights.

[3] Article 476 of the Military Justice Law of 1955.

Palestinian defendants of their right to a fair trial.[4] This report will address these shortcomings only insofar as they contribute to an environment in which abuses by interrogators go unpunished and tainted confessions are accepted into evidence.

Separate systems of law apply to Palestinians and Israelis in the occupied territories. Palestinians are charged according to the security legislation applied by the military government. Except when the offense is viewed as an ordinary criminal matter,[5] the defendant is tried in a military court. By contrast, Israeli settlers are charged according to the Israeli Penal Code and tried in civilian courts inside Israel, where the rights of defendants are better protected.[6] Palestinian residents of Israel and Israeli-annexed East Jerusalem are also tried in civilian or, in some security-related cases, in military courts inside Israel or East Jerusalem.

---

[4] Lawyers Committee for Human Rights, *A Continuing Cause for Concern: The Military Justice System of the Israeli-Occupied Territories* (New York: Lawyers Committee for Human Rights, February 23, 1993); and *Lawyers and the Military Justice System of the Israeli-Occupied Territories* (New York: Lawyers Committee for Human Rights, May 7, 1992); Amnesty International, *The Military Justice System in the Occupied Territories: Detention, Interrogation and Trial Procedures* (London: Amnesty International, July 1991); B'Tselem, *The Military Judicial System in the West Bank* (Jerusalem: B'Tselem, July 1989) and *The Military Judicial System in the West Bank: Followup Report* (Jerusalem: B'Tselem, May 1990); International Commission of Jurists, *Inquiry into the Israeli Military Court System in the Occupied West Bank and Gaza* (Geneva: International Commission of Jurists, December 1989); and al-Haq and the Gaza Centre for Rights and Law, *Justice? The Military Court System in the Israeli-Occupied Territories* (Ramallah: Al-Haq, February 1987).

[5] In practice, many offenses not clearly linked to "security" have been tried by military courts. Many of these offenses relate to unauthorized construction, licensing infractions, nonpayment of taxes, and motor-vehicle offenses. In 1967, military legislation empowered these courts to adjudicate all criminal offenses recognized by the Israeli authorities, whether under previously enacted law or under the military government's own legislation. (Israel Defense Forces, Military Advocate-General's Unit, *Israel, the "Intifada" and the Rule of Law*, p. 86.)

[6] See B'Tselem, *Law Enforcement vis-a-vis Israeli Civilians in the Occupied Territories* (Jerusalem: B'Tselem, March 1994), in Hebrew; English-language summary available.

The Military Courts in the Occupied Territories

The military courts in the occupied territories are divided between courts of first instance and a court of appeals. The former are presided over either by a single judge or by a three-judge panel. Judges can be career army officers or reservists. Judges who try cases alone, or who serve as presidents of three-judge panels, must be officers of the rank of captain or above, and have legal training. The president of the panel appoints the two other members from the ranks of the IDF; they need not have legal qualifications.

Single-judge courts, in which the vast majority of Palestinians are tried, may impose sentences of up to ten years.[7] Three-judge courts can pass any sentence, although their convictions and sentences must be endorsed by the IDF regional commander.

A military court of appeals was created in 1989, at the urging of the Supreme Court. Both defendants and prosecutors may appeal convictions or acquittals, as well as sentences decided upon by the military courts. Palestinians have an automatic right to appeal sentences passed by a three-judge panel. If the sentence is less than three years' actual imprisonment, or the combined period of actual and suspended imprisonment is less than five years, the defendant must apply for permission to appeal. The appeal can be based on a challenge to facts, procedure, or the appropriateness of the sentence.

In practice, a defendant cannot appeal a sentence if it was decided upon in fulfillment of a plea-bargain agreement. If the plea bargain concerned only the list of offenses to which the defendant pled guilty, rather than the sentence, then the defendant can conceivably challenge the sentence imposed.

Legal Procedures Governing Arrest and Interrogation in the Occupied Territories

International law provides detainees certain rights that help to safeguard against ill-treatment and arbitrary or unlawful detention, and help to insure that any eventual trial proceedings are fair. These rights include, among others:

---

[7] Military Order 378, as amended in July 1991.

- The right to be "brought promptly before a judge or other officer authorized by law to exercise judicial power,"[8] and

- The right to adequate and timely access to legal counsel.[9]

In contrast to the situation inside Israel, these rights are systematically violated for Palestinian security suspects. They are usually told nothing at the time of their arrest about the accusations against them (see Chapter Six). Then they are commonly held incommunicado by security forces for two weeks or longer (except for a meeting after two weeks with a delegate of the International Committee of the Red Cross), unable to communicate with lawyers or relatives, and brought before no judicial authority for up to eight or eighteen days, depending on the nature of the case.

If eventually charged with a security offense, most suspects are denied bail; they are remanded in custody until the end of proceedings against them.[10] Detainees who do not quickly agree to a plea-bargain, or

---

[8] Article 9 of the ICCPR.

[9] Article 14(3)(b) of the ICCPR requires that any defendant charged with an offense be given "adequate time and facilities for the preparation of his defense and to communicate with counsel of his own choosing."

The U.N. Body of Principles for the Protection of All Persons under Any Form of Detention or Imprisonment, adopted by the General Assembly in 1988, states in Principle 17.1 that a detained person "shall be informed of his right [to legal counsel] by the competent authority promptly after arrest and shall be provided with reasonable facilities for exercising it." Principle 18 requires that detainees be entitled to "communicate and consult" with counsel "without delay," except "in exceptional circumstances, to be specified by law or lawful regulations, when it is considered indispensable by a judicial or other authority in order to maintain security and good order."

Article 72 of the Fourth Geneva Convention provides that accused persons "shall have the right to be assisted by a qualified advocate or counsel of their own choice, who shall be able to visit them freely and shall enjoy the necessary facilities for preparing the defense."

[10] The IDF blamed the denial of bail in cases where it might otherwise be warranted on conditions prevailing during the intifada:

who do not have the option of a "quick trial," are likely to wait in jail for months before their trial begins.

The Right to be Brought Promptly before a Judge

Until 1992, arresting authorities were permitted to hold suspects for eighteen days before they were required to bring them before a military judge.[11] Amendments in that year shortened to eight days the limit for certain categories of suspects, primarily persons accused of relatively light offenses, such as "disturbances of public order." If a suspect has not been charged by the end of pertinent period, the authorities must either release him or obtain authorization from the military judge for further detention.

While HRW welcomes the reduction of the maximum period of detention prior to judicial review, the new policy is inadequate on several counts:

•   A substantial percentage of detainees continue to be held for eighteen days before seeing a judge;

•   Even eight days is too long to hold detainees incommunicado. It is four times the maximum initial period allowed inside Israel for holding an adult suspect; and

> Arresting an individual suspect was a difficult task, requiring a large contingent of troops to guarantee safety. Many local Palestinian policemen had resigned under the pressure of "Intifada" intimidation, making the task of arresting individuals that much more difficult. Thus, once suspects were actually in custody, releasing them on bail or bond represented a real problem. In the prevailing atmosphere of violence and rebellion accompanied by an effective breakdown in the traditional authority structure, it was likely that many persons released on bail would not appear for their trials. Rearresting them would be an extremely difficult task in the circumstances then prevailing.

(Military Advocate-General's Corps, Israel Defense Forces, *Israel, the "Intifada" and the Rule of Law*, p. 93.)

[11] In the West Bank, the legislation is section 78 of Military Order 378.

- When a detainee is finally brought before the judge — whether after eight or eighteen days — the hearing is a perfunctory affair, in which the judge almost always approves the interrogators' request for extending the detention, despite the absence of formal charges.

Ex-detainees described to HRW how their extension-of-detention hearings violated their rights to legal representation and substantive judicial review of detention. Some said they were not even aware that they were in a court of law. Extension hearings were often held in makeshift chambers located in rooms adjoining the interrogation wings, reinforcing the impression of some detainees that the extension hearing was another stage of the interrogation process. Their lawyers were typically absent from the hearings, since, according to several attorneys we interviewed, they had not been informed in advance by the authorities of the time and date of the session. With the exception of the detainee and, if present, his lawyer, nearly all persons attending the extension hearing wear uniforms, including the judges, prosecutors and guards. The translation of the proceedings into Arabic was inadequate, they said, and they were informed neither of their right to counsel nor of the fact that what they said or did not say might later be used against them in court.[12]

---

[12] Their testimony echoes criticisms made by several of the human rights organizations cited in the fourth footnote to this chapter, but is contradicted by the IDF's claims about extension hearings:

> [Extension] hearings are held only after the lawyer has been notified by either the police or the appropriate military court for the purpose of coordinating the time and place of the hearing....Should the detainee appear before a judge at such a hearing without a lawyer, the judge immediately informs the detainee of his rights to have a lawyer and to file a bail application....[M]ilitary judges, like all other judges, ask detainees if they wish to be represented by counsel...."

IDF Judge Advocate-General's corps, "Reply to Lawyer Committee Report," [sic] July 1992, p. 4, contained as an appendix in Lawyers Committee for Human Rights, *A Continuing Cause for Concern: The Military Justice System of the Israeli-Occupied Territories.*

Some of the ex-detainees said that they had felt either too intimidated or unclear about their rights to demand that the written record ("protocol") include their denial of the accusations. Some said that they had not been aware that their response to the accusations read to them at extension hearings could be used as decisive corroborating evidence against them at their trial (see Chapter Eighteen).

Ramallah lawyer Ibrahim Barghouti, spokesman for the West Bank Lawyers Association, summarized, in an interview with HRW, the due process shortcomings of the extension courts:

> First, in 95 percent of the cases, lawyers are not present at the hearing. The only people present in addition to the detainee are soldiers or policemen, and the defendant has no independent witnesses who can dispute the military's version of events.
>
> Second, many defendants do not even know they are in a courtroom; they are taken, usually hooded, from the interrogation wing to another room in the same facility, which has been turned into a court. How are they supposed to know where they really are?
>
> Third, the court protocols are rarely precise. The defendant's exact words are not always taken down carefully.

The perfunctoriness of the extension hearings was described to HRW by Tal Raviv, the Israeli reserve sergeant who served as a guard at al-Far'a detention center:

> One day I brought sixty [detainees from the interrogation wing] to the extension-of-detention court. It's not really a court, it's just a booth in the prison. They went in, three by three, and after three minutes they came out. Within one hour we had finished with everyone. That can't be a real court, because how can they deliberate about whether to extend in one minute?

The Right to Adequate and Timely Access to Lawyers

According to HRW's interviews with detainees and defense lawyers, Palestinians under IDF or GSS interrogation are routinely denied access to lawyers during the course of their interrogation, particularly if their interrogation ends in one month or less. But even detainees interrogated for longer than thirty days are also sometimes denied access to a lawyer. This contrasts with the practice in Israel, where the denial of prompt access to a lawyer is rare.

By the time detainees are permitted their first meeting with a lawyer, many have already given and signed a statement or provided information that helps to convict others. This practice taints the entire judicial process. Detainees are denied independent advice concerning their rights, risks and options under interrogation, as well as a key opportunity to have an outsider observe and act on evidence of any physical or psychological mistreatment that occurred during interrogation.

According to Military Order 378, a Palestinian in investigative detention has the right to see a lawyer if he or she requests one, or if a family-appointed lawyer requests to see the detainee. However, the person in charge of the investigation may issue a written order preventing access to a lawyer for fifteen days "if in his opinion it is necessitated by the security in the region or for the sake of the investigation." Access to counsel can be prevented for a further fifteen days by a higher officer. It can then be denied for sixty days longer by order of a military court judge. This ninety-day limit on prevention of access to a lawyer contrasts with the limit inside Israel of thirty days.

Official interpretations of this provision make clear that the denial of access to a lawyer is to be reserved for "exceptional circumstances when it is believed that such a meeting will prejudice the investigation."[13] But of the twenty-one Palestinians we interviewed who were permitted to meet their lawyers during their interrogation, the average length of time before the first meeting was twenty days. (At least thirteen other GSS and IDF detainees in our sample were prevented from meeting with a lawyer throughout their interrogation; see data in Chapter Two.)

In a small victory for defendants' rights, the Israeli Supreme Court in 1993 affirmed that the authorities have an obligation to inform a

---

[13] See, e.g., Ministry of Justice, Human Rights and International Relations Department, "Fact Sheet" on the case of Ahmed Salman Musa Qatamesh, File 164.1-'75, December 10, 1992, p. 2.

The Military Courts in the Occupied Territories

detainee of his right to see a lawyer, even if they are preventing him from exercising that right.[14] However, the Court did not explicitly rule that the authorities are also required to fulfill a prisoner's request to inform his lawyer of his place of detention, even if the attorney is blocked from meeting the client. (Such a requirement would give substance to the prisoner's right to challenge the denial of his right to see a lawyer.)

The denial of legal counsel to a person under interrogation can be challenged to the Supreme Court, sitting as the High Court of Justice.[15] The Association of Civil Rights in Israel has petitioned the High Court of Justice on many occasions over the last several years, and succeeded in winning lawyers' access for suspects in all but three cases.[16] Such challenges, however, are often not feasible. In most cases, defense lawyers are not promptly informed that a detainee's access to a lawyer is being denied. If a defense lawyer does receive this information but is not a member of the Israeli bar, he or she must enlist a lawyer who is a member to petition the High Court of Justice. This requirement adds time and expense to the process of contesting the denial of counsel. In the end, many, if not most, detainees do not see their lawyers until they have confessed or have been released.

---

[14] HCJ 3412/91, *Sufian Abdullah v. Military Commander, Gaza Strip*, unpublished decision of June 7, 1993. The case was filed on behalf of the petitioner by the Association for Civil Rights in Israel.

[15] In its capacity as the High Court of Justice, the Supreme Court rules on petitions challenging measures taken by administrative authorities.

[16] HRW interview by telephone with ACRI attorney Dan Yakir in Tel Aviv, April 28, 1994. See also B'Tselem, *The Interrogation of Palestinians during the Intifada*, p. 98.

9
METHODS OF INTERROGATION: INTRODUCTION

"If you look through Western eyes, there is brutality, there is torture against people that are terrorists or could lead us to terrorists. This every country will justify, look at Britain with the IRA. With all the unpleasantness, with [the Israeli rights group] B'Tselem and others, and with Amnesty [International] writing [about torture] — and they have a right to do so and they have a place to do so, so those people who are dealing with it [interrogators] will be afraid, and will know that there are limits."

— Lieutenant Colonel (Reserve) Nathan Ronen, formerly in the Gaza Civil Administration[1]

Part Two of this report examines the techniques employed by interrogators of the General Security Service (GSS) and the Israel Defense Forces (IDF). The techniques are divided according to two basic criteria:

- The **timing** of their utilization, i.e. whether they are used **during** the questioning sessions, or **before and between** the questioning sessions. This criterion generally correlates with location, i.e., methods used inside the interrogation room vs. methods used outside the interrogation room; and

- The **nature** of the method, i.e. whether it is primarily **physical** or **psychological**.

The findings presented in the next six chapters rely almost entirely on the following:

---

[1] Israel Radio, December 12, 1992, 1:00 PM English-language news, as transcribed by the Associated Press.

- Thirty-six interviews conducted by HRW in 1993 and 1994 with ex-detainees who had been interrogated between 1992 and 1994;

- Five interviews conducted by defense lawyers with Palestinians still in detention who had been interrogated during 1993;

- Four interviews conducted by HRW with Israeli reservists who served in IDF detention centers and who had some connection to the interrogation process;[2] and

- Documentation from military court trials in which defendants challenged their confessions, including medical records, declassified GSS interrogation logs, and the testimony of GSS interrogators and the defendants.

DURING VERSUS BETWEEN QUESTIONING SESSIONS

The typical image of an interrogation, in which a suspect is questioned in a room by interrogators, does not apply to the Israeli-occupied territories. In both the GSS and IDF interrogation systems, the face-to-face confrontation with the interrogator is only one stage in a round-the-clock process that continues with little respite until the end of the interrogation period.

Methods used before and between questioning sessions are aimed at disorienting and debilitating interrogation subjects and inducing a sense of dread. These methods aim to "dry out" the detainees, as IDF reservist Tal Raviv put it, in preparation for their meeting with the interrogator in the questioning room.[3]

The methods used during the questioning sessions — including threats, violent shaking, choking and beating — are intended to complete

---

[2] One of the reservists, Avshalom Benny, was by the Association for Civil Rights in Israel, on September 14, 1992, and by HRW on July 29, 1993. Most of the quotes from
Benny cited in this report are taken from the ACRI affidavit.

[3] See the Appendix of this report for Raviv's full testimony.

the breakdown process, inducing the detainee to provide information or a statement.

In addition to the testimony of detainees, other kinds of evidence, presented below, underscore the critical role played by the abuse inflicted between interrogation sessions. The evidence includes admissions made by GSS interrogators during the trial of Muhammad Adawi (see Chapters Twelve and Eighteen), who challenged his confession on the grounds that it had been coerced. Adawi's argument relied primarily on what he had experienced between, rather than during, questioning sessions.

The evidence also includes testimony by soldiers about what authorities term the "waiting" period. The next chapter, for example, contains IDF paramedic Avshalom Benny's description of how detainees at Dhahiriya were, between rounds of questioning, made to stand or locked in closet-like stalls for prolonged periods.

PHYSICAL VERSUS PSYCHOLOGICAL ABUSE

Psychological abuse, as practiced by IDF and GSS interrogators, includes a wide range of deprivation techniques, including social deprivation (isolation), sight deprivation (hooding/blindfolding), sleep deprivation, space deprivation (confinement in tiny enclosed), personal hygiene deprivation, toilet-related abuses and humiliation, subjection to round-the-clock loud music, and threats.

Physical abuse is of two basic types: impact abuse, such as beating a detainee or holding him by the collar and violently shaking him back and forth; and non-impact abuse. Beatings are administered by interrogators and, to a lesser extent, by Palestinian collaborators (see Chapter Fifteen). Interrogators usually use their fists and boots and, occasionally, blunt instruments such as plastic clubs. The arresting soldiers and prison guards also sometimes beat detainees (see Chapter Six, on violence during arrests). Non-impact physical abuse refers to methods such as abusive body positioning and exposure to drastic temperature changes.

10
ABUSIVE BODY POSITIONING

The most common methods of physical abuse outside the interrogation room in both GSS and IDF interrogation wings is the chaining, handcuffing, shackling, confining or otherwise constraining of detainees in painful positions for hours or days. Some of the positions are painful from the outset. Others grow painful over time, due to restricted circulation, straining of limbs, cramps, numbing, itching, and the friction of chains, handcuffs or legcuffs.

These methods, applied at what can be termed position-abuse stations, leave few marks. If the detainee refuses to confess, interrogators can resume the position abuse and try again.

In GSS interrogation facilities, the presence of the following specially designed equipment at position-abuse stations indicates the degree to which the abuse is premeditated and systematized:

- **"Kindergarten chairs,"** as they are called by ex-detainees, are small chairs with low backrests, to which detainees are shackled for days at a time, with only a few brief respites per day. Ex-detainees estimated the height of the seat to be twenty centimeters (about eight inches) off the ground. They noted that the rear and front legs of the chairs are sometimes different heights, adding to their discomfort.

- **Rings or pipes attached to the wall** are used by the GSS to shackle detainees' hands and, sometimes, their feet.

- **"Closets,"** as they are called by ex-detainees, are small, enclosed stalls in which detainees are confined at GSS and, less often, at IDF facilities. In some cases, GSS "closets" are fitted with "kindergarten chairs," wall rings or pipes.

Abusive body positioning continues for long periods of time. Most of the GSS interrogation subjects interviewed for this report experienced position abuse for more than five consecutive days, with respites only during questioning rounds, trips to the bathroom, or occasional, brief rest spells. The overall strategy appears to be, in the words of a U.N. mental health professional working in the occupied territories, to "eliminat[e] any chance victims might have to rest their minds and bodies between the traumatic experience of the interrogation sessions."[1]

Psychologists point out that persons can often reduce physical pain and discomfort by distracting themselves from what is happening to their bodies.[2] GSS interrogation techniques appear designed to impede this process through a combination of sensory deprivation (hooding/blindfolding and confinement) and loud, relentless music. Ex-detainees said these measures ensured that they could think of nothing but the physical discomforts they were enduring.

"Waiting"

GSS agents employ the euphemism "waiting" when referring to the combination of hooding, sleep deprivation, and abusive body positioning. But even their own toned-down descriptions of "waiting" reveal that it is not a neutral holding phase but rather a regime of deliberate discomfort.

A GSS interrogator code-named "Thompson" testified at the trial of Muhammad Adawi that interrogators have some discretion in selecting the positions that detainees are forced to assume between questioning sessions:

> On June 10, 1992, at 7:00 P.M., he [Adawi] was admitted to the prison and put into a situation of waiting. This is a situation in which the interrogatee waits for interrogation. He can be handcuffed, he can be with a hood on his head, and sometimes can also be sitting on a normal chair, which

---

[1] HRW interview, March 12, 1993, in Jerusalem. The official spoke on condition of anonymity, since he is not permitted to give on-the-record interviews.

[2] Ronald Melzack and Patrick D. Wall, *The Challenge of Pain* (New York: Basic Books, 1983), pp. 37-38.

is either low or high, according to the interrogator's discretion.[3]

"Gabi," another GSS agent, described "waiting" in his testimony at the Adawi trial:

> In the [interrogation] facility, interrogatees sit there and wait for interrogation. Some of them are tied and some are not. When the man is sitting there, it is uncomfortable for sleeping, but if he wants to doze, we don't bother him. He sits there and therefore it is naturally difficult for him to sleep because he is sitting.[4]

According to Israeli attorney Avigdor Feldman, the concept of "waiting" has its roots in an investigative procedure that had once been sanctioned by Israeli courts. Interrogators had been permitted by the courts to hood detainees for brief periods while they waited outside the interrogator's office, in order to prevent them from identifying one another. But, said Feldman:

> This authorization was maliciously converted into permission to use moderate physical pressure [sic], which is reflected, among other things, in the placing of hoods on the detainee's head for the long hours of "waiting."[5]

---

[3] Hebron Military Court, case 2332/92, June 30, 1993 session, p. 75 of the protocol. The trial is recounted in greater detail in Chapters Twelve and Eighteen.

[4] Hebron Military Court, case 2332/92, April 20, 1993 session, p. 11 of the protocol.

[5] Avigdor Feldman, "Welcome to the Modern Inquisition," *Haaretz* weekend supplement, July 16, 1993.

ABUSIVE BODY POSITIONING — GSS INTERROGATIONS

For detainees under GSS interrogation, position abuse is interrupted during the week only when detainees are being questioned in the interrogation room and during short bathroom/eating breaks. Position abuse generally continues, five to six days a week, for the duration of the interrogation.

A weekly respite from position abuse appears to be a relatively standard GSS practice. Most GSS interrogation subjects are permitted to rest from Friday afternoon until Sunday morning. A few of the ex-detainees we interviewed were given breaks during the week; and a few said they sometimes spent seven or more days in position-abuse stations without a break.

During the rest periods, detainees are locked in small cells, sometimes with other prisoners. Although these cells were described by the ex-detainees as dark and filthy, they provide a respite from the regimen of interrogation, abusive body positioning, hooding, monotonous music, sleep deprivation, and restricted toilet access.

GSS Abuse Station #1:
The "Kindergarten Chair" (See illustration)

> They put the hood back on my head and took me to a room with a small chair. The chair is fixed to the ground. They tied both my feet to the chair legs, each foot to a different chair leg. They tied my hands through the chair's backrest.
>
> The chair is like a baby chair. The seat is sloped down and the-27 backrest is angled into your back....The chair was right next to the door. One of the legs is fixed to the ground. There is a hook in the ground and a ring on the chair leg. There is a long padlock fixing the chair ring to the floor hook.
>
> "Captain Cohen" came up to me while I was on the chair, lifted the hood, and said, "You have been in interrogation

before. I don't want to have to use other measures. Start talking."

— Sh. Z., a student interrogated for fifteen days at Ramallah prison in December 1992

The most common method of GSS position abuse is the shackling of detainees to small wooden or hard plastic chairs. Thirteen of the seventeen GSS detainees we interviewed reported being forced to sit for prolonged periods on child-sized chairs. The other four said they were restrained for prolonged periods on ordinary chairs. Chair shackling was consistently used in conjunction with hooding, loud music, and sleep deprivation.

The "kindergarten chairs" appear to be of standard dimensions in all of the GSS wings discussed in this report, with the exception of Tulkarm. Three of the Tulkarm detainees did not mention experiencing the small chair.

As described by former detainees, the chair's seat is fifteen to twenty centimeters high and about twenty centimeters square (eight by eight inches). The chair has a low backrest that reaches only to the center of an average adult's back. It is not known whether the chairs are standard-issue children's school-chairs, or are made to order for GSS interrogations. In some cases, the front or the back legs of the chair have been shortened, causing the chair to slope forward or backward. Twenty-six-year-old Abd A., who was interrogated for fifty days, recalled his time on the chair:

> I had a hood over my head. The front legs of the chair had been sawed off so that they were lower than the back legs. Because the chair sloped forward, the pain was in the wrists and shoulders.
>
> I was not beaten, unlike my previous interrogations. There was *shabeh* [prolonged sitting or standing while hooded], music, and interrogations. All the time I was being taken from *shabeh* to interrogation and back to *shabeh*....Sometimes I sat for as long as two straight days on the chair without being interrogated.

Illustration #1

"KINDERGARTEN CHAIR" — GSS detainees are typically shackled for days at a time to undersized chairs, barely able to move, with only short breaks. Confinement to the chair grows increasingly painful to the back and limbs. Some "kindergarten chairs," such as the one shown here, slope forward due to shortened front legs. This increases the strain on the legs and wrists.

Illustration #1

While on the chair, GSS detainees reported, they were continuously hooded. They were not allowed to speak with other detainees shackled to chairs nearby, or to talk with guards, other than to ask permission to use the toilet or see a doctor. Detainees' hands were typically chained together behind them, in many cases, attached to the chair's backrest and/or to a ring built into the wall.

When the handcuffs are attached to the backrest, they are usually attached together to one side, forcing the detainee to twist his abdomen. In some cases, detainees' legs are chained together and then tied to the chair. In other cases, each leg is chained to a separate chair leg, so that the detainee's legs are parted and his groin is exposed.

It is debilitating to sit on a "kindergarten chair." Restful sleep is impossible, given the uncomfortable position and the practice some guards have of slapping or shouting at detainees who appear to nod off. Blood circulation problems cause cramping and discomfort to the detainees' backs, shoulders and arms. When the chair slopes forward or the detainee leans back, the backrest digs into his back. The short seat of the chair digs into the back of his thighs, eventually causing abrasions that are aggravated by sweat, dirt and chafing.

Some ex-detainees reported that the small chairs caused sharp spinal and lower-back pains. This happened frequently at Hebron prison, where detainees' hands were tied behind their bodies to rings attached at chest level to the wall, forcing them to bend forward while on the chair.

Ribhi Qatamesh, who spent most of his twenty-three-day interrogation at Hebron prison on a "kindergarten chair," recalled:

> When you are on the chair, it as if your arms are being torn away. When you get a minute to eat, you can't move your arm to get the food. To move is very painful. When you are tied and then all of a sudden released, you want not to be released. When you are chained you lose all feeling. You prefer to remain that way, because once you are released and then tied up again soon after, it takes two to three hours to lose feeling again. You can't straighten your spine, you can't straighten your knees, they hurt so much.

M. R., an unemployed college graduate in the social sciences, was interrogated for eight days at Gaza prison. Most of his time was spent chained to the "kindergarten chair." He said:

> When you are on the chair, every part of your body hurts. You cannot concentrate on anything after ten or twenty hours. I could not even finish one thought. The chair destroys your ability to think.
>
> During my first two days there, every part of my body felt ill. If the guard thinks you are sleeping, he makes you stand. You never sleep on the chair. The guard was always walking around between us.

Ahmed al-Batsh, forty-seven, spent most weekdays on a small chair during his seventy-five-day interrogation at Ramallah prison in 1992. He recalled:

> All of your body hurts you in *shabeh*: your legs, your bottom, your back, everything....You sit alone, you talk with the floor, you laugh to yourself. [The interrogators] would say to me, "You can only dream about us hitting you, we won't hit you, it's more difficult for you this way." You get hysterical....
>
> During the first two weeks, my legs were shackled to the chair. I had a constant gash on the back of my legs from the seat of the chair. You are so filthy, and the salt from your sweat gets into your wounds. It hurts so much that you think you will never be able to keep sitting.

At the trial of Muhammad Adawi, GSS agent "Gabi" described the chair in which the defendant had been confined:

> During the waiting period, the accused was tied up. Most of the time he was tied....During waiting, the accused sits on a chair that is...about ten to fifteen centimeters lower

than a usual chair. Its width is thirty-five to forty centimeters.[6]

"Mousa," another GSS agent, described Adawi's position in the chair as follows:

> The suspect sits while cuffed, with a hood on his head, in waiting. Sometimes I received the accused with his hands cuffed. Sometimes cuffed in front, sometimes cuffed in back. There is a space between the cuffs, there is a chain between them....In some cases, the accused sits in waiting with his hands cuffed behind him.[7]

HRW had an artist sketch the "kindergarten chair" as it was described by the ex-detainees we interviewed (see illustration). This sketch was given to Adawi's attorney, Shlomo Lecker, who asked "Mousa" whether it accurately represented the position that detainees were placed in while "waiting" in Hebron prison. "Mousa" looked at the illustration and stated:

> According to the [HRW] sketch there is no opportunity [for the detainee] to move his legs because of the leg cuffs....With us [the GSS interrogation wing in Hebron], there is a space between the leg cuffs, and a man can walk with them on. We don't cuff the legs every time someone is in waiting.[8]

During the June 30, 1993 court session, agent "Mousa" testified that detainees in "waiting" "can move their legs, but they can't move their hands. They cannot walk around."[9]

---

[6] Hebron Military Court, case 2332/92, April 20, 1993 session, p. 11 of the protocol.

[7] Ibid.

[8] Ibid., p. 376.

[9] Ibid., June 30, 1993 session, p. 71.

H. M., interrogated at Ramallah, said he was not allowed to get off the "kindergarten chair" even during his twice-daily rounds of questioning:

> I sat on the kindergarten chair from Sunday morning until Friday. Even when I went into the interrogation room for questioning, they kept the chair tied to my hands, and I remained sitting on that same chair. They only took the hood off to talk to me. The interrogators would sometimes sit behind their desks, sometimes with their feet on my legs or on my chest. Sometimes they slapped me, knocked me off the chair, and then pulled me up and put me back on it.

Despite being hooded, detainees caught occasional glimpses of their surroundings through rips in the hood or — on rare occasions — by rubbing the hood against the wall until they could see under its hem. They provided the following accounts of the arrangement of the chairs:

Ramallah and Gaza

At Ramallah and Gaza, the "kindergarten chairs" are lined up in a long indoor corridor outside the interrogation rooms. There can be up to thirty persons shackled to "kindergarten chairs" at one time. They are forbidden to talk with one another.

In the Gaza interrogation wing, the corridor, called "the Bus" by detainees, contains three separate rows of chairs stretching the length of the corridor: one along each wall and a third row down the middle.

Hebron

Ex-detainees reported that the chairs at Hebron were located in narrow cells or in concrete "closets." They were thus physically isolated from other detainees (see below, under "Closets").

Petach Tikva

At Petach Tikva, most "kindergarten chairs" line the wall of an open courtyard in the middle of the interrogation facility, according to the one ex-detainee interviewed for this report who was interrogated there. He said that additional chairs are located in concrete "closets."

Ashkelon

There are "kindergarten chairs" at Ashkelon, according to detainees interviewed by attorney Tamar Pelleg-Sryck. We do not know where they are located.

Tulkarm

At Tulkarm, ex-detainees said, "kindergarten chairs" were not in use. But three ex-detainees said they were forced to sit, handcuffed behind their backs and hooded, on plastic vegetable boxes not much higher than small chairs. The criss-crossed plastic slats of the boxes made prolonged sitting painful for the detainees, who were unable to shift their weight or stand up.

Respites from the "Kindergarten Chair"

The ex-detainees we interviewed typically spent days and nights on the chair. In general, they were unchained for the following reasons only:

> *To go to other position-abuse stations.*
> *To go for questioning in the interrogation rooms.*
> *To go to the toilet and to eat meals.*

Detainees were typically freed to eat and go to the toilet three times a day. The short walk provided little exercise or relief from the sitting position.

Many of the seventeen GSS interrogation subjects interviewed by HRW said they were forced to eat their meals while in the toilet stall (see Chapter Twelve). As a rule, detainees were given three to five minutes in the stall; during this time, they had to relieve themselves, wash their hands, drink water from a faucet (usually their only opportunity to drink during the day), and eat their meals, which were put in the toilet stall on a tray.

To lie down for brief rest periods. At the trial of Muhammad Adawi, GSS agents testified that "rest" meant unshackling the detainees and permitting them to lie down in empty interrogation rooms for several hours. Detainees often said they remembered these rests only dimly, due to their exhaustion. The log that the GSS kept of its interrogation of Adawi indicates that he received only five hours "rest" during a 109-hour-long period of being hooded, confined to a chair, and repeatedly questioned.

To take weekend rests. From Friday afternoon to Sunday morning (the Israeli weekend), detainees were usually released from the chair and put in cells, where they were allowed to sleep. In some centers, such as Hebron, detainees were sent to isolation cells during these weekend breaks. In other centers, such as Ramallah, detainees reported being locked into crowded cells containing up to five prisoners.

GSS Abuse Station #2:
Shackling to Rings or Pipes Embedded in the Wall (See illustrations)

Ten of the seventeen GSS interrogation subjects reported being shackled to pipes or rings built into the walls during their interrogation. There are two basic variations: some detainees are shackled to the wall while seated on a "kindergarten chair"; others are made to stand or crouch in awkward positions while chained to the rings or pipes.

Shackling to rings or pipes while standing

Six of the seventeen GSS interrogation subjects reported that during their interrogation, they were taken off chairs and chained to iron rings fixed to the wall or to pipes running either parallel or perpendicular to the floor. The duration of these spells ranged from four hours to, in one case, three days, with short breaks for eating and using the toilets.

In most cases, the implements are located at an uncomfortable height, so that the detainee must reach up or semi-crouch in a way that grows painful over time to their arms and legs. The discomfort is exacerbated by chaining the detainees' ankles to rings in the wall in a way that allows them only a few centimeters of movement. They are thus unable to shift their weight to relieve cramps and pains. Movement also causes the wrists to be pinched by the tight-fitting cuffs.

Three of the six detainees we interviewed who had been interrogated at Ramallah said they had been attached to arm and leg rings built into the wall of a cell. For periods they described as lasting from four to six hours, they were hooded, with their backs to the wall, their wrists and ankles chained to rings. The wrist rings were either below waist-level or high up, near their shoulders.

Ramallah ex-detainees also described a pipe that runs vertically along a wall that has two sets of rings attached to it, one for hands and the

ILLUSTRATION #2

PIPE SHACKLING (1) — Detainee is shackled to an immovable object fixed to the wall, forcing him to remain hunched over for long periods. This method is used most commonly by the GSS, but was also reported in some IDF centers. Here, the detainee's head is covered with a sweater; hoods are also used during pipe shackling.

Illustration #2

other for legs. Again, the hand rings are located below an average man's waist, forcing detainees to hunch over in a way that grows increasingly painful. Ahmed al-Batsh said he was twice chained to wall rings, once for three days:

> In the courtyard...[t]hey shackled me to the iron rings. When they do that you can't stand, you can't sit. You are bent over, with your arms behind you, up near the height of your shoulders. Your legs are shackled together. I was once on this wall for three straight days, with only a few breaks for the toilet and eating.

S. R., interrogated for thirty-eight days at Ramallah prison in 1992, described pipe-*shabeh* there:

> There are rings in the wall, higher than your shoulders, and your hands are chained with metal handcuffs to them. Your legs are also tied to the wall. The legs are jammed up against the wall, tied to a pipe. The pipe runs perpendicular to the ground, behind your back, so you can't lean back on the wall, because the pipe digs in all along your spine. I was in this position for four to five hours at a time.

S. R. was chained in the same room in another contorted position involving two chairs. He was forced to sit on one chair, and then had his hands handcuffed to rings in the wall with the second chair between him and the wall. His legs were chained to the legs of the second chair.

Three of the four former Tulkarm detainees said they were locked hand and foot to a pipe located in an old toilet stall for periods ranging from four hours to two days. The wrist cuffs are attached to rings welded to the pipe, so that detainees cannot move downward to relieve the pain. While chained to the pipe, detainees remain hooded. The music is extremely loud in the stall, which has a hole in the ground for human waste. Ad. M., who was interrogated for forty-seven days at Tulkarm in 1992, recalled:

> The pipe at night was the worst. Your legs are very tired, but the cuffs are so tight to the pipe that you can't move.

> You are wedged up in the corner of the toilet stall, legs and feet fixed to the pipe, [held tight] all the way back. When he [the interrogator] opens the door, it slams you in the face.

U. Gh. was interrogated at Tulkarm for twenty-four days in 1992. He said that at one point during the first few days of his interrogation, after standing hooded for several days in the hall outside the interrogation rooms, he lost control and began to scream hysterically. In response, he recalled:

> The interrogator took me to a small toilet stall which has a vertical pipe attached to the wall. He chained my hands to the pipe and chained my legs together. I stayed that way for about four hours.

Ribhi Qatamesh was interrogated for twenty-three days at Hebron in 1992. He said his hands were chained behind his back to a pipe built horizontally into the wall at chest level. Qatamesh was thus forced to stand on tiptoe, with his hands pulled upward behind his back. He told HRW that he was chained in this position on three or four occasions, each lasting seven to eight hours. During that time he was continuously hooded.

Seven of the seventeen GSS interrogation subjects reported being chained to "kindergarten chairs" while also being shackled to wall pipes or rings. The rings are built into the wall behind the chair, at the height of the back of an average man sitting in the chair. The height of the rings forced the detainee's hands up behind their backs, and his head and shoulders forward and down.

B. Ah., an unemployed twenty-three-old, described his experience on a small chair in a "closet" at Hebron:

> The chair is fixed to the wall. The ring was about sixty centimeters high, at about the level of my shoulders. So my hands were raised behind my back, which was very painful. I was forced to bend over with my face toward the ground, and my hands were higher than my head. All the pain was on the disk in the center of my back.

> During the week, you leave the closet only for interrogation sessions or for the bathroom. When you want to go to the bathroom, you have to call for the guard and plead. On average, he takes you about twice a day. If you ask for water, when he comes, if he comes, he lifts the sack up a little and lets you drink from a plastic cup.
>
> [When food is brought to the "closet"] the guard will take off one cuff. If he is really nice, he takes off both. He opens the door and shoves the tray in with his leg, and then he closes the door....You have to search around in the dark with your hand for the tray, since you can't see anything. You don't know what you are eating.

During the trial of Muhammad Adawi, GSS agents confirmed that detainees in Hebron prison were chained to rings or bars attached to the wall. During the May 17 court session, agent "Mousa" said, "There are places where the cuffs are wrapped around a pole, so that the accused can't move."[10] "Mousa" described the position assumed by detainees shackled to wall pipes or rings, explaining:

> Sometimes [when cuffed behind], one of the cuffs is wrapped around the backrest of the chair. Sometimes the cuffs on the interrogatee's hands are attached to a second pair of cuffs, which are attached to a bar in the wall.[11]

Police Superintendent Menachem Nidam, chief warden of the Russian Compound police jail in 1990, confirmed that detainees at the GSS wing of the Russian Compound were shackled and hooded for hours at a time, a practice he said violated police rules regarding the treatment of detainees. He told the Jerusalem District Court in November 1992:

> The detainees usually are outside of the cells, in a small yard. Some of them [have their hands] tied behind their

---

[10] Hebron Military Court, case 2332/92, May 17, 1993 session, p. 36 of the protocol.

[11] Ibid.

> backs, and some in front [of their bodies]. Sometimes they are tied to an iron bar attached to the wall, with a covering over their heads....
>
> It is difficult for me to estimate the time [they were in that position] because I wasn't there [in the interrogation wing] for a long time. Sometimes I saw the detainee stand there for hours, but I don't know if it was for an entire day.[12]

At one point during the trial, the defense attorney prompted Nidam, "You described a hook to which detainees were tied in the courtyard." Nidam replied:

> It [the hook] is fixed at different heights. It can be low, it can be at the height of a man standing, or [at the height] of a man sitting while he is bound.[13]

GSS Abuse Station #3:
Confinement in "Closets" (See illustration)

Several GSS detainees reported being locked in small, enclosed spaces that they called "closets" (*hazana* in Arabic). "Closet" confinement was often employed in combination with other methods: detainees would be placed inside while hooded or unhooded, shackled or unshackled. Some "closets" are fitted with cooling devices and rubber insulation around the door. These "closets" become what the detainees call "refrigerators" (see Chapter Eleven).

In court testimony, Police Superintendent Menachem Nidam described a tiny cell in the GSS wing of the Russian Compound. Asked about the smallest cell in the GSS wing, Nidam said:

---

[12] Jerusalem District Court, case 576/91, November 17, 1992 session, p. 797 of the protocol.

[13] Jerusalem District Court, case 576/91, November 17, 1992 session, p. 801 of the protocol.

> [It is] something like — it's hard for me to estimate — very small....It is hard to lie down in. You can barely sit there. It is both narrow and I don't know how low [the ceiling is]. It is narrow, but the height, I don't remember. It's very narrow.[14]

Israeli lawyer Avigdor Feldman collected testimony from several Palestinians interrogated by the GSS at the Russian Compound in 1991 who referred to a particular cell as "the grave." That cell may be the same as the one described by Superintendent Nidam. Feldman included testimony from Medhat Amin Najidi in his petition to the Supreme Court challenging the GSS's interrogation guidelines (see Chapter Three). Najidi stated:

> I was in "the grave" for a long period of time. There is a terrible stench in there. I was in there with my hands tied, but not with my legs tied. The size of it is like that of the witness stand, the same length and a little higher. There are two seats in it.
>
> Inside, there is a pool, with some kind of terrible stench, I don't know what kind of smell it is. They put it in there to torture....The stench stuck to me. My legs were plastered with it. We call this place the grave. They call it a cell....
>
> All night I stood there in the grave with my hands tied behind my back. Every time I tried to sleep, a guard came and hit me so that I wouldn't fall asleep.
>
> ....They open the door and put you inside, it is one meter by one meter. You are entirely cut off from the world, you can't even see [as far as] your own finger....It is a closed

---

[14] Jerusalem District Court, case 576/91, November 17, 1992 session, p. 797 of the protocol.

space, very frightening, there is a door, but you can't see anything. There are no openings.[15]

During his interrogation, Najidi signed a statement that he belonged to a group of youths that had burned a number of cars in East Jerusalem. He was subsequently convicted of arson.

Petach Tikva

According to the one Petach Tikva detainee we interviewed, there is a "closet" approximately fifty centimeters wide, one meter long, and two meters high. From September 17 until October 26, 1992, journalist Rashid Hilal was interrogated at Petach Tikva and then at Ashkelon, before being released without charge. He said that while in the "closet" at Petach Tikva, he was hooded and chained to a "kindergarten chair." The "closet" was extremely hot and stuffy, he said, and he had to plead many times before being given access to the toilet. When he tried to remove the hood by rubbing his head against the wall, he said, guards came and punched him in the head and upper body.

Hilal estimated spending as long as twenty-four consecutive hours in the cell, although he said he could not keep track of time with any precision. He recalled:

> The "closet" is made of very rough cement. There are no windows, and no place for air to come in, except through the air conditioner.
>
> The "closet" is a form of intense pressure. In other types of *shabeh* you can breathe, and if you push the hood off a little, you can see something. In the "closet," however, you can't breathe. There is a small light inside the "closet," and if you remove the hood, it shines right in your eyes.
>
> Your hands are tied through the backrest of the chair. Sometimes they tie you crosswise, so that you are twisted in the chair.

---

[15] HCJ case 2581/91, supplementary petition submitted by the petitioner, p. 10, section 27.

ILLUSTRATION #3

PIPE SHACKLING (2) — Detainee is hooded and shackled hand and leg to immovable rings on a pipe or wall, prevented from standing up straight or sitting down. Ex-detainees reported enduring this method at Ramallah's GSS wing for periods ranging from four hours to, in one case, three days, with only brief respites.

ILLUSTRATION #3

The guards come and disturb you every few minutes. You can't breathe, you can't even think about sleeping, only about breathing.

Hebron

During his trial, Muhammad Adawi testified about being confined in a "closet" at Hebron. GSS agent "Gabi" countered that the small spaces in which detainees were kept were not enclosed cells, but rather, small alcoves, "like bathroom stalls without doors."[16] GSS agent "Mousa" concurred that the spaces in question were doorless stalls. When asked by Adawi's attorney if the size of the stall was approximately one meter by eighty centimeters, "Mousa" concurred.[17] The agents' testimony contradicted both the defendant's and that of B. Ah., quoted above, that Hebron prison does contain "closets."

Tulkarm

Ex-detainees interrogated at Tulkarm did not refer to specially designed interrogation "closets." All of them reported, however, being chained inside a stall to a pipe running perpendicular to the ground.

Ramallah

At Ramallah, the closet-like cells seem to be used mostly as "refrigerator" cells (see Chapter Eleven).

Gaza

At Gaza prison, none of the former detainees interviewed for this report said they had been placed in "closets." (See, however, Chapter Eleven for testimony on "refrigerators" at Gaza.)

---

[16] Hebron Military Court, case 2332/92, April 20, 1993 session, p. 15 of the protocol.

[17] Hebron Military Court, case 2332/92, May 17, 1993 session, p. 6 of the protocol.

ABUSIVE BODY POSITIONING — IDF INTERROGATIONS

Both the IDF and the GSS resort systematically to abusive body positioning between rounds of questioning. But the IDF's methods are less systematic, sophisticated and abusive, and IDF detainees are normally not subjected to position abuse at night.

IDF Abuse Station #1:
Enforced Standing

Among the GSS detainees we interviewed, only two, both of whom had been held at Tulkarm, reported being forced to stand for long periods. In IDF interrogations, by contrast, enforced standing is the most common form of position abuse. All three IDF interrogation centers have large, concrete-paved yards used as "standing areas" for prisoners (*shabeh* yards). Fifteen of the nineteen IDF interrogation subjects interviewed by HRW were made to stand for long periods, most of them outside in *shabeh* yards and a few in narrow "closets." They reported being forced to remain standing whether it was hot, cold, or raining.

Prolonged standing causes physical exhaustion and pain in the feet, legs, and lower back. It can eventually cause swelling and even bleeding. It is also a method of sleep deprivation.

When standing, most detainees are blindfolded. Some reported being hooded, and one had his shirt pulled over his head in lieu of an army-supplied head-covering. Nearly all are handcuffed behind their backs with painfully tight metal cuffs. While standing, prisoners are sometimes ordered to stand erect and are not allowed to speak with one another or with the guards, except to request access to the toilet. These requests often are refused, forcing detainees to wait for hours before being led to the toilets. Meals are usually taken in the cells, in "closets," or in the standing area itself. During meals, prisoners are usually permitted to sit down for several minutes.

Avshalom Benny, the IDF reserve paramedic, described what he saw in Dhahiriya:

> Along the wall of the stone building, in front of the waiting cells, interrogatees stand facing the wall, their hands tied behind their backs, their eyes blindfolded. They can stand that way for hours. Every five hours or so they are given a rest. I don't remember if they were permitted to sit down

> during the break, but their blindfolds were taken off, they were led to the toilets, and they were allowed to drink. [The guards] made sure the detainees would not see each other.
>
> The interrogation process can be different from interrogatee to interrogatee, according to the instructions of his interrogator. I saw people standing like that both during the day and during the night, all hours of the day. I do not know how long people stand there.[18]

IDF reservist Tal Raviv recalled what he saw from the guard post above the interrogation center in al-Far'a:

> Once, I went up there [on the roof of the interrogation wing] during the day to talk with the guard about something. I saw about twenty people standing there in the yard, with their hands tied behind their backs. Usually, when I was there during the night, they would sit with their hands tied. I was amazed to see them all standing there, all together like that, so many. At night, there are only two or three standing at a time, sometimes five.[19]

D. B., an Israeli reservist, was interviewed by B'Tselem in August 1993 about the thirty-day reserve duty he had served in the spring of 1993 at al-Far'a. D. B. said he worked as a military policeman patrolling the open area where most of the position abuse takes place. He told B'Tselem that the guards were instructed to keep detainees standing for defined periods of time:

> When new detainees would come, especially at night, they were often made to stand up, handcuffed and blindfolded for three or four hours, but in any case, not more than five hours.

---

[18] Affidavit given to ACRI on September 14, 1992, section 10.

[19] HRW interview, Tel Aviv, June 16, 1993.

The regulations about waiting were that they could be in that position for five hours, and from there they would take them in to interrogation. Then they could then be sent back to waiting. After that, it began all over again.[20]

D. B. said that guards were ordered to give prisoners water every thirty to forty minutes, contradicting the testimony HRW took from ex-detainees. In all three IDF facilities, they reported, their requests for water were repeatedly turned down, and unless they persisted they were not allowed to drink outside of mealtimes. Patrolling guards threatened and sometimes hit detainees with their gun butts, boots and fists if they tried to sit down, move about, or speak with others, detainees said.

According to former detainees, periods of enforced standing ranged between one and twenty-four hours at a time, but averaged eight to ten hours per day. Standing was interrupted only by questioning sessions, meals and toilet breaks. At al-Far'a, standing alternated with prolonged sitting on concrete blocks. At al-Far'a and Dhahiriya, "closets" were used as well (see below).

I. K., a twenty-year-old Gazan, was interrogated for twenty-nine days at the Beach facility during the winter of 1992–1993, and then released without charge. After each round of questioning, he said, he stood in the *shabeh* yard:

> I had iron cuffs on my hands. I was blindfolded. I was not allowed to lean against anything. If I asked to go to the bathroom, they said no.
>
> ....How long you stand depends on what the interrogator says. The longest time I stood was six hours. Other times it was two, three, four or five hours. Mostly it was about three to four hours. It was winter, and it was raining...and very cold.

Ah. al-M., an unemployed laborer from Bethlehem, was interrogated at Dhahiriya for fifty days in May-June 1992, and then

---

[20] B'Tselem interview by telephone, August 8, 1993. The name of the soldier is on file with B'Tselem. HRW translated his remarks into English.

released without charge. Ah. al-M. said he was routinely made to stand in *shabeh* until 11:00 P.M. or midnight. During the day, he recalled:

> You are under the sun, which is shining directly on you. The handcuffs bother you, they are tight, and they cut into your skin....Over my eyes I had about five blindfolds. It was like a joke for the guards; every guard who happened to be around put one over my eyes....
>
> Your legs hurt while you are standing. Your hands also. You can't breathe. When you are standing, guards sometime come and hit you. If you ask for water, they say no. If you ask to go to the toilet, they say no. I would say "*sherutim*" [Hebrew for toilet]....Whether they let you go or not depends on their mood....Some prisoners went to the bathroom in their clothes.

At al-Far'a some of the ex-detainees said their standing periods alternated with prolonged sitting on concrete blocks located in the middle of the standing area. Muhammad R., thirty-one, from near Jenin, was held under interrogation for forty-five days in early 1993. He recalled:

> The main thing is your legs. You are standing, you try to move your feet. There are many flies swarming around and on your hands and legs, and you can't swat them, because your hands are cuffed behind you.

Muhammad R. recounted one incident that occurred in the *shabeh* yard:

> Next to me were a couple of guards sitting with girls, women soldiers from the military base, who were in uniform. They were sitting there and laughing. I could see the girls from under my blindfold. I called to them and said, "My cuffs are too tight."
>
> The guard said to me, "I'm not on duty now." I said, "So bring me someone who is on duty." I was speaking in Arabic. He came up to me and punched me in the nose and said, "Talk to me in Hebrew!"

IDF Station #2:
The "Closet"

The IDF detention wing at Dhahiriya contains "closets" similar to those in use at GSS interrogation wings. We found no evidence of "closets" at the Beach facility or al-Far'a prior to late 1993. Beginning sometime in the second half of 1993, however, "closets" were reportedly built and put into use at al-Far'a.

Interrogation subjects described their time in the cramped "closets" as extremely uncomfortable. Only three body positions were possible:

- Sitting on the ledge, which was too narrow for comfortable sitting and too high to rest one's legs fully on the ground;

- Standing up straight; or

- Sitting on the ledge with one's legs jackknifed in the air, with the knees resting against the door.

To minimize discomfort, detainees in IDF "closets" continually shifted among these positions and were thus unable to sleep or rest. Two detainees from Dhahiriya said that guards ordered them to remain standing in the "closet," threatening that if they were caught sitting they would be beaten. They said the guards pulled open the "closet" doors every few minutes to check on them.

Most of the Dhahiriya detainees we interviewed said they had been locked in "closets" for several hours at a time; one said he had once been confined for twenty-four hours. To use the toilet, ex-detainees said they had to plead with the guards to escort them.

At mealtimes, guards opened the "closet" door, placed the food inside, and closed the door. Former detainees reported that at dinnertime it was too dark inside to identify the food they were served.

IDF reserve paramedic Avshalom Benny described the "closets" in Dhahiriya, referring to them by the IDF euphemism of "waiting rooms":

> In the interrogation wing there is a yard. When you enter, on your left you can see a row of waiting rooms for interrogation. They are made out of metal and measure about eighty centimeters wide, eighty centimeters deep, and about two meters high. There is a stone ledge inside.

Illustration #4

"CLOSET" — A small enclosed space in which many GSS and IDF detainees are confined for hours and sometimes for days, with only short breaks. In some GSS closets, detainees are hooded and chained to a "kindergarten chair," as pictured here, and bombarded with loud, grating music.

ILLUSTRATION #4

> The metal door has a small window, about 20 centimeters by 20 centimeters, which permits guards to peek inside. I don't know how air can get in. There is no light inside unless you open the door or the window from outside. There is no water in these cells and no bucket for going to the bathroom....
>
> A detainee would go into the waiting room, would be called at some point to interrogation, and then would go back.[21]

Benny's description resembles that of H. D., who spent many hours in Dhahiriya's "closets" during his forty-day interrogation in the winter of 1992–1993:

> I was taken straight to a closet. It is about fifty centimeters deep, eighty centimeters wide, and two meters high. Inside there is a concrete bench. The door is made of two tin or thin metal sheets with something heavy, like wood, in between. The closet is painted white; the door is black.
>
> There are five or six holes in the bottom of the door, each one about two centimeters in radius. The holes are for light and air.
>
> The closet is made of five slabs of concrete; one on each side, one in back, the roof, and the door. Everything is held together by screws. There are spaces between the slabs, and a little light comes in from there.

According to IDF reservist D. B., "closets" were under construction during 1993 at al-Far'a. D. B. told B'Tselem:

> They are now building cement waiting cells. These cells are about ninety by ninety centimeters (I measured them with a ruler), and they are about two meters high. There is a concrete ledge inside for sitting. The door is made of

---

[21] Affidavit given to ACRI on September 14, 1992, section 7.

metal, and there is a shutter about fifteen by twenty centimeters large, but as a rule, it is supposed to be shut.

Ventilation comes from the two-centimeter crack between the floor and the door. The idea, according to what I heard in the prison, is that the detainees are to stay in there for about twelve to fourteen hours at a time. I heard this from the second in command of the interrogation wing.[22]

Al-Far'a's "closets" were in use during early 1994, according to ex-detainees we interviewed (see, for example, the testimony of N.S. in Chapter One of this report).

At both Dhahiriya and al-Far'a, when winter daytime temperatures frequently drop to 5º celsius (41º fahrenheit), the "closets" get very cold. H. D. described the "closet" where he was confined during the winter of 1992-1993:

It was freezing in there. We used to put bread between the slits to stop the cold air from coming in. I kept trying to move myself, to keep the blood flowing. The whole time I was wearing a sweatshirt and heavy jacket that my mother had given me before I left. My hands were very cold. I used to put them in my pockets. I used to stomp my legs to try to keep warm.

IDF Abuse Station #3:
Pipe-Shackling

One ex-detainee described a form of position abuse at Dhahiriya that resembled GSS techniques, but was not reported by any other IDF detainees we interviewed. Muhammad Abu Hikmeh, a twenty-one-year-old history student at Birzeit University, told HRW that for the first ten or twelve days of his 1992 interrogation, he spent daytime intervals between questioning sessions in the "closet." For the next ten or so days, Abu Hikmeh said, he and others were tied to metal pipes in an external corridor bordering on the *shabeh* yard, in one of two positions:

---

[22] B'Tselem interview by telephone, August 8, 1993.

- His hands were tied above his head to a metal pipe, while his jacket covered his head. Although his feet were just on the ground, the pipe was high enough that some of his weight hung on his wrists and shoulders; and

- His hands were tied behind his back to a metal pipe protruding from the wall. The pipe was at mid-back level, forcing him to hunch forward, with his head at waist level.

Abu Hikmeh told HRW:

> It was a continual rotation between the interrogations, the pipe and, at night, the cell....When they first tie you to the pipe, you are in real pain. One minute is like a year. Eventually, you get used to it. You may even prefer pipe-*shabeh* to questioning. They cover your head with a piece of cloth or with your jacket, and you can even fall asleep sometimes.

IDF Abuse Station #3:
Prolonged Sitting on Concrete Blocks

In the interrogation wing at al-Far'a, one of the more common practices is to force detainees to sit on concrete blocks in the *shabeh* yard. The blocks are twenty by twenty centimeters wide, former detainees said, and are about fifty centimeters high. This method is used primarily during the day.

Three of the al-Far'a detainees we interviewed recounted being forced to sit on such blocks. While seated, they were blindfolded, handcuffed behind their backs, and ordered to sit erect. This caused cramps, back and shoulder pains, and exhaustion. Detainees said that they were forced to sit on blocks for up to fifteen hours, but more often, the block-sitting alternated with enforced standing and questioning sessions throughout the day. O. T., a twenty-three-year-old university student, was interrogated for twenty-five days at al-Far'a in 1992. During that time, he shuttled between standing, interrogation sessions, and the concrete blocks. He said:

> They usually take you at 8:00 A.M. to *shabeh*, and you stay there for hours, depending on the interrogators.

> Sometimes you stand, sometimes you sit. It depends on the interrogator.
>
> You get very tired on the concrete block. You can't lift your head; you must keep it lowered all the time. Your lower back begins to hurt, and your eyes hurt, because you are always blindfolded. Your legs also hurt, because your blood does not circulate. There is pain in your hands, because of the cuffs, which are tight and dig into your wrists.
>
> *Shabeh* is exhausting and nerve-wracking. You become very bored. They almost never let you go to the toilet or drink. You can only go when you get food, which comes in the morning and at night.
>
> I couldn't see the others, but I think there were about thirty in there with me. If you try and raise your head and look under the blindfold, they hit you.

IDF reservist Tal Raviv, who served as a guard on a rooftop overlooking al-Far'a's *shabeh* yard, told HRW:

> The regular army soldiers called the detainees' stint in the yard *yibush* [Hebrew for drying out]. Most of the torture is not in the interrogation rooms, it is being tied, blindfolded. It's frightening, and they are helpless, all tied up, and then they are hit in the yard by the guards. Their arms are pulled back, and you can see that it hurts.
>
> Some detainees asked for their cuffs to be removed, and the guards did it. Others didn't. The cuffs are very tight, and are placed high up on the arms so that the elbows are joined together behind their backs. It goes on for a long time, that's the whole point, that's the torture.[23]

---

[23] HRW interview, Tel Aviv, June 16, 1993.

D. B., the reserve military policeman who served at al-Far'a in the spring of 1993, told B'Tselem:

> The detainees who were in waiting would usually sit, their hands tied with cuffs behind their backs and their eyes covered with a strip of flannel cloth.

Twenty-one-year-old A., of Jenin, was interrogated at al-Far'a during August 1992. He described being made to sit on concrete blocks and to stand during the day, always blindfolded and tightly handcuffed behind his back. He told HRW:

> It never happens that you go straight from the cell to interrogation. You first go to *shabeh*, and only later, you go to the questioning session — once, twice, and even three times a day. When you finish the questioning session, you go back to *shabeh*. The guards walk around all the time, and you are not allowed to talk.
>
> You sit there for hours on these blocks, not moving, for as long as fifteen hours at a time. But days and evenings only: I never spent a night in *shabeh*.
>
> When you ask for water, they don't give it to you, even though you ask again and again, calling out to the guards. Sometimes it seems as if they have forgotten you in *shabeh*. You sit and sit, then, all of a sudden the interrogator comes and says, "Let's talk." But if you say nothing, he leaves you there in *shabeh*.
>
> For the first day, there is no problem. On the second or third day you begin not to feel your arms and hands, as if they are dead. When the guards want to hurt you, they come up to you and tighten the cuffs even more. The cuffs have ratchets, so the guards can cinch them tighter. They do it when the interrogator tells them to, for more pressure. This happened to me three times. When I got to the cell I couldn't use my hands because they had completely lost all feeling.

11
SUBJECTION TO TEMPERATURE EXTREMES

Between questioning sessions, both IDF and GSS interrogators expose detainees to harsh weather conditions for which they are not properly clothed. These include summer heat and winter rain, cold and even snow. In some cases, the exposure is inflicted through the use of special equipment, including fans and refrigeration units.

The April 25, 1993 affidavit submitted by the State Attorney to the Supreme Court stated that the revised GSS interrogation guidelines explicitly prohibited the "abandonment" (*hafkara*) of detainees to heat or cold (see Chapter Three). It is not clear whether "abandonment" rules out limited exposure of detainees to temperature extremes. Such abuse is apparently continuing, according to Palestinians interrogated by the GSS in late 1993 and by the IDF in early 1994.

MECHANICALLY INDUCED TEMPERATURE CHANGES

The GSS

The inducing of temperature changes by technical means appears to be primarily a GSS phenomenon. Of the seventeen GSS detainees we interviewed, five reported having been confined in deliberately over-cooled rooms ("refrigerators"), most of them at Ramallah. Two others were exposed to cold weather without adequate clothing, and one was placed in a hot and poorly ventilated cubicle, under circumstances that strongly suggested that the discomfort was intentional.

From the ex-detainees' descriptions, it is often not possible to know whether the source of cold air is in fact an air conditioner or simply fan-driven vents. Whatever the case, the devices blew cool air on detainees who were often ill-clad and unable to move their bodies much because they were shackled or confined.

Ramallah

A. Z., a twenty-three-year-old student, was held at Ramallah for eighteen days during October and November 1993. He said that while hooded and chained to a "kindergarten chair" in an interrogation room, he was exposed to cold air flowing from a vent:

> "Another simple and effective type of pressure is that of maintaining the temperature of the cell at a level which is either too hot or too cold for comfort. Continuous heat, at a level at which constant sweating is necessary in order to maintain body temperature, is enervating and fatigue-producing. Sustained cold is uncomfortable and poorly tolerated.
>
> "...The effects of isolation, anxiety, fatigue, lack of sleep, uncomfortable temperatures, and chronic hunger produce disturbances of mood, attitudes and behaviour in nearly all prisoners. The living organism cannot entirely withstand such assaults. The Communists do not look upon these assaults as 'torture.' Undoubtedly, they use the methods which they do in order to conform, in a typical legalistic manner, to overt Communist principles, which demand that 'no force or torture be used in extracting information from prisoners.' But all of them produce great discomfort, and lead to serious disturbances of many bodily processes: there is no reason to differentiate them from any other form of torture."
>
> Lawrence Hinkle Jr., M.D., and Harold Wolf, M.D., "Communist Interrogation and Indoctrination of 'Enemies of the State'" paper submitted for publication on May 31, 1956, American Medical Association, *Archives of Neurology and Psychiatry*, pp. 129-130.

> There is a vent in the ceiling of the room, that blows cold air in. Sometimes they left me in there all day and night. It happened on five or six separate days. I was wearing a buttoned shirt and regular pants. It was very cold. Sometimes I would beg the guard to button my shirt so that the collar would be closed.

Four other former Ramallah detainees reported being placed in "refrigerator" cubicles, of which there were seven or eight, according to the detainees. Fans built into the ceilings blow cold air inside, they said. Some of the "refrigerator" cells contain concrete ledges, while others have no seats, so detainees must stand or sit on the floor. The doors are typically made of metal with a rubber lining around the edges.

Detainees were typically forced to remain in the "refrigerator" for several hours at a time. Some said that while inside they were confined to "kindergarten chairs"; some were hooded, others not; some had handcuffs and leg chains, others did not.

Sh. Z., who was interrogated at Ramallah for fifteen days during December 1992, said:

> I was put in seven or eight different refrigerators while I was there. Some of them are larger than others. They are made of concrete, and are painted grey inside. They have a bucket that you can use as a toilet.
>
> The longest I spent in the refrigerator was three days straight. It was dark: the lightbulb didn't work and there was no window. You could hear the music, but it is less loud than in the *shabeh* corridor, where the chairs are.
>
> You can hear the other young men calling to each other, or reciting the Quran. Some of them were groaning, as if they were in pain. They were also in refrigerators. When you are in there, you feel as if your body is like a block of solid ice on the chair. You have pain in your hands and neck. I wasn't always hooded while in the refrigerator. If you are, that is worse.

S. R. was put in the "refrigerator" at Ramallah several times, usually for periods of about five hours. On one occasion, he said, he was held in one for twenty-four hours. He recalled:

> The refrigerator is a dark room....It has a refrigerator door, not a regular door. If you knock on it, they don't hear you from the outside. It has no chair, just a ledge, about twenty centimeters wide and fifty centimeters high, made of concrete. It's barely large enough to sit on.
>
> I sat there with my hands tied behind my back. Most of the time, I was there without a hood, but sometimes I was wearing one. When the guard brings the meal, they raise the hood a little over your face. The guard checks up on you in there every five or six hours, sometimes only at mealtimes.
>
> During the occasions I was in there for five or six hours, they put the air conditioner on for two to three hours. I felt as if I was in the snow, completely naked. The air conditioner is in the middle of the ceiling, so I would try to squeeze into the corner to get away from the current of cold air.

Tulkarm

At Tulkarm, none of the ex-detainees we interviewed had been placed in a "refrigerator." However, one detainee reported being ordered to stand on two occasions in front of a powerful air conditioner. Ad. M. recalled:

> "Captain Shalom" stood me in front of the air conditioner, for an hour or two, when I was still sweating a lot from being shackled. He would leave me in the room and say, "Don't move." The hood was on my head, and I was afraid to move because he could suddenly come back into the room without my knowing.

Subjection to Extreme Temperatures

Petach Tikva

The one Petach Tikva detainee we interviewed was not placed in a "refrigerator." However, he reported being locked in a small, extremely hot closet for as long as twenty-four hours (see Chapter Ten).

Gaza

Gaza prison had, until its closure in 1994, working "refrigerators," according to reports by other human rights organizations.[1] HRW interviewed a Gazan who described his experience in a "refrigerator" at the GSS wing in January–February 1991. Yousef Haddad, a Gaza City lawyer accused and later convicted of nonviolent activities on behalf of Hamas, recalled:

> At intervals, while I was on "the Bus," [the *shabeh* corridor] they put me in the refrigerator. It's a closet about sixty centimeters by one hundred centimeters, with a ceiling fan and rough, bumpy walls. There is no light inside. I was not wearing a hood, but I was handcuffed....While inside I was not allowed to sit down. The sessions in the refrigerator lasted two to three hours, except for once when it lasted about twelve hours.[2]

Hebron

At Hebron, there do not appear to be "refrigerators," according to our interviews with five ex-detainees.

IDF Facilities

HRW interviewed three young men detained at al-Far'a in early 1994 who charged that interrogators had confined detainees in a deliberately over-cooled corridor. We found no evidence of fans or air conditioners used abusively at Dhahiriya or the Beach facility.

The three recent al-Far'a detainees, all university students in the West Bank, said that between questioning sessions they were shackled to

---

[1] See, e.g., B'Tselem, *The Interrogation of Palestinians during the Intifada*, pp. 61-62.

[2] HRW interview, Gaza City, October 24, 1992.

chairs in a long corridor outside the interrogation rooms. One reported that his chair was tiny, like the GSS's "kindergarten chairs"; the other two said they sat on normal chairs. As they sat shackled in the corridor, dressed only in thin prison shirts and pants, they felt cold air from vents in the wall blowing onto their backs and necks. One of the three, twenty-one-year-old Sh. S., recalled:

> After interrogations, they would put the blindfold back on, and put me on a wooden chair next to the interrogation room, in a corridor. I would sit in the corridor. It had about twenty chairs, lining both sides. There were other prisoners there, I could see them when I looked up from under the blindfold every now and then.
>
> There were air conditioners[3] in the corridor. I can't say exactly how many. I think there was one above every chair, and they were blowing very cold air. The ceiling slopes down, and the vents of the conditioners are where the ceiling meets the wall. It is aimed right at you while you sit there, and is positioned maybe one meter from you.
>
> I used to sit there in the corridor for anywhere from fifteen minutes to three hours. Between interrogation sessions I sat there, sometimes four times a day. While I sat there under the cold air, the back of my neck and head began to freeze. It was like ice.

EXPOSURE TO ADVERSE WEATHER

Most of the ex-detainees interrogated in the fall, winter, or spring said that they had been exposed to harsh weather without proper clothing. The exposure seemed deliberate. Abd R. described his stay at al-Far'a, in the hilly northern West Bank, during February and March 1994:

---

[3] It is not clear whether blindfolded and confined detainees would be in a position to distinguish an air conditioner from other devices that blew cool air. See above.

Subjection to Extreme Temperatures 153

> When we checked in, they gave us a prison uniform, very lightweight, and too small. The pants only went down three-quarters length, and the sleeves were short, like for an undershirt. It was not enough for that time of year.
>
> Of the eight days I was in interrogation, I spent four standing in *shabeh* and three in the "closet." *Shabeh* was mostly standing in the courtyard, for about eight to twelve hours at a time. It was winter, and I had on only the uniform, with a T-shirt underneath. When it rained I still had to stand there.

Ali Radaydeh, interrogated at Hebron prison in January–February 1993, said that after one round of questioning, he was placed, hooded and chained on a "kindergarten chair," into a tiny cell containing a leaky window:

> I spent about three days there, in a cell about sixty centimeters by one meter. The cell was located high up. There was wind coming in; it was very cold.

Radaydeh's exposure to cold in the closet-like cell appears to have been deliberate. If the window were open, the guards or interrogators could have closed it. If it were broken, it could have been repaired or the detainee could have been placed elsewhere.

IDF reservists we interviewed confirmed that Palestinian detainees undergoing interrogation were denied adequate clothing and protection from the cold. Reserve Sergeant Tal Raviv, who served as a guard at al-Far'a in the winter of 1992–1993, said of the detainees in the *shabeh* yard:

> The clothes they were wearing were very thin....At night, it was about 5º or 6º centigrade (41–43º fahrenheit). Some of the people are left there in the yard throughout the night.

Reserve First Sergeant Shimon M. told HRW that when he served at the Beach facility as a military policeman in the winter of 1990, he wondered how the detainees survived:

> I would stand guard in the tower, freezing, wearing an overcoat, gloves and a scarf. And they would be down there, in the courtyard, wearing only the shirts they had been arrested in. I don't know how they did it.

On February 4, 1992 Mustafa Akawi, thirty-five, died while under interrogation in the GSS interrogation wing at Hebron prison. The immediate cause of Akawi's death was heart failure related to chronic arteriosclerosis. An independent pathologist acting on behalf of Akawi's family, Dr. Michael Baden, concluded that the fatal heart attack was "precipitated by the physical, psychological, and environmental abuse" Akawi suffered under interrogation, including being hooded and handcuffed in a chair located in a bitterly cold exterior hallway on the night he died. Dr. Baden visited the hallway four days after the death and said he felt cold while dressed in street clothes and a raincoat. At night, he said, the temperature was at most 0° centigrade [33° fahrenheit]. The windows in the corridor were broken, allowing cold air to flow in from outside. His reconstruction of events, based on the testimony of GSS interrogators and paramedics on the scene, left little doubt that the exposure of Akawi to cold was deliberate. (See Chapter Nineteen, on deaths in detention.)

12
PSYCHOLOGICAL ABUSE AND SLEEP DEPRIVATION

[While a paramedic in Dhahiriya] I got the impression that there are two stages to the interrogation. In the first stage the interrogation is intensive: there are many hours of questioning, of standing, and of being in the waiting room.

In the second stage there is usually a deep internal crisis. [The detainees] try to go to the clinic, there is lots of crying, they call you and say they can't breathe, there are those who kiss your hands and feet. "I can't breathe" is the complaint you hear endlessly from everyone. There were times when the doctor diagnosed this as an "uncontrolled hysterical reaction," and prescribed valium for them.

Interrogators told me that hysteria and fear is part of the detainees' game. The interrogators worry only about problems that are physical.

— IDF reserve paramedic Avshalom Benny[1]

On the third day, four interrogators came into the room and said, "We are going to kill you. You will not come out of here alive. The only way you can leave is to confess, or to die or go insane. Trust us."

Everything is planned to make you go crazy....You sit alone, you talk with the floor, you laugh to yourself....I could hear others in the corridor laughing, crying, reciting verses from the Quran....You become completely hysterical.

—Ahmed al-Batsh, describing his seventy-five days under interrogation at the Ramallah GSS wing

---

[1] Affidavit given to the Association for Civil Rights in Israel, September 14, 1992, section 22.

For a person who is arrested and facing questioning anywhere in the world, a certain degree of stress and dread is almost inevitable. If nothing else, the detainee is removed from familiar surroundings, placed under the authority of strangers, and may be at risk of conviction and imprisonment. If he or she expects harsh methods of interrogation, the anxiety is that much greater.

The IDF and GSS select techniques that are calculated to exacerbate the stress and dread felt by detainees. These include isolation; prolonged sight, sleep and toilet deprivation; and, at GSS centers, bombardment with grating music. While some of these methods — such as blindfolding — have a rationale in the interrogation process, they are used in a manner that is more abusive than functional.

HOODING/BLINDFOLDING: THE DEPRIVATION OF SIGHT

Prolonged sight deprivation instills a feeling of disorientation, isolation, and dread in persons undergoing interrogation. It can distort one's sense of reality, make it difficult to concentrate, and cause visual sightings (illusionary flashes) and hallucinations.[2]

GSS Interrogations

The GSS employs sight deprivation more systematically than the IDF. All seventeen GSS detainees interviewed for this report said they were hooded during most of their time in the interrogation wing. Hoods remained over detainees' heads around the clock, five to six days per week, throughout the interrogation period, with the exception of questioning sessions, a few respites and weekend breaks (see below).

---

[2] Hallucinations, in contrast to visual sightings, involve the belief that what is seen is real.

Psychological Abuse and Sleep Deprivation

"It is helpful to consider the individual man as a living system entirely dependent upon maintaining a satisfactory relationship with his total environment. A man's life is dependent upon his ability to maintain a satisfactory body temperature; a satisfactory intake of food, fluids and air; a satisfactory elimination of waste products; and a satisfactory amount of rest and activity. It is equally necessary for him to maintain a satisfactory relationship with the other human beings in his environment....

"When any of these necessary relationships between a man and his environment are disturbed, there develop within him feelings which are unpleasant, and which stimulate him to take whatever action is necessary to bring them to an end. Among these unpleasant sensations are hunger, thirst, fatigue, sleeplessness, excessive warmth or coldness, and all sorts of pain. These sensations originate within the human body as a result of disturbances of bodily processes. There are other unpleasant feelings, such as anxiety, fear, anger, loneliness, sadness and dejection, which arise out of disturbed relations to the total environment and the people in it. When beset by these feelings, man is strongly motivated to make whatever adjustments in his relation to his environment that are necessary....

"[In interrogation,] the subject is faced with pressure upon pressure and discomfort upon discomfort, and none of his attempts to deal with his situation lead to amelioration of his lot....When a man is at the "end of his rope," he accepts avidly any help that is offered....His own intense needs have prepared him to accept suggestions which he previously would have rejected.

"....Not only are his mood and behaviour disturbed, but profound and potentially dangerous alterations to his bodily processes occur also. Thus, the power which the interrogator possesses in dealing with the prisoner is great; his ability to manipulate both the physical and the interpersonal aspects of the prisoner's environment place his victim in a highly vulnerable position.

"....It is readily understandable that the prisoner ultimately adopts the suggestions of the interrogator."

Hinkle and Wolf, "Communist Interrogation and Indoctrination," pp. 170-173.

The Impact of Blindfolding during Torture

"[B]lindfolding during torture is a common practice which not only helps the torturers remain unidentified, but also appears to increase the impact of torture.

"Blindfolding is highly aversive even when not combined with other forms of torture. Loss of visual monitoring of the environment distinctly intensifies feelings of helplessness and introduces a significant element of unpredictability regarding imminent aversive events. When blindfolding is combined with other forms of torture, it appears to potentiate their effects....For the detainee the blindfolding magnifies a realistically minor threat into an apparently life-endangering situation."

Metin Basoglu and Susan Mineka, "The Role of Uncontrollable and Unpredictable Stress in Post-Traumatic Stress Responses in Torture Survivors," in *Torture and its Consequences*, ed. Metin Basoglu (Cambridge: Cambridge University Press, 1992), p. 203.

Psychological Abuse and Sleep Deprivation

Hooding is justified by security agencies in many countries as a means of preventing suspects from identifying one another or their interrogators. For the GSS, however, hooding is primarily a means of psychological and physical pressure. This is shown by the fact that some detainees were hooded even while inside "closets" or "refrigerators," where they were in no position to be identified or to identify others. Sometimes, interrogators re-hooded detainees in the middle of questioning sessions, an act that could only be explained as a means of turning up the pressure. (For the most part, GSS interrogation subjects were permitted to see the faces of their interrogators.) Moreover, the failure of the GSS to launder the hoods on a regular basis seemed to be a means of making the hooding experience more unpleasant than necessary.

The GSS-issue hood is a shroud-like garment made of dark green canvas or rough cotton. It is of a standard size and cut, according to detainees' descriptions. The hood reaches down to the wearer's upper chest, with slits at the shoulders to keep it from bunching up at the neck. When standing, detainees said, they could see their feet through the opening in the bottom. The hood reportedly has a sponge-like substance lining the inside top, so that it remains in place while resting on the head. There are no nose- or mouth-holes; air enters through the opening in the bottom and through small rips found in some of the hoods.

According to ex-detainees interviewed by HRW, hoods were, in general, removed in the following situations only:

- **When detainees were being questioned in the interrogation room.**

  However, five detainees reported being re-hooded when interrogators were dissatisfied with their answers, after which the questioning continued.

- **When detainees were taken from the position-abuse station to the toilet, usually three times daily.**

  Guards removed the hood at the entrance to the toilet stall, and placed it back over the detainee's head when he re-emerged, usually no more than three to five minutes later.

- **On weekends, when most interrogation subjects spent some thirty-six hours in cells.**

The detainee was unhooded upon entering the cell, and re-hooded at the end of the rest period, as he was brought back to a position-abuse station or interrogation room.

- **Often, when interrogation subjects were placed in "closets" or "refrigerators."**

- **When detainees were taken to see a military judge, ICRC delegate, lawyer, or prison doctor or medic.**

Many ex-detainees said that because they remained hooded nearly all of the time, they could not sketch the facility in which they had been held. Twenty-three-year-old U. Gh., who said he was hooded throughout his twenty-four-day interrogation at Tulkarm, said:

> There are three ways of telling where you are: the color of the floor, whether or not there is music, and the guard. It is the guard who brings you from the interrogation area to the cell, but it is the interrogator who puts you in *shabeh*. There are electric doors and codes they must punch in when they move between the cells and the interrogation area.

Some GSS detainees reported that small tears in the hoods enabled them to discern the shapes of other detainees shackled nearby and of their general surroundings. They could also sense when guards were nearby.

Breathing Difficulties

Some ex-detainees said that the hoods fit so snugly over their faces that the thick material clinged slightly to their noses and mouths each time they inhaled. Sometimes, interrogators used the suffocative feel of the hoods to terrorize detainees. Two of three Tulkarm detainees reported that, on at least one occasion, interrogators had come up and tightened the hood at their necks, by pulling the drawstring found in some hoods. Ad. M. recalled:

> Sometimes, "Major Shalom" put a very tight hood on my head, a different one, with a cinch, and tightened it very

tight. I couldn't breathe. I would suck it into my mouth with every breath. He did this during questioning.

Some detainees held at other facilities said interrogators sometimes crept up and suddenly covered their nose or mouth through the hood. Although the interrogators invariably let go before long, these surprise attacks were a constant source of dread.

Dirty Hoods

Responding to allegations by human rights groups that the GSS used dirty or wet hoods to intensify the discomfort of detainees, State Attorney Dorit Beinish reportedly told the U.N. Committee against Torture in April 1994 that the practice was forbidden, and that disciplinary actions had been taken against interrogators who employed it.[3]

At the trial of Muhammad Adawi, GSS agent "Billy" was asked by the defense whether it was true, as Adawi had alleged, that his hood was dirty and bad-smelling. "Billy" replied, "I don't know if the hood was washed sometimes. We have many hoods."[4]

The overall impression we gathered from detainee testimony is that they are frequently assigned hoods that have not been washed, whether by design or negligence. Many ex-detainees complained that their hoods smelled of the breath and saliva of other prisoners, or, sometimes, of gasoline or excrement. Three GSS detainees accused the guards of deliberately dropping their hoods onto the floor when they brought the detainees to the toilets.

Ahmed al-Batsh said he judged the kindness of the guards at Ramallah by the way they handled his hood when escorting him to the bathroom. The "nice" guards did not grasp it and pull him "like a donkey," or drop the hood on the floor when al-Batsh used the toilet. As for the other guards:

---

[3] U.N. press release, "Committee against Torture Begins Review of Report of Israel," HR/CAT/94/11, April 25, 1994.

[4] Hebron Military Court, case 2332/92, April 20, 1993 session, p. 27 of the protocol.

> When they take off the hood for the bathroom, they throw it on the ground, into the excrement and urine that's all over the floor. Then you put the same hood back on.

S.R., also interrogated at Ramallah, told HRW:

> They don't use the same hood all the time. Some hoods have no smell. Usually, however, they smell like someone else's breath. When I went to the toilet, the guard tossed the hood onto the floor, and it would get wet and dirty from the floor.
>
> When it was hot, I sweated a lot in the hood. My hair would get in my eyes. I itched inside the hood all the time. It is possible to breathe, but it is not normal breathing, not comfortable.

B. Ah. said he was hooded for much of three weeks while chained to a chair in a "closet" at Hebron prison. He recalled:

> I had a headache all the time in the "closet." I was unable to think or to concentrate on anything. Part of the pain was from my eyes; I never saw light, or anything; the hood makes you lose your sight.
>
> If the guard opens the door and catches you rubbing the hood off your head against the wall, he hits you in the face or curses you. This happened to me many times. I couldn't bear the hood, the smell was so awful and disgusting...as if they use it for cleaning the floor, wiping tables, everything, and then put it on your head. Sometimes, it smelled like gasoline. Other times, like sewage.
>
> You get a different hood every Sunday morning. Some hoods are better than others. But the new ones on Sunday weren't necessarily any cleaner, they just smelled differently from the others.

IDF Interrogations

All nineteen IDF interrogation subjects interviewed for this report said they were blindfolded with strips of cloth during daytime position abuse; two reported also being hooded at certain times.

Detainees were blindfolded throughout the day, except when they were being questioned, using the toilets, or, in Dhahiriya, placed in "closets." During the night, when detainees were placed in cells, guards removed the blindfolds.

The blindfold causes less discomfort than the GSS hood, since it does not interfere with breathing or force the wearer to inhale foul odors. But like hoods, blindfolds isolate detainees from the outside world, and increase their feelings of anxiety and vulnerability.

SLEEP DEPRIVATION

> In the head of the interrogated prisoner a haze begins to form. His spirit is wearied to death, his legs are unsteady, and he has one sole desire: to sleep, to sleep just a little, not to get up, to lie, to rest, to forget....Anyone who has experienced this desire knows that not even hunger or thirst are comparable with it.
>
> I came across prisoners who signed what they were ordered to sign, only to get what the interrogator promised them. He did not promise them their liberty. He promised them—if they signed—uninterrupted sleep! And they signed....And having signed, there was nothing in the world that could move them to risk again such nights and such days....The main thing was — to sleep.
>
> — Former Israeli prime minister Menachem Begin, recalling his experience in a Russian prison in 1940.[5]

---

[5] Menachem Begin, *White Nights: The Story of a Prisoner in Russia*, trans. Kafie Kaplan (Jerusalem: Steimatzky, 1977).

> With respect to prevention of sleep, any detainee who wants to talk can go to sleep immediately thereafter. If I wanted him [Adawi] to sleep, I would have sent him to sleep. That is our position.
>
> —GSS agent "Thompson," testifying at the trial of Muhammad Adawi.[6]

Sleep deprivation is a key tactic in GSS and IDF interrogations. Like abusive body positioning, sleep deprivation undermines a detainee's concentration and self-control. And, because it leaves no lasting physical traces, sleep deprivation is difficult to prove after the fact. This complicates the task of detainees who wish to prove later that prolonged sleep deprivation coerced them into signing a statement.

Israel's techniques for depriving sleep involve position abuse, constant noise, and harassment by guards. The accounts below of long-term sleep deprivation do not exclude the possibility that, during such periods, detainees dozed off occasionally. But, as the ex-detainees testified, the methods used guaranteed that what sleep they got was brief and troubled.

GSS Interrogations

Sixteen of seventeen GSS detainees interviewed for this report said they had been deprived of sleep for long periods, lasting as long as six consecutive days. The chief means was to confine them to a position-abuse station that made sound sleep impossible. In addition, some detainees reported that when their heads dropped as they nodded off, guards would shake, hit, or yell at them.

In most cases, interrogation subjects were kept at position-abuse stations day and night, all week, with brief interruptions, until the beginning of the weekly rest period that began Friday evening, the beginning of the Jewish sabbath. They were then confined in cells until

---

[6] Hebron Military Court, case 2332/92, June 30, 1993 session, p. 77 of the protocol.

[7] The seventeenth, Bassem Tamimi, was not held long enough to be subjected to this method for a prolonged period: his interrogation ended in its second day, when he was hospitalized with a head injury. See Chapter One.

"The effects of isolation, uncertainty, and anxiety are usually sufficient to make the prisoner eager to talk to his interrogator and to seek some method of escape from a situation which is intolerable. But, if these alone are not enough to produce the desired effect, the officer in charge has other simple and highly effective ways of applying pressure. Two of the most effective of these are fatigue and lack of sleep....It is easy to have the guard awaken the prisoner at intervals. This is especially effective if the prisoner is always awakened as soon as he drops off to sleep. The guards can also shorten the hours available for sleep, or deny sleep altogether. Continued loss of sleep produces clouding of consciousness and a loss of alertness, both of which impair the victim's ability to sustain isolation. It also produces profound fatigue."

— Hinkle and Wolf, "Communist Interrogation and Indoctrination of Enemies of the State," p. 129.

Sunday morning. In a minority of cases, the GSS transferred detainees from position-abuse stations to cells at night at times during their interrogation.

Detainees reported that the five-to-six-day cycles of sleep deprivation were repeated throughout the interrogation, so that during a thirty-day interrogation there would be at most six days during which they could sleep soundly. Some detainees said that interrogators promised them sleep if they signed a confession or provided sought-after information.

During position abuse, most detainees said, they were rarely able to get more than a few minutes' sleep at a time. On "kindergarten chairs," many nodded off, only to be awakened by the guards or by the pain of the chair seat and tight cuffs. When they were shackled to wall rings or pipes, sleep was more difficult.

GSS Court Testimony on Sleep Deprivation

Muhammad Adawi's trial at the Hebron Military Court revealed much about the practice of sleep deprivation. GSS agents acknowledged that Adawi had been subjected to three extended periods in which sleep was effectively impossible, the longest of which lasted more than four days, interrupted by only two brief respites. One agent tacitly admitted that agents made sleep contingent upon the detainee's willingness to talk (see the comments of "Thompson," quoted above).

Another agent, "Mousa," suggested that the interrogators did not closely monitor the time detainees spent without sleep. Defense counsel Shlomo Lecker asked "Mousa" whether he was aware that when he questioned Adawi on June 23, 1992, the detainee had not slept "throughout the waiting period, for thirty-nine hours straight, and that he was physically exhausted." "Mousa" replied:

> I don't check how long a person sits in waiting [before interrogation]. I simply bring him into interrogation....I did not know that the accused had been in waiting for thirty-nine hours before he was brought in to me. I don't count how many hours the accused sits in waiting....I don't add up the number of hours....The number of hours the

Psychological Abuse and Sleep Deprivation

accused sits in waiting is not relevant to the interrogation.[8]

The GSS's log of its interrogation of Adawi was turned over to attorney Lecker. It shows the times and dates that Adawi was brought into the interrogation room, and notes the content of the interrogation. It gives the time that each interrogation round ended, and where the detainee was then sent — in Adawi's case, to one of three places: "waiting," "rest" and "cell." The log is reproduced in English translation in the Appendix to this report.

Waiting

As mentioned in Chapter Ten, "waiting" is the interrogators' euphemism for the periods between questioning sessions in which the detainee is almost invariably subjected to a combination of abusive body positioning, hooding and sleep deprivation.

Rest

According to the log, Adawi was sent on several occasions for two to three hours of "rest" during prolonged periods of "waiting." GSS agent "Gabi" described it thus:

> "Rest" is when I let the accused sleep and put a mattress and blankets down for him. That's called rest.
>
> [During rest,] the accused can sleep in the interrogation facility. He goes into the room, where he can sleep and rest.[9]

"Gabi" said he did not remember whether Adawi's hands remained cuffed during "rest" periods.[10]

---

[8] Hebron Military Court, case 2332/92, May 17, 1993 session, pp. 71-72 of the protocol.

[9] Hebron Military Court, case 2332/92, April 20, 1993 session, p. 11 of the protocol.

[10] Ibid., pp. 25-27.

Adawi told his lawyer that he was not permitted to rest for the full period specified as "rest" in the log. The time it took to transfer him to and from the "rest" station consumed some of the period logged as "rest." He was also taken to the toilet and fed during "rest," which also reduced the time available for sleep. Adawi told his lawyer that he estimated sleeping for just over one hour during a two-hour "rest" period.[11]

Cell

According to the GSS agents who testified at the trial, "cell" in Adawi's case refers to a cell located outside the interrogation wing in the section of Hebron prison that is administered by the Israel Prison Service. Since the GSS has no formal authority over that section, the agents said they could not speak to the size and condition of Adawi's cell.

According to the GSS log, Adawi was sent to a "cell" three times during his June 10–25, 1992 interrogation. He was sent there first from Friday, June 12 until Sunday, June 14 in the morning. The second time was from the afternoon of Thursday, June 18 until the evening of Tuesday, June 23. The third time was in the afternoon of Thursday, June 25, after he had signed his second and final confession.

The timing of the first period Adawi spent in the cell appears consistent with what other ex-detainees told HRW regarding weekend breaks from questioning and abusive body positioning. Adawi's second period in the cell, however, lasted longer than the average weekend rest periods described to HRW. This may be due to the head injury he incurred on Thursday, June 18 (see Chapter Sixteen), the day he was transferred to a cell.

Adawi's third and final respite in the prison cell is consistent with accounts by other interrogation subjects: once they signed the sought-after confession, the interrogation ended and detainees were sent to cells in the general section of the prison.

The GSS log provides an account of where Adawi spent his time during interrogation (see the Appendix). According to the log, Adawi was deprived of proper sleep for long periods of time on three occasions:

---

[11] HRW interview with attorney Shlomo Lecker, Hebron Military Court, June 30, 1993.

Psychological Abuse and Sleep Deprivation

1. 55 hours, between Wednesday, June 10 and Friday, June 12

Upon his arrival at Hebron, Adawi was placed in the "waiting" mode and thereby deprived of proper sleep for forty-one hours. He had been awake for fourteen hours before his arrival, according to his court testimony.

2. 109 hours (with two short breaks), between Sunday, June 14, and Thursday, June 18

During this time, Adawi remained in the "waiting" mode or in questioning for 105 hours, with the exception of two breaks that lasted two to three hours each.

On June 17, during this period of prolonged sleeplessness, Adawi signed his first confession, stating that he was an activist in Hamas.

On June 18, the routine was disrupted by Adawi's head injury, the cause of which was debated in court (see Chapter Sixteen). After the injury, Adawi was taken to the cell and permitted to rest for four days, during which time he was taken to the doctor and given medication.

3. 55 hours, between Tuesday, June 23 and Thursday, June 25

According to the log, the GSS kept Adawi in "waiting" or under interrogation for forty-two hours. Adawi told his lawyer that the actual period of sleeplessness was closer to fifty-five hours, since he had been awake for over twelve hours in his cell before being taken back to the interrogation wing on June 23. Towards the end of these fifty-five hours, Adawi agreed to sign his second and final confession. (At the trial, the charges stemming from the second confession were dropped as part of a plea bargain. See Chapter Eighteen.)

***

Abd al-Qader Seif al-Din Mon'em al-Khatib was arrested on May 5, 1992, and interrogated by the GSS at Ramallah prison and the Russian Compound. He was charged with membership in an illegal organization, possessing weapons, and recruiting others to carry out shooting attacks, none of them successfully executed, on IDF and civilian vehicles in the West Bank.

Al-Khatib signed a confession following interrogation, but contested its validity during his trial in the Ramallah Military Court,[12] saying it had been extracted through coercion. He said interrogators handcuffed him for long periods, beat him, hooded him, deprived him of sleep, and made threats against himself and his family, including a threat to demolish his family's home. (For more on his trial, see Chapter Eighteen.)

During the trial, according to al-Khatib's lawyer, Abed Asali, GSS agents acknowledged confining the defendant to a chair for long periods, handcuffed and hooded. Al-Khatib contended that virtually all of the "waiting" time was spent under these conditions, and that the chair was a "kindergarten chair."

According to Asali, the GSS agents denied that these methods amounted to impermissible pressure. Rather, they said they were designed to prevent the defendant from escaping or identifying other detainees between rounds of questioning. They categorically denied having beaten or threatened al-Khatib.[13]

The GSS interrogation log presented as evidence during the trial show al-Khatib spending long periods in "waiting" during his first ten days in detention, punctuated by questioning sessions and brief rest periods. The log, made available to HRW by Asali, does not reveal where al-Khatib spent every minute of his time. But it strongly suggests that he spent at least five periods, each between nineteen and forty-eight hours long and some possibly longer, in the "waiting" mode, prevented from sleeping. The log depicts the following sequence of events:

> Al-Khatib was admitted to the Ramallah GSS wing on May 5, 1992 at 11 P.M. and was sent directly to "waiting." He appears to have remained there for twenty-four hours. He was then allowed to sleep for five hours, until 4:00 A.M. on May 7. Al-Khatib's first round of sleep deprivation thus was twenty-four hours, in addition to the fifteen hours he said he had been awake before admission to the facility.

---

[12] Ramallah Military Court, case 4614/92.

[13] HRW interview with Abed Asali, Jerusalem, July 18, 1993.

Psychological Abuse and Sleep Deprivation

Al-Khatib's second round of "waiting" began at 4:00 A.M. on May 7 and ended at 4:00 A.M. on May 9. He was then allowed to sleep for another five hours, until 9 A.M. that morning.

On May 9 at 9 A.M., al-Khatib was sent back to "waiting." On May 10, at 3:30 P.M., after an additional thirty and-a-half hours of "waiting," al-Khatib began to supply his interrogators with names of purported associates in his activities.

Al-Khatib was returned to the "waiting" mode at 7:00 the same evening (May 10), where he remained until 1:50 the following afternoon (May 11). At this point, al-Khatib had apparently been prevented from sleeping for over two full days. He was then brought to the interrogation room and questioned for over two hours. During this session he provided additional information, according to the GSS log.

Al-Khatib was then returned to the "waiting" mode. On May 11, according to the log, al-Khatib was transferred "from Room Six to Room Three, handcuffed in front, with two blankets and no hood." The form was signed by a person named "Moti."

On May 13, at 8:40 A.M., al-Khatib was questioned again and gave his interrogators more information, according to the log. At 5:30 the same afternoon, he was again sent to "waiting," where he stayed until May 14 at 3:20 P.M., when he was led back into interrogation.

At 5:20 P.M. on May 14, after two hours of questioning, al-Khatib was sent to a cell, where he was presumably allowed to sleep.

EFFECTS OF SLEEP DEPRIVATION

According to ex-detainees, the lack of sleep, combined with position-abuse, hooding and grating music, undermined their ability to concentrate, reason, or form complete thoughts. S. R., twenty-five, was interrogated by the GSS at Ramallah for thirty-eight days. He recalled:

> I would begin to imagine things from the lack of sleep. Nothing precise. I was neither quite awake nor asleep. I would say things, but I don't remember what. When I most wanted to sleep, I began to imagine that I was home. But then, after a few minutes, I would feel a tug, my head would bob, and I would realize where I was: in *shabeh*. It was like dreaming, but without sleeping.
>
> Or I would begin to fall asleep on the chair, and my body would begin to slump. But my hands were tied, and in the few seconds between falling asleep and when the handcuffs dug into my wrists, I hallucinated.

M. R. said that after several days on a "kindergarten chair" at Gaza prison he began to break down:

> It gets to the point where the pain and the fatigue is so bad that you must sleep, at any price. You just collapse. If you can't stand up, the guard will hit you....You are in confusion all the time. You ask yourself, What will the interrogator ask you? Have other people said things against you? When you meet the interrogator you cannot control yourself, you cannot answer as you want, you totally lose control.

IDF Interrogations

The IDF uses techniques of sleep deprivation that differ from those of the GSS. During the night, most detainees are returned to cells from the daytime position-abuse stations. The cells were described by the detainees as small, dirty, damp, foul-smelling, stuffy in summer, and freezing in winter. Still, the detainees said, they would have slept easily — if the guards

Psychological Abuse and Sleep Deprivation

left them alone. Most of the IDF detainees, particularly those held at Dhahiriya and al-Far'a, said that guards woke them periodically through the night, banging on the door and ordering inmates to call out their prisoner numbers. Nineteen-year-old Abd R., interrogated at al-Far'a during early 1994, said that, at night:

> They took me to a cell, 1.30 meters by two meters, with two people inside, including me. It had a metal door and a small window. Every night, the guard would come maybe twenty times, to wake us up. He would open the shutter and yell at us, and we had to stand up and say, "Yes, Captain."

Twenty-three-year-old Ah. al-M., a resident of Bethlehem, was interrogated at Dhahiriya for fifty days in 1992. He recalled:

> You don't sleep through the night, because the guards have orders to disturb you. They beat on the doors with a stick. If you are about to fall asleep, this wakes you. The guards make rounds, waking everybody up. They came every few minutes. Then at 5:00 A.M., they come to take you to *shabeh*.

IDF reserve paramedic Avshalom Benny recounted how guards at Dhahiriya routinely disturbed the sleep of a particular detainee:

> At night, while he [Abd al-Ghani] was in his cell, the order was given to wake him up every quarter of an hour, which was done for several days. If a guard didn't carry this order out to the letter, others made sure to do it.[14]

Y. D., twenty, was interrogated at Dhahiriya for eighteen days in December 1992. He said interrogators offered to let him sleep if he provided a statement:

---

[14] Affidavit given to the Association for Civil Rights in Israel on September 14, 1992, section 23.

> During the eighteen days I spent under interrogation, there were only three days during which they allowed me to sleep. I was always very tired....The interrogators said to me on several occasions, "If you confess, you will go to a nice room, you will leave the cell, and you can sleep. You are like a log of wood stuck in the closet. Confess, and you can sleep."

Isolation

Isolation of detainees from one another and from the outside world is central to Israeli interrogations. Contact is denied with fellow prisoners and with outsiders who might provide comfort and fortitude, such as lawyers, family members, and other visitors.

Under Israeli military law, the detaining authorities can prevent a suspect from seeing a lawyer for two consecutive fifteen-day periods, after which a military judge must approve continued denial (see Chapter Eight). Among the detainees we interviewed, access to a lawyer was provided an average of twenty days after the arrest, not counting the thirteen detainees who were released from interrogation without having seen a lawyer at all. Family visits are almost always denied during interrogation.

GSS Interrogations

Throughout the GSS interrogation, most detainees had contact with no one but the facility's staff, except for those who shared cells during weekend rests. During the week, they were forbidden from speaking to other detainees. The only communication permitted was to ask guards for permission to use the toilets or receive medical treatment. The sense of isolation was reinforced by the wearing of hoods.

B. Ah. told HRW that the authorities took pains to isolate him, during both position abuse and the weekend rests:

> There were maybe twenty-seven cells at Hebron prison, but I never talked with anyone while in there. It is hard to hear. When I was in the "closet" during the week, I knew that there were other closets, maybe thirty of them, and that there were other prisoners. I couldn't talk to them,

however, because if the guards catch you, you are in big trouble.

IDF Interrogations

IDF interrogation practices on isolation are less stringent than those of the GSS. During the day, ex-detainees said, they were forbidden to speak with others while at the position-abuse stations. Roving guards enforced the policy.

At night, some were placed in solitary cells, others in shared cells. Those in shared cells were often inhibited from talking with cellmates out of fear that there might be informants among them.

Some IDF detainees spent several days locked in isolation cells before the interrogation began. I. K., interrogated at the Beach facility, recalled:

> They put me in cell number eleven. At first I was alone. They released my hands and uncovered my eyes. I was in the cell for two days. No one spoke to me. This is a policy. They let you stay by yourself, you become scared, you ask yourself what will happen. I heard from people in the general section that you should expect that this is going to happen to you, and be prepared for it.

Another ex-detainee said that the suspense was so great during the initial isolation period that he grew eager for the interrogation to begin.

SUBJECTION TO LOUD, CONTINUAL NOISE

The GSS subjects nearly all detainees to loud, grating music in a deliberately abusive manner. A government official acknowledged in 1993 that GSS interrogators used music during interrogation, but, in response to a complaint by a detainee's attorney, stated that the music played "was not excessively loud."[15]

---

[15] Letter from Rachel Sukar, deputy to the State Attorney, to lawyer Tamar Pelleg-Sryck, dated August 18, 1993. Sukar was responding to a complaint filed by Pelleg-Sryck on behalf of detainee Na'im Ibrahim abu Seif, who had been interrogated at Ashkelon prison in February 1993.

The music was quite loud, according to all seventeen GSS detainees we interviewed. It was also broadcast day and night. Some said they believed it to be Western classical or operatic music, but most found it bizarre and unfamiliar. On the basis of their descriptions, it was clear that the program varied among interrogation wings.

A. M., interrogated at Tulkarm, said the music was especially loud when he was chained to a wall pipe in an alcove:

> When you are tied to the pipe, and it is very quiet, you hear the music and you feel like you are going to die. You are standing, hood on your head, and the music is very loud, and you are very scared. The music is strange, like you are in a nightmare, unnatural. You can't hear anything else of what is going on in the other rooms. I still dream often of the "terror music." Sometimes, I wake up hearing it.

Hassan Zebeideh, who was in a catatonic state for months after his interrogation at Tulkarm (see below, this chapter), said of the music:

> There was a large speaker next to me, all the time. There was a voice with girls screaming, screaming in Hebrew. It was screaming, not music, not songs.

At Ramallah, detainees said there were several speakers in the corridor housing most of the "kindergarten chairs." S. Z., interrogated at Ramallah, said:

> Throughout the time there, there was loud music. I can't describe it because it's not real music. Sometimes they had sounds of women playing with children.

> It sounds like what is used in horror movies. It is quiet, and then suddenly loud, about fifty musical instruments all playing at the same time. Each one has a different tempo. I have never heard anything like this before. "Captain Cohen" [one of the interrogators] would ask me how I liked the music, and then would dance to it.

At Hebron, according to B. Ah.:

> Every closet had a speaker above it. All the time it played music, terrible music. It was like classical music, but terrible, special. I never heard music like that before, not on television, not on the radio, never.
>
> It was a cassette. I knew because when it ended, they would turn it over and it would begin again. It had drums, guitar and I don't know what else. Sometimes the tempo was very fast, other times slower. It was always at the same volume.

One ex-detainee said the music at Gaza prison was a fragment of a piece of classical music, "quick and loud, with a high-pitched and weak voice." He said prisoners were rotated from one "kindergarten chair" to another so that everyone would have a spell directly under the speaker.

TOILET DEPRIVATION AND HUMILIATION

> In the yard [at Dhahiriya], I saw violence against detainees. Some of them want to go to the toilet, and they aren't allowed. When they ask they get hit. It is usually the interrogators who do the hitting. They stink from going in their pants.
>
> — IDF reservist Tal Raviv

In both IDF and GSS interrogations, detainees were often denied permission to go to the toilet, other than at widely spaced intervals. Their discomfort was exacerbated by the painful body positions they were forced to maintain. The situation was yet more difficult for GSS detainees: they depended on guards around the clock for access to the toilet, because, unlike IDF detainees, they usually spent nights in position-abuse stations rather than in cells.

Reserve paramedic Avshalom Benny said that at Dhahiriya, written regulations specified that detainees undergoing interrogation should be permitted to use the toilet every few hours. In practice, however, access depended on the instructions of individual interrogators. He told HRW:

> I would hear the detainees calling out from the waiting rooms, "*Sherutim! Sherutim!*" [Hebrew for toilets] Often the guards would open the shutter and yell in, "Shut up! You just went!"
>
> At a certain stage of the interrogation, the interrogators told the guards what to do about toilet access. In some cases, they told the guards, "I don't want you to open the door of that cell," meaning that the guards shouldn't let them out for anything, including the toilet.
>
> I know for a fact that many of the detainees went to the bathroom on themselves, in their clothes. For some, it was probably from fear. For others, however, the problem was that they weren't being allowed out to use the toilet.
>
> Many of the detainees stank really badly, most from not washing, but some as a result of going to the bathroom on themselves.

As a general practice, detainees were allowed to go to the toilet two or three times a day. In some cases, access to the toilet was routinely given during mealtimes. But if detainees needed to use the bathroom more frequently than their allotted opportunities, their pleas were often turned down.

Some detainees said they believed interrogators used access to the toilet as a means of pressure, conditioning access to the toilet to cooperation with the interrogation. Ah. al-M., who was interrogated at Dhahiriya in 1992, told HRW that, while standing, blindfolded and handcuffed:

> I would ask for the bathroom, [and] they said no. I called out in Hebrew, "*Sherutim.*" It's what we were all calling out. But whether they let someone go depended on their mood. When all the guys insisted, they gave in. They used this in the interrogation. Once, I was calling for the bathroom. The interrogator came up to me and said, "If you want to go to the bathroom, you must confess." Others went to the bathroom in their clothes.

Psychological Abuse and Sleep Deprivation

U. Gh. said he was interrogated by an interrogator named "Tzadok" at Tulkarm. Once, he said, while sitting on a "kindergarten chair":

> I needed to go to the toilet. He wouldn't allow me, so I went in my pants. He left me sitting there like that. After a while, he came back and said, "You did it in your pants? Oh, that's great."

Abd A., interrogated at Hebron, recalled:

> Sometimes I sat for as long as two days on the chair without being interrogated. When I begged, they let me go to the bathroom. It took hours. They would first reply, "Shut up!" The second time, they hit me. The third time, nothing happened. Sometimes on the fourth time they took me. There was no rule concerning this. Some guards immediately take you, others won't, no matter what. I think it is the interrogators who decide when you go.

Unlike in GSS facilities, most IDF detainees spend nights in cells. Those cells, according to ex-detainees, usually contain buckets or soft-drink bottles in lieu of toilets. A. A., an Aida refugee camp resident who was interrogated at al-Far'a in November 1993, described the consequences of this degrading practice:

> At 11:00 P.M., I was brought from *shabeh* and put in a solitary cell. There was a bottle for urine, nothing for excrement. Since the guards would not take me to the toilet, I had to move my bowels in the bag they had brought the bread in.

Many of the detainees interviewed for this report reported that fellow prisoners had soiled their clothing, but only two admitted to having done so themselves. This phenomenon was probably under-reported by the detainees.

When permitted to use the toilet, detainees were often given inadequate time. Detainees held at Hebron and Ramallah said they were expected, during five minutes in the bathroom, to both relieve themselves and eat their meals, which guards placed in the toilet stall as they entered.

In many cases, detainees reported being ordered out of the stall before they had relieved themselves or finished eating.

A. Z., interrogated at Ramallah in October and November, 1993, told HRW that access to the toilet was quite restricted during his eighteen-day interrogation. He said that during the week, when hooded and shackled to the "kindergarten chair":

> I was allowed to get up and go to the toilet only once or twice a day. Sometimes we would call them to let us go, but they wouldn't come and take us. Our meals were given to us in the toilet. They said we had five minutes to eat and to move our bowels, but it was really less. Once, I had just started to eat, and the guard banged on the door and said "Let's go!"

Giving detainees their meals in the toilet stalls is a practice that can only be understood as deliberately degrading. The detainees we interviewed from facilities other than Ramallah and Hebron did not report this practice.

DEPRIVATION OF PERSONAL HYGIENE

> He [a Palestinian detainee at Dhahiriya named Abd al-Ghani] had one set of clothing and underclothing. For an entire week he neither showered nor changed his clothes. When I pointed this out to the interrogator, I was told that he was on strike and was refusing to take a shower. I asked Abd al-Ghani if he wanted to shower and he immediately said that he did, and said they hadn't allowed him to do so. I asked the military policeman, the guard and the interrogator what he could wear if he were to wash his clothes, and their answer was, We're not interested. They said he could receive clothes only after the interrogation was over. He really stank, so I sent him to the shower. When I wanted to clean his clothes, I realized that I had to boil them, they were so dirty.
>
> — Avshalom Benny, IDF reserve paramedic

Psychological Abuse and Sleep Deprivation

In both GSS and IDF interrogations, detainees were prevented from keeping clean. Many aspects of hygiene deprivation appeared deliberate, rather than due to budgetary constraints or indifference. Detainees said that hygienic conditions were unsanitary and humiliating.

Most of the GSS detainees reported being denied permission to change their clothes during their entire interrogation. As mentioned earlier, among the GSS detainees interviewed for this report, the average length of interrogation was twenty-nine days.

Detainees at Ramallah, Hebron, and Petach Tikva said they remained in their street clothes. By contrast, Tulkarm detainees said they were issued new sets of prison uniforms once a week.

The distress caused by dirty clothing was reinforced by limits on access to showers and other washing facilities. While the majority of detainees reported being able to take one quick shower per week, several said they were prevented from showering throughout their interrogation.

At GSS facilities, showers were taken in isolation; detainees were led, one by one, into the shower room, where they cleaned themselves under the watch of a guard. After showering, former detainees were given towels many described as filthy.

The IDF detainees we interviewed were generally permitted weekly showers. The facilities were described as filthy rooms with water pipes jutting out of the wall without shower heads. Soap was often provided.

Many detainees said they were bothered by their own body odor during interrogation. For some, the suffering was worsened immeasurably by having soiled their clothes. A few reported that interrogators or guards commented on detainees' body odors when passing nearby.

While using the toilet, prisoners were not given adequate means of cleaning themselves. The stalls in most facilities were described as containing a jar of water but no soap, running water, or toilet paper. The stalls were often filthy, their waste holes clogged.

SPACE DEPRIVATION

Throughout their time under interrogation, detainees experience various methods of space deprivation. "Closets" and "refrigerators" are described in Chapter Ten. Here we discuss the conditions in which IDF detainees are housed at night and GSS detainees are housed on weekends.

In contrast to inmates in the general sections of Israeli prisons, detainees under interrogation are denied opportunities to exercise or walk in outdoor courtyards. Thus confined, detainees are prevented from alleviating much of the stress and discomfort that builds during the days of position abuse and interrogation.

GSS Cells

The majority of GSS detainees we interviewed reported that, from Friday afternoon until early Sunday morning, they were placed in cells. They described the cells as dirty, foul-smelling and cramped. Some contained hole-in-the-floor toilets. In others, detainees were given plastic containers or buckets to serve as toilets.

At Ramallah, ex-detainees said, there were both shared and solitary weekend cells. Ahmed al-Batsh said he was placed in a shared cell:

> On Friday, they put you in the cells. There were four or five other people, in a very small cell. There are two mattresses for everyone. The length of the cell was about two meters. There was a hole for the toilet, and no soap, toilet paper or water.
>
> The guards responsible for the cells were the worst. The cells are absolutely filthy....They would say to us, "You are in a five-star cell. Some cells don't have a hole, they only have a bucket. You are lucky."

Abd A., who was placed in isolation on the weekends at Hebron, said:

> I was taken to a cell that was about one meter by 1.75 meters. There is a toilet in there, a hole in the ground. There was no running water. There were three blankets and a mattress. The cell had a terrible smell, like something rotten mixed with sewage. There is no opportunity to go out of the cell. The isolation cell was the worst, because then you are completely alone, even worse than *shabeh*.

IDF Cells

Detainees in all three IDF interrogation wings were usually placed in cells during the night. The cells vary in size. Most common is a single-person room, about one meter wide by two meters long. In some cases, interrogation subjects were placed in shared cells. This happened most frequently at the Beach facility and al-Far'a; Dhahiriya's interrogation wing appears to have more isolation cells than the other centers.

The cells were described by ex-detainees as dirty and often damp in the winter. They were either dark or lit by a ceiling bulb that shined throughout the night.

Shimon M., an IDF reservist who served as a guard at Dhahiriya in 1993, once entered a collective cell in the interrogation wing. He recalled:

> The smell in there was something like I have never smelled before. It was like sticking your head into a full garbage can. There were about ten detainees in there, in a very small place. I couldn't have lasted in there for two minutes, it smelled so terrible.

In the cells there is typically a pail detainees use as a toilet. There is no toilet paper; in some cases, there is a jar or bucket of water which detainees use both to clean themselves as well as a source of drinking water during the night. The cells contain several blankets and, in many cases, sponge mattresses, which take up most of the floor space. Some detainees described the blankets and mattress as torn and dirty, as if they had not been replaced in years.

Most cells are cold in winter and hot and stuffy in summer. In some cells there are small windows covered with a thick mesh. The windows provide neither a view nor much fresh air.

A., who was interrogated at al-Far'a in August 1992, recalled:

> I used to be in the cell from eight at night to seven in the morning....You are very dirty in there, and there are rotten blankets and mattresses, and it is very hot.
>
> Sometimes I was with another person in there. The cell is about 1.5 meters by two meters, and we had to sleep very close together. It's disgusting in there, it smells like sewage. The toilet bucket is right next to your head, and

when the other person uses it you cover your head, the smell is so bad.

It's so hot you can't be in there with your clothes on. There is a window, very small, twenty by twenty centimeters, but no air gets in, because a metal sheet covers it. Air can only get in from under the door. I think that if you had asthma you would die in there.

The Case of Hassan Zebeideh:
Acute Catatonia Follows GSS Interrogation

Hassan Zebeideh, a thirty-four-year-old grocer from the West Bank town of Anabta, was arrested at his home on the night of September 25, 1992. He was taken to the GSS wing at Tulkarm, where, he later told his family, he was interrogated about alleged links to Hamas. Thirty-three days after his arrest, Zebeideh was freed without charge in a state of catatonia.

Upon his release, Zebeideh was examined by Dr. Ruhama Marton, a psychiatrist who heads the Association of Israeli-Palestinian Physicians for Human Rights (AIPPHR). On December 12, 1992, Dr. Marton wrote:

> [According to Zebeideh's family, the patient] was physically and mentally healthy until his detention. He did not suffer from any form of disturbances, in his communication with others or in any other way....[According to the family] there is no history of mental disease in his extended family.
>
> After thirty-three days in detention he was returned to his home in a state of stupor, and in fact a state of catatonic stupor, one which is not schizophrenic.
>
> He was unable to react to any form of environmental stimulation, was unable to control his sphincter, did not speak, was unable to eat without help, or to help himself in any way. His movements were stiff and frozen.
>
> With his family's support and with medication, his condition has slightly improved. But today, seven weeks

after his release, he is still unable to remain alone or to take care of himself in any way.[16]

Unlike the other detainees interviewed by HRW, Zebeideh was unable to detail the methods he experienced while under interrogation. On May 16, 1993, five-and-a-half months after Zebeideh's release, a HRW researcher, who is not medically trained, visited him at home. His body movements were slow, and he appeared withdrawn and barely aware of his surroundings. In response to questions regarding his experiences during interrogation, Zebeideh uttered only a few disjointed words and sentences, including, "They hit me...all over," and "Music, terrible music, women screaming." He also mentioned threats made against his life. In a May 1993 interview with the AIPPHR, he stated that his interrogators had badly beaten him on the head and choked him.

The Justice Ministry announced an investigation into the case. In February 1994 the office of the State Attorney responded to an inquiry about the investigation as follows:

> My investigation deals with the period in which Zebeideh was in the [Tulkarm GSS] facility, September 24, 1992 to October 16, 1992. For this period I found that there were no incidents or deviations in his interrogation.
>
> As to his strange conduct during his detention, he was sent for a medical examination, and was checked by three doctors in a civilian hospital...and all three found nothing requiring urgent treatment.[17]

On October 14, 1993, Dr. Marton conducted a follow-up examination on Zebeideh and found an improvement in his condition. However, she predicted that "at best, with continued psychiatric care, his disability level will not drop below 70 percent."

---

[16] Medical Evaluation Form, signed by Dr. Ruhama Marton, December 16, 1992.

[17] Letter signed by Rachel Sukar, deputy to the State Attorney, and addressed to AIPPHR director Neve Gordon, dated February 6, 1994.

Zebeideh's family retained an Israeli lawyer, Dan Assan, to file a civil suit to recover damages for the injuries Zebeideh allegedly suffered in prison. With details of Zebeideh's treatment under interrogation still murky, Assan requested that the state provide the plaintiff with all documents relevant to his case, including the classified appendix to the Landau Commission report. Zebeideh's civil suit was pending before a district court in Tel Aviv as of early May 1994.

13
BEATING AND VIOLENT SHAKING

Beatings in both the GSS and IDF centers appear to be administered with some care and calculation. According to the testimonies we collected, interrogators avoid hard blows to faces, where the blows might show, and concentrate primarily on the torso and groin. Most beatings are carried out using fists or kicks, although in a few cases, implements such as clubs or metal rulers were used. Of the nineteen IDF detainees, thirteen said that their testicles were beaten or squeezed. Although painful and frightening, this method leaves no marks as long as the impact or pressure is limited.

As discussed in Chapter Three, the GSS appears to have reduced the frequency of beatings compared to earlier periods. Beatings still occur, but are less routine than the grueling combination of psychological and non-impact physical abuses that virtually all GSS detainees experience. At IDF interrogation centers, nearly all detainees continue to be beaten. However, the violence appears to have become more standardized: Reported incidents of bone-breaking brutality are less common than in previous periods.

GSS INTERROGATIONS

Nine of the seventeen GSS detainees interviewed for this report were beaten severely or moderately. From our sample, it was not possible to tell whether the use of direct violence was random or associated with particular case characteristics, such as the seriousness of the charges under investigation, the urgency with which information was being sought, or the failure of other methods to elicit information. This question can be answered only by interviewing a larger sample that includes a sufficient number of persons who were convicted and imprisoned for serious offenses.

We include as beatings the most common form of direct violence experienced by GSS detainees we interviewed, which is not blows or kicks, but vigorous shaking or whiplashing by interrogators who clutch detainees by their collars or shoulders. This method is sometimes combined with choking. Ex-detainees described the shaking as so vigorous and protracted that they lost consciousness or suffered severe neck pains for days.

Bassem Tamimi was subjected to this technique at the GSS wing of Ramallah in November 1993 and ended up in the hospital. His experience is recounted in detail in Chapter One. The direct cause of the cerebral hemorrhage he suffered is not known, but its severity suggested that Tamimi may have been thrown head-first against the floor or wall. Tamimi later gave statements to units from the IDF and the State Attorney's office investigating his injury. As of mid-March 1994, no results of these inquiries had been disclosed, according to Tamimi's lawyer, Jawad Boulos.

Another detainee held at Ramallah, Sh. Z., described the violent shaking he experienced:

> An interrogator called "Captain Benny" stepped on the chain linking my legs, while my hands were tied behind my back. He grabbed my shirt collar, bent me backward at a 45º angle, and begin to shake me very hard.
>
> When he did this I felt as if I was choking. I couldn't feel my neck, as if it was not even there. The first time he did this I fell to the ground and fainted. "Benny" did this almost every day, mostly during nighttime interrogations. It hurt my spine from my neck down to the small of my back.

S. R., interrogated at Ramallah in 1992, said:

> [The interrogator] grabbed me by the collar and shook me many times. When he did that, my head flapped backward and forward and lost all feeling. When I was put back in the chair, it hurt a lot. I couldn't control my head for two or three hours afterward. If I tried to move it forward even a little, my head flopped forward. My muscles just couldn't control my head.

A few GSS detainees said that interrogators slammed their heads against the wall during questioning. None reported this occurring more than two or three times per questioning session, suggesting that the

Beating and Violent Shaking

interrogators may have been wary of causing serious physical injuries. B. Ah. recalled the violence at Hebron:

> The one who did most of the beating was a huge interrogator, very tall and wide. He was blond or red-haired, with blue eyes. I don't remember his name. He had silver fillings in all of his teeth and looked like he was from Russia. He spoke good Arabic like everyone else, but you could see he wasn't from here because of his silver fillings.
>
> When the interrogator got angry because I didn't talk, he hit me. He picked me up like a child from the shoulders and slammed me against the wall. He also came up and slammed my head against the wall, holding me by the hair. Then he grabbed me by the hair, kneed me in the groin, hit me with a karate chop in the kidneys, and kicked me in the stomach.

Muhammad Adawi, also held at Hebron in 1992, alleged during his trial that interrogators had slammed his head into the wall (see Chapter Sixteen).

Testicle beating, common in IDF interrogations, was also reported by two detainees interrogated at the GSS interrogation wing of Tulkarm. Hassan Zebeideh, whose case is described at the end of Chapter Twelve, said he was beaten in the groin while handcuffed and hooded. Another Tulkarm detainee, Ad. M., said interrogators "Major Shalom," "Captain Jimmy" and "Captain Tzadok" beat him regularly during much of his forty-nine days under interrogation, including on the testicles. In one instance, he said, "Major Shalom" forced him to lie on his back with his hands cuffed behind his back. Then "Major Shalom" lifted Ad. M.'s legs back over his head, so that his knees hung over his ears and his backside and groin were in the air. Then, Ad. M. said:

> ["Major Shalom"] stood behind me, holding my legs down near my ears, and pounded on my testicles. He did this while he asked me questions. For half an hour, he kept hitting me and asking questions about the Islamic Jihad [organization], and whether I was planning operations for them.

> After it was over, my testicles were swollen. I couldn't sit, walk or go to the bathroom without feeling pain. They still hurt a month after I was released.

Ad. M. said that on other occasions he was beaten while cuffed hand and leg. An interrogator placed him on a stool with no backrest and ordered him to sit erect with his feet raised off the ground. The interrogator then placed his fist near Ad. M.'s neck, so he was unable to lean forward without feeling pressure on his windpipe. When his stomach muscles could no longer support him and Ad. M. fell backward, the interrogator kicked him in the stomach and testicles, and ordered him to get back onto the stool.

IDF INTERROGATIONS

> Twice during my detention, the interrogator hit me with open palms on my ears. When he did this, I felt a shaking, trembling sensation from head to foot, like an electric shock going through my body. It lasted for two minutes, and it took a while before I could even see again.
>
> —Twenty-one-year-old A., interrogated at al-Far'a

Sixteen of the nineteen IDF detainees interviewed for this report said they were beaten inside the interrogation room. The beating techniques used in all three IDF facilities appeared relatively similar, suggesting that IDF interrogators work according to a set of guidelines. (In a recent court-martial of IDF interrogators for beating detainees at Dhahiriya, the court justified seemingly lenient sentences in part by explaining that the interrogators had been led to believe that a certain measure of violence was permissible during interrogation. See Chapter Twenty.)

Most IDF beatings involved punches, karate-style chops, and kicks. The blows were aimed at the testicles, throat, stomach, back and shins. At the Beach facility, interrogators also used the edge of a heavy metal ruler to strike detainees in the foreheads, shins and knees. The blows to the face with the ruler were painful, but left no lasting marks. Detainees were often handcuffed behind their backs when assaulted during questioning sessions, and occasionally also blindfolded.

The assaults in the genital area involved either punches or kicks, or the application of pressure by an upward motion with an open hand or both hands clasped together. In other cases, interrogators squeezed one or both testicles between thumb and forefinger.

Two reserve soldiers interviewed for this report said they believed beatings were taking place in the facilities where they served. Tal Raviv, who spent a month at al-Far'a, said:

> I did guard duty four or five times in what we called the "Shabak roof" post.[1] That is on the roof of the interrogation rooms. Each time I spent about four hours there. It was always at night. While [on the roof]...you hear people being hit, and you hear them screaming and crying.
>
> During those times, I heard the hitting, and the crying, each time. It was intermittent. The interrogators yell and then you hear slaps and punches.

Avshalom Benny made regular rounds in the interrogation wing as a reserve paramedic at Dhahiriya in 1992. He recalled:

> I don't know what happens in the interrogation offices, because I didn't see them. But I heard screams coming from there almost every day....I heard from detainees what goes on in the interrogation room: they cover their eyes and hit them in the testicles, in the head, in the throat, and tell them to hop on one leg and to do all kinds of exercises that make their muscles cramp, and then they make them stand for long periods against the wall.[2]

---

[1] *Shabak* is the Israeli acronym for the GSS. However, many soldiers use it to refer to all intelligence agents in the occupied territories, including IDF interrogators.

[2] Affidavit given to ACRI on September 14, 1992, section 21.

According to ex-detainees, IDF interrogators work in relays; one interrogator takes a suspect for one or more days, and then, if he fails to elicit the desired information or statement, passes him onto another interrogator. Twenty-three-year-old Ah. al-M., interrogated at Dhahiriya, recalled an interrogator named "Amir," who he says he encountered only in his tenth day of interrogation:

> When I came into the room, "Amir" stood up and said, "Now you have come to the person who takes souls." Then he slammed me against the wall and I fell down. He told me to stand up, and began to hit me. He punched me in the stomach, and then kicked me between the legs, and then punched me in the face....When he was hitting me in the head and the testicles, I felt as if I would explode from pain.

Seventeen-year-old I. M. was interrogated at the Beach facility during January 1993. At one interrogation session a person he described as a "beating specialist" was brought in:

> I was taken out of the interrogation room and sent to *shabeh* for fifteen minutes, and then a short, fat, and dark-featured man came. He took me into another interrogation room. He uncuffed my hands, took off my jacket, and then recuffed me. He said, "You have no idea what the Israeli government is. Now I will show you."
>
> I was standing. He hit me four times with his fists in my stomach. When I doubled over, he hit me with both hands clasped together on the back of my neck. I couldn't see or know what was going on around me. It was very painful. I couldn't breathe, I couldn't see. I was dizzy.
>
> I sat down on the floor. He started kicking me in the hip, quite hard. He asked me no questions; he just kicked me that way for about five minutes. Then he pulled me up by the shoulders, so I was standing, and he swung up his open hand and hit me right in the testicles. I fell back into the

wall. He grabbed my hair from the back and slammed my
head against the wall, twice. I fell down. Then he left.

Many IDF detainees reported being told to remain either seated in a chair or squatting on the floor, in both cases with their hands cuffed behind their backs. Sometimes, they were forced to maintain positions that quickly grew painful or exhausting, such as sitting on their kneecaps. The interrogator would then sit in a chair facing the detainee, usually with his boots resting on the floor in front of the detainee's legs. M. N., an eighteen-year-old student interrogated at the Beach facility in October 1993, said:

> When they brought me into the room for questioning, they took off my blindfold. My hands were still cuffed. The interrogator, a huge blond with pimples named "Abu Jalal," made me sit in a chair. He read me a list of charges, and questioned me for about five minutes. Then he hit me in the stomach five times. He made me sit on the floor, on my knees, right in front of him, with my legs spread. He punched me in the chest, stomach and sides, swinging both his hands clasped together.
>
> This went on for forty-five minutes. When it was over I could not rise because my knees hurt so much. The interrogator kicked me a few times to get me to stand up. I had to use my elbows to lift myself.

"The Gas Pedal" (see illustration)
In several cases, IDF interrogators sat on desks facing the detainee's chair, resting their boots on the detainee's crotch. They would then press their foot down when detainees did not cooperate. Detainees likened this method to a driver pressing on the accelerator.

Twenty-one-year-old Muhammad Abu Hikmeh, interrogated at Dhahiriya, described this technique as administered by "Captain Mike":

> "Captain Mike" is the biggest person I have ever seen. He started off by talking to me. Then he began to punch me in the stomach while I was kneeling in front of him. Then he stood me up, pushed me against the wall and tripped

me. I was lying on my face, hands tied, and he stepped on my back and hands.

[Later,] I was sitting on the chair. He sat on the table facing me, and he put his foot between my legs and started pressing as if on a gas pedal. I tried to close my legs. When he saw me doing that he forced my knees apart again and kept on pressing. The pressing hurt more than the kicking.

Twenty-year-old I. K., interrogated for twenty-nine days at the Beach facility, recalled that on the fourth day of his interrogation:

> I sat down on the chair in the interrogation room. My hands were tied behind my back. The interrogator took off my blindfold, and sat close. He put his knees between my legs, on the insides of my thighs, and used his knees to push my legs apart.
>
> He said to me, "Tell the story." I asked, "What story?" He said,"You are accused of membership in the Arab Liberation Front." I replied, "I have no connection to them."
>
> Then he reached out and grabbed one of my testicles between his two fingers. He began to press his fingers together, squeezing for about ten or fifteen seconds. I was wearing sweatpants. I couldn't stand the pain and pushed myself off the chair in order to stop it.
>
> He pulled me back up and did it again. Then he punched me in the throat, I don't remember how many times. It made it difficult for me to breathe.

Several of the detainees said that interrogators choked them to the verge of fainting. In most cases, interrogators forced the detainee's back up against a wall, held his throat between two fingers, and applied pressure to the windpipe or carotid artery.

Twenty-two-year-old Yasir Abdullah Salman Mughari was interrogated at the Beach facility during November 1992. He described one such incident:

> I was put on a chair. The first interrogator came in, and slammed my head against the wall many times, I can't remember how many. Then he threw me on the ground.
>
> He asked, "Don't you want to confess?" While I was lying on the floor, he grabbed my windpipe between his thumb and forefinger, and squeezed. He did that three or four times. I felt as if I couldn't breathe. I was screaming and crying. I am sure that everyone could hear me.

O. T., interrogated at al-Far'a for twenty-five days in 1992, said that during one questioning session:

> I was blindfolded. They stood me in the corner and grabbed my windpipe, pressing their thumbs into my throat. Once, when they did this without the blindfold, I saw the interrogator timing himself on his watch. He did it for...maybe thirty seconds. Then they punched me in the sides, and kneed me in the testicles. Then they asked, "So, have you thought about it?" I said no, and the beating resumed.

H. D. said he was beaten during questioning rounds at Dhahiriya:

> The interrogators hit me often. Once, one of them pulled my head down and kicked me with his heel on the back of my head. Other times, they kicked me with the point of their boots in my stomach, and hit me there as well. They once knocked out some of my false teeth, which were bonded into my jaw. For three days I couldn't even eat from the pain. I went to the doctor, but all he did was give me Acamol (acetaminophen). I also told him I could barely stand because my back muscles were tight like rocks. He asked, "From what?" I replied, "From the interrogation."

ILLUSTRATION #5

"GAS PEDAL" — Interrogator sits on his desk and rests his boot on the crotch of the detainee, whose hands are cuffed behind him. The interrogator then presses his foot down when the detainee does not cooperate. Ex-detainees likened this method to a driver pressing on an automobile's accelerator pedal.

ILLUSTRATION #5

He said, "That's OK, don't worry, that's what interrogations are like."

The interrogators also kicked me in the testicles with the point of their boots during six or seven of the questioning rounds. Later I got these waves of pain in my groin that lasted for fifteen or twenty minutes. My testicles were all blue, and they felt like they were on fire. I used to sprinkle water on them to cool them off.

Chapter Sixteen describes the case of Nader Qumsiyeh, in which there is documentary evidence to support his contention that interrogators at Dhahiriya beat him on the testicles.

14
THE USE OF THREATS

The first day I was in interrogation they did not beat me. I was questioned for four hours, and he cursed me all the time. He said, "Your mother is a cunt. You mother is fucked by many men, and your sister is a whore. Your sister gets fucked, and I want to fuck your mother." Later, he warned, "I will torture you. We will use electric shock and a lie detector. We will paralyze you. We will beat you in the balls. We know everything. You will be here for a hundred days, and at the end, you will confess."

— H. D., interrogated at Dhahiriya

The Israeli Penal Code strictly forbids the use of threats by interrogators. Article 277 provides for a prison sentence of up to three years for any public servant who:

> threatens any person, or directs any person to be threatened, with injury to his person or property or to the person or property of anyone in whom he is interested for the purpose of extorting from him a confession of an offense or any information relating to an offense.

Threats against person and property are utterly routine in both IDF and GSS interrogations. They are practiced with apparent impunity, despite their illegal nature. No GSS agent has ever been criminally prosecuted for threatening a Palestinian under interrogation. Nor, to our knowledge, has any IDF interrogator, although details of the court-martials of IDF interrogators are not always disclosed in detail.

The commonplace use of threats by GSS interrogators raises the suspicion that they may be authorized by the agency's classified guidelines. Threats could fall within the scope of the Landau Commission's recommendation that GSS interrogators use methods involving "nonviolent psychological pressure...with the use of stratagems, including acts of deception."[1] To our knowledge, however, no government official has ever disclosed if threats by GSS interrogators are permissible "stratagems" or "acts of deception."

The effect that threats have on individuals depends on various factors, including their personalities, their impression of Israeli interrogation practices, their legal sophistication, and the context in which the threats are made. For a Palestinian under interrogation, the context is usually a situation of incommunicado detention, no access to a lawyer, uncertainty over whether his family knows where he is, prolonged sight and sleep deprivation, position abuse, and, for some, subjection to physical violence.

The threats made by Israeli interrogators generally fall into the following categories:

- Indefinite incommunicado detention;
- Death;
- Insanity;
- Severe bodily harm, including causing impotence;
- Sexual abuse, including rape;
- Abuse of relatives, most commonly, rape of sisters and mothers;
- Ominous unspecified abuses.

The most common threat is that of indefinite incarceration. Detainees are told the interrogation will continue until they sign a confession. Interrogators assure them that the military judges will approve requests to prolong the detention for as long as it takes to get the sought-after statement.

A. M., interrogated at Tulkarm for forty-nine days, said he was at one point shown a document by "Major Shalom," who told him, "This is from the chief of interrogations. It says the interrogation must go on. You have two choices: to die or to confess." A. M. said another Tulkarm interrogator, "Captain Jimmy," said to him at one point, "I will kill you by putting an electric wire here and here [on the testicles] for seven seconds." Interrogators also threatened to prevent him and his family from obtaining the permits required to travel to Jerusalem or abroad.

Interrogators exploit Palestinian awareness that several young men have died while under interrogation. One ex-detainee said that at Hebron

---

[1] Paragraph 4.7. See Chapter Three.

prison, interrogators boasted of having killed Mustafa Akawi, who died there in 1992 (see Chapter Nineteen). At Tulkarm, interrogators told some detainees they had killed Mustafa Barakat, who also died in 1992. Many Palestinians believe, correctly or not, that these deaths were homicides, and that interrogators can kill with impunity.

Ahmed al-Batsh told HRW that, early in his seventy-five-day interrogation at Ramallah:

> Four interrogators came into the room and said, "We are going to kill you. You will not come out of here alive. You will leave here only dead or insane. Trust us."

He said that, at another point:

> Someone came into the interrogation room and said, "What's with this son of a bitch?" The other interrogators said, "He is stubborn." So he said, "You son of a whore, I am going to kill you. You will see. I killed Mustafa Akawi, I killed Hazem Eid.[2] What street do you want them to name after you in Ramallah?" I said, "I want a street in the Old City."
>
> He told me to get up. I did. I was without the hood, but my hands were tied. He lifted my chin, grabbed my collar, rolled it up until it was thin like twine, and then pulled it tight around my throat. He began to shake my neck from the collar. He shook me very hard twenty, thirty times, for three or four minutes, until I lost consciousness....
>
> When I woke up, they said to him, "It's OK, now he will talk, he's all right." I said, "I have nothing to say." "Major Chaim," the one who shook me, picked up a chair as if he was going to hit me with it. The others told him, "Don't do it, he will talk, don't do it."

---

[2] Eid, like Akawi, died at Hebron while under interrogation. His death was ruled a suicide by Israeli officials. See Chapter Nineteen.

> "Major Chaim" rolled up my collar again and began to choke me....I didn't think I was going to come out of it alive....Then they said, "Rest up. Think. We will be back." Then they put me back in the corridor.
>
> The next day, "Major Chaim" returned and did the same thing again. He screamed at me hysterically, "You will go insane! No one leaves from here without speaking, either from the mouth or from the ass! You will see, in the end you will talk."

Muhammad Abu Hikmeh described one questioning round at Dhahiriya:

> On about the seventeenth day, "Captain George" came back and hit me on my side with his fist, many times....My hands were not tied, and I made as if I was going to hit back.
>
> He tied my hands, grabbed my neck and began to choke me....Then he slammed me against the wall, grabbed my windpipe between his fingers, and threatened that he would disfigure my face. He held me against the wall with one hand and traced a design on my face with the other, saying, "I will cut here, here and here."

Interrogators often swing between friendly and violent approaches, or collaborate with one another in "good cop-bad cop" ploys. Y. D. related one incident at Dhahiriya:

> "Captain Jerry" told me to sit in the chair. He did not cuff my hands. He recited the accusations against me: throwing stones, Molotov cocktails, membership [in a banned organization], and interrogating suspected collaborators. He was speaking nicely. When I replied, "I don't know anything," he suddenly started screaming and yelling, and cuffed my hands and forced me to sit on my knees. He shouted things like, "Your mother's cunt! Your sister's

cunt! You fuck your mother, you fucker! I will break your head, you fucker, I will hit you if you don't confess!"

Y. D. said that on the next day he was brought back before "Major Jerry":

> I immediately had my hands tied and was ordered down on my knees. He read me the same accusations and I denied them. He began to yell and scream at me, and spat in my face. Then he grabbed my throat and said, "Now I'm going to kill you." He began to squeeze. It hurt, and I couldn't breathe. I thought at first he was really going to kill me, but later I realized that he wouldn't.

Y. D. added that an interrogator code-named "Captain Sami" asked him, "Have you ever seen blood come from your ass?" Y. D. recalled, "I thought he meant it, that they would use bottles or a stick. I was very scared."

A few ex-detainees said they had been threatened sexually.[3] U. Gh. said he was fondled at Tulkarm by an interrogator whom he described as "fat, with glasses and dark hair":

> He asked, "Are you a homosexual? You look like a woman. Have you ever fucked a woman?" Then he came up to me very close. He put his hand down my shirt and touched my chest, then my cheeks and hair, and was talking as if to a girl. Then he turned off the lights and kept on touching me. My hands were cuffed behind my back, but I kept on trying to twist my chest away from his hands. He kept pulling me straight. He touched me like that for about ten minutes. Then he said, "I can bring a woman soldier for you here."

In cases where IDF interrogators beat a detainee in the testicles, they sometimes threatened to continue until the person could no longer

---

[3] On the sexual harassment by male GSS interrogators of Palestinian women detainees, see Teresa Thornhill, *Making Women Talk: The Interrogation of Palestinian Women Security Detainees by the Israeli General Security Services* (London: Lawyers for Palestinian Human Rights, 1992), pp. 28-34.

father children. The threat appeared credible to some of the detainees, in light of the pain, swelling, and other symptoms.

Interrogators frequently threatened to imprison, injure or otherwise abuse the detainee's relatives. Many detainees reported that threats and insults were directed at their mothers and sisters. Among the most common such remarks were: I want to fuck your sister/mother; I will bring your sister/mother here to the interrogation wing; and Your sister/mother is fucked all the time by other men.

Interrogators frequently threatened unspecified abuses, along the lines of "The worst is yet to come," and "This is nothing, wait until tomorrow." Ribhi Qatamesh, a thirty-seven-year-old lawyer who was interrogated several times by the GSS, described the interrogators' strategy:

> They give you the idea that you will spend months in the world of interrogation if you don't confess. They say that since you will confess eventually, you might as well do it now, to save yourself. They ask you over and over, "What you've seen so far is only an introduction. There is another stage ahead, which will be terrible." You always think about this unknown, what they might do, and how terrible it will be.

15
THE ROLE OF PALESTINIAN COLLABORATORS IN INTERROGATIONS

Both IDF and GSS interrogators use Palestinian collaborators[1] to obtain information from detainees under interrogation. These collaborators use deception, threats and sometimes direct violence against detainees.

Detainees do not always know who is a collaborator, and the reticence of authorities in discussing interrogations is even more pronounced when it comes to the contribution of collaborators to the process. Little is known with certainty about the number of collaborators involved in interrogations, the roles that they play, and whether in practice they obtain much information or function chiefly to frighten detainees placed in their midst.

In January 1994, a Justice Ministry official acknowledged that collaborators worked with the GSS in interrogating Palestinians, but denied any pattern of abuse. Rachel Sukar, a deputy to the State Attorney, said that collaborators are instructed to "obey the rules," but did not disclose those rules. She said her office had investigated reports of abuse by collaborators working for the GSS. "When we are informed of an incident in which the

---

[1] Collaborators are generally referred to by Palestinians as *'umala'* (singular: *'ameel*). Those who collaborate with the authorities in detention facilities are known as *'asafir* (singular: *'usfour*), or "birds." The Hebrew term for collaborator is *meshatef pe'ula* (abbreviated as *mashtap*).

The phenomenon of collaboration with the occupation authorities raises many human rights issues, including the manner in which Palestinians have been pressured and/or blackmailed into collaboration by the GSS; the abuses that collaborators have been responsible for perpetrating; and the way that suspected collaborators have themselves been targeted for assault and assassination by Palestinian activists. See, for example, B'Tselem, *"Collaborators" in the Territories During the Intifada: Violations and Abuses of Human Rights* (Jerusalem: B'Tselem, January 1994), in Hebrew.

rules are violated, we make sure that justice is done to the perpetrators," she said.[2]

Sukar's statement came in response to a report by the rights group B'Tselem charging that collaborators use threats and "violent methods and torture in order to extract confessions from detainees."[3] A recent example documented by B'Tselem concerns a Palestinian who said that during his interrogation at the Russian Compound in August–September 1993, collaborators in his cell burned him with cigarettes, apparently because he had refused to disclose information they suspected him of concealing from his interrogators.[4]

Even when collaborators do not resort to threats or violence, their known participation in the interrogation process sharpens the feeling of isolation and paranoia felt by detainees under interrogation. It makes them distrustful not only of all security force personnel but also of the few Palestinians with whom they come into contact.

According to testimony collected by HRW and other organizations, collaborators often appear to play roles in ruses coordinated by the interrogators. In a typical stratagem, the detainee is removed from the place of interrogation, sometimes after being told that the interrogation is over, and is sent to a prison cell containing collaborators posing as inmates. The "prisoners" greet the newcomer, offering him hot drinks, fresh vegetables, and cigarettes, and share with him their experiences under interrogation. Eventually, one or more of the "prisoners" takes the newcomer aside and explains that they are members of the prisoners' internal security apparatus, and need to verify the newcomer's credentials as an activist. They ask him to report the accusations against him, what he has confessed to under interrogation, and more important, what he has *not* confessed to. This way, the members of "internal security" explain, activists outside the prison can keep track of what the Israeli authorities know.

The collaborators' apparent objective is to get the detainee to disclose information about offenses and/or accomplices beyond what he has

---

[2] Tuvya Tzimooki, "Collaborators Torture Persons Under Interrogation," *Yediot Achronot*, January 9, 1994.

[3] B'Tselem, *"Collaborators" in the Territories*, p. 60.

[4] B'Tselem, *The "New Procedure" in GSS Interrogation: The Case of 'Abd a-Nasser 'Ubeid* (Jerusalem: B'Tselem, 1993), pp. 10-15.

already provided to the Israeli interrogators. The ex-detainees we interviewed said they believed that statements obtained in this manner are turned over to the interrogators, who use them to carry out further arrests or to pressure detainees to confess in writing to the newly mentioned offenses.

Of the Palestinians interviewed for this report, two of the GSS detainees and one of the IDF detainees said they had been interrogated by collaborators. All three said that they recognized the deception.

H. D. said he was transferred from Dhahiriya to a collaborator cell in Ramallah Prison on the twenty-second day of his interrogation:

> I knew I was going to the *'asafir* [prisoner-collaborators], because you never go to a central prison [i.e. from interrogation at a military detention center] unless it is for the *'asafir*. When I entered into the cell, the men gave me cigarettes and tea and said I was a hero. Then they talked to me about conditions in the prison.
>
> Later on, they took out a piece of paper and said, "Write down here what you confessed to in interrogation." I refused to write anything down. They wanted me to write. They forced me into a corner, so I was trapped between the wall and the bed. Then they said to me, "You are violating the rules of the organization [i.e. the Palestinian organization] if you don't write on the paper."
>
> Then they beat and kicked me....I was so tired, I agreed to write down that I had participated in intifada activities — throwing stones, writing graffiti and raising flags. I was so tired, I just wanted to be left alone and to rest.

H. D. said his statement was not detailed enough for the collaborators:

> They told me to write down things like, in 1989 I was a member of a group, in 1990 I wrote graffiti on the walls, in 1992 I didn't do anything because I was studying for my *tawjihi* [baccalaureate]; on intifada anniversaries I went out

and wrote graffiti; and I did the same on Fatah day and on [Palestine] independence day.

H. D. refused to write down any specific information, and the pressure to confess continued for several hours. The collaborators finally left him alone, but he was too sore and frightened to sleep, he said. The next day, H. D. was taken back to the interrogation wing at Dhahiriya, where he was brought to see "Captain Rami," one of his interrogators:

> Captain Rami asked me, "So, where have you been?" I said, "With the *'asafir*." He laughed, showed me a piece of paper, and said, "This is what you wrote in that cell. You must write it down here, again."

H. D. said he refused, and the interrogation resumed.

16
THE COMPLICITY OF MEDICAL PERSONNEL IN TORTURE AND ILL-TREATMENT

Experts have identified several possible forms of participation by medical professionals in torture or ill-treatment, including:

- Directly participating or assisting in abuse, such as in the case of dentists applying dental torture, or doctors injecting abusive drugs;

- Attending torture sessions in order to intervene, as in a boxing ring, when the victim's life is in danger;

- Developing abusive methods to produce the results desired by the interrogators, such as psychiatric techniques;

- Providing indirect assistance and legitimacy to abuse, by monitoring the health of victims undergoing torture or ill-treatment, or examining and/or treating victims before and after torture sessions, without attempting to stop the abuse; and

- Failing or omitting to correctly diagnose sequelae of torture, thereby frustrating attempts at documenting evidence of abuses.[1]

HRW found no evidence to suggest that Israeli physicians or paramedics participate directly in abusing Palestinians under interrogation. However, some are complicit in torture and ill-treatment in the fourth and fifth ways delineated above. By examining and treating detainees while turning a blind eye to evidence that they are undergoing torture or ill-treatment, these medical personnel violate their ethical duty not to countenance or condone such abuses.

According to both detainees and officials, doctors and/or paramedics make regular rounds inside interrogation wings, observing,

---

[1] This list is based partly on one provided in Eric Stover and Elena O. Nightingale, M.D., eds., *The Breaking of Bodies and Minds: Torture, Psychiatric Abuse, and the Health Professions* (New York: W.H. Freeman, 1985), p. 13.

talking to, examining and treating detainees. In those same wings, detainees are commonly subjected to prolonged sleep and sight deprivation, handcuffing, and forced standing or sitting in painful positions. A large subset of detainees is beaten or violently manhandled, and most also experience one or more of the following: confinement in closet-like spaces, long periods of toilet deprivation, and deliberate exposure to extremes of temperature. These abuses often continue, with only brief respites, throughout interrogations lasting three weeks or longer.

"[T]he task of every physician is to assure the health of the patient in any circumstances, and to *not* serve any other interests," Dr. R. Yishai, chair of the Ethics Committee of the Israel Medical Association, has stated.[2] As this chapter argues, many doctors and paramedics serve less the interest of the patient than the interest of the interrogation agency in continuing the interrogation: rather than ensuring that their patients are not subjected to illegal or health-endangering ill-treatment, these medical personnel tend to intervene in the interrogation process only in order to avert permanent injuries or deaths. Even so, the negligence of medical staffers has contributed to the deaths of some of the Palestinians who have died while under interrogation (see Chapter Nineteen).

It is heartening to find Israeli medical personnel who have spoken out about their experiences in interrogation centers (for example, paramedic Avshalom Benny, who is quoted in this report). However, the small number who have done so is disappointing, particularly since, in contrast to the situation in many repressive countries, Israeli physicians do not risk imprisonment or worse for whistle-blowing.

INTERNATIONAL BANS ON MEDICAL INVOLVEMENT IN TORTURE

The World Medical Association's Declaration of Tokyo states, in its first paragraph:

> The doctor shall not countenance, condone or participate in the practice of torture or other forms of cruel, inhuman

---

[2] Dr. R. Yishai, in letter to B'Tselem, reprinted in B'Tselem, *The Death of Mustafa Barakat in the Interrogation Wing of the Tulkarm Prison* (B'Tselem: Jerusalem, September 1992), p. 18.

or degrading procedures, whatever the offense of which the victim of such procedures is suspected, accused or guilty, and whatever the victim's beliefs or motives, and in all situations, including armed conflict and civil strife.[3]

The Tokyo Declaration is widely accepted as the definitive statement of professional ethics relating to medical participation in acts of torture and ill-treatment. The Israel Medical Association, as a member of the World Medical Association, accepts the Declaration of Tokyo and considers it binding on every physician in all circumstances.[4]

In 1982, the U.N. General Assembly adopted a code of medical ethics drafted by the Council of International Organizations of Medical Sciences, which applies to all medical and health personnel, not only to doctors. This code is pertinent to the situation in Israeli interrogation centers, where a paramedical staff fulfills many of the health-care duties. Principle Four of the code states:

> It is a contravention of medical ethics for health personnel, particularly physicians:
>
> (a) To apply their knowledge and skills in order to assist in the interrogation of prisoners and detainees in a manner that may adversely affect the physical or mental health or condition of such prisoners or detainees and which is not in accordance with the relevant international instruments.
>
> (b) To certify or to participate in the certification of, the fitness of prisoners or detainees for any form of treatment or punishment that may adversely affect their physical or mental health and which is not in accordance with the relevant international instruments, or to participate in any way in the infliction of any such treatment or punishment

---

[3] The Declaration of Tokyo was adopted by the twenty-ninth World Medical Assembly in Tokyo, Japan, in 1975.

[4] Ibid.

rights] instruments.[5]

CABINET MINISTER: DOCTORS NEED NOT KNOW WHAT THEY ARE CERTIFYING DETAINEES FOR IN GSS INTERROGATIONS

According to the present government of Israel, doctors who examine detainees undergoing GSS interrogation are not formally apprised by the authorities of what this process entails.

On December 1, 1992, Member of Parliament Naomi Chazan submitted a list of questions to Prime Minister Rabin regarding medical involvement in GSS interrogations. In sum, her questions focused on whether:

1. Doctors are authorized, on medical grounds, to prevent detainees from being interrogated;

2. Doctors are authorized to order that interrogators restrict their methods of interrogation, the length of interrogation, or the conditions of detention;

3. Doctors know the contents of the classified interrogation guidelines;

4. Paramedics, when acting in the place of a doctor, have the same powers as doctors with respect to interrogations.

In February 1993, Environment Minister Yossi Sarid, replying to Chazan on behalf of the prime minister, stated, "In reply to your first and second questions, both are within the doctor's authority. The doctor's decision is binding, and is not merely a recommendation."[6]

---

[5] *Principles of Medical Ethics Relevant to the Role of Health Personnel, Particularly Physicians, in the Protection of Prisoners and Detainees against Torture and other Cruel, Inhuman or Degrading Treatment of Punishment*, ST/DPI/801, 1982.

[6] Knesset session of February 15, 1993, Questions and Answers.

As to doctors' knowledge of the interrogation guidelines contained in the classified Landau report, Sarid stated:

> The doctor is not briefed as to the report's contents. Medical examinations are carried out according to accepted medical standards and do not take into account the requirements of the interrogation. The doctor has the authority to restrict the length or conditions of interrogation.

Sarid also gave assurances that interrogators were informed of their duty to allow detainees to see a doctor if they request it, and that doctors regularly monitored the detainees:

> In the detention and interrogation centers a doctor goes through once every twenty-four hours and sees all the detainees as well as all persons under interrogation. If, in addition to this visual check, a detainee or person under interrogation complains and wants to see a doctor, he is taken for an examination with the doctor.

Medical authority over interrogators extends even to paramedics, Sarid said. "A paramedic is authorized to determine that a detainee's health conditions require a doctor's examination, and in this way to restrict his interrogation."

The authority vested in doctors and paramedics to halt or limit interrogation methods would seem to provide a basis for holding them accountable under Article 322 of the Penal Code, if they knowingly or negligently allowed a patient to undergo methods that injured the patient's health. Article 322 provides that a state agent responsible for another person's well-being will be liable for the consequences to that person's life or health if the state agent fails to provide for that person (see Chapter Five).

Thus, a doctor who encounters evidence that a detainee under his care is suffering from ill-treatment or torture is obligated by the ethics of the profession and, arguably, by Israeli law not only to treat the patient but to order a halt to the interrogation or to limit its methods.

In Israeli interrogation centers, there is a basic conflict between the doctors' duty to serve exclusively the health interest of the patient[7] and their supposed ignorance of the harsh conditions to which they are sending the patient. If they do not know the rigors to which they are sending detainees under interrogation, prison doctors have an ethical duty to learn what they are, especially when they are responsible for patients whose health makes them especially vulnerable to exceptional conditions.

Minister Sarid stated that prison doctors are not privy to the classified interrogation guidelines. But the doctors, according to Minister Sarid, see all of the detainees under interrogation during their daily rounds. If they instead diagnosed and treated detainees outside the interrogation wing itself, they would probably hear some of their allegations of abuse. They might also receive information from the paramedics who make rounds inside the interrogation wing. Finally, in Israel's politically open culture, they would likely be exposed to some of these troubling issues just by reading the daily press or following the news on Israeli radio and television. It thus seems that a doctor who examined detainees at a particular interrogation center over any length of time and who remained utterly ignorant of the abusive techniques in use there would have to be making a concerted effort not to know.

MEDICAL EXAMINATIONS

Doctors who examine Palestinians undergoing interrogation are typically reservists or career officers in the army, employees of the Israel Prison Service (IPS), a semi-autonomous division of the Police Ministry that runs many of the prisons containing GSS interrogation wings. In addition, Israeli civilian doctors working in civilian hospitals frequently treat Palestinians who are brought in from interrogation facilities. These doctors

---

[7] Article 4 of the Declaration of Tokyo states:

> A doctor must have complete clinical independence in deciding upon the care of a person for whom he or she is medically responsible. The doctor's fundamental role is to alleviate the distress of his or her fellow men, and no motive, whether personal, collective or political shall prevail against this higher purpose.

The Complicity of Medical Personnel in Torture and Ill-treatment

are also sometimes complicit in abuse (see the case of Nader Qumsiyeh, below).

Upon admission to military or IPS detention centers, Palestinian detainees are examined by Israeli physicians or paramedics. Avshalom Benny, an IDF paramedic who served at Dhahiriya, described the procedure:

> When a detainee is received in the interrogation wing a medical examination is carried out. There is a form that a doctor or medic fills out, which the doctor must sign. The detainee is asked about his health, whether he requires special medication, if he has allergies, and everything is written down. They are asked if they smoke. The depth of the examination is different from medic to medic.
>
> The doctor decides whether the detainee is fit for detention. If the doctor, or the medic in the doctor's absence, says that the detainee is not fit for interrogation, they will put the interrogation off, until they receive the doctor's permission.[8]

According to many ex-detainees, the medical check-in exams are usually perfunctory. The doctor or paramedic takes the detainee's blood pressure and asks about personal and family medical histories and whether the patient is taking medication. When departing from the interrogation wing, detainees are given another medical exam.

During interrogation, ex-detainees said, medical personnel visited frequently, asking them whether they had any ailments. (HRW does not know how often physicians performed these visits; detainees were not always able to distinguish between paramedics and physicians.) According to the ex-detainees, the medical staff almost invariably gave them aspirin or other mild pain-relievers in response to complaints, and told them to drink plenty of water.

---

[8] Affidavit given to the Association for Civil Rights in Israel, September 14, 1992, section 14.

THE SCANDAL OVER MEDICAL FITNESS-FOR-INTERROGATION FORMS

In 1993, a prison medical form came to public attention that indicated doctors were evaluating the ability of detainees to withstand specific forms of abuse under interrogation. The form was obtained by attorney Tamar Pelleg-Sryck of the Association for Civil Rights in Israel during her representation of Ribhi Shukeir, who had been interrogated at the GSS wing of Tulkarm prison. According to a sworn affidavit taken by Pelleg-Sryck, Shukeir was beaten, hooded, bound in a "kindergarten chair" and in other painful positions for long periods of time, held in a tiny cell, and deprived of sleep.[9]

On the medical form, the examining physician is asked to state whether the patient is medically fit to undergo four different techniques during interrogation: prolonged isolation, tying, wearing a head or eye covering, and prolonged standing. The existence of a standard-issue form suggests that these four techniques are among the methods permitted interrogators according to the GSS's classified guidelines.

The following is a translation of the medical form submitted by the doctor who examined Shukeir:

Publication of the certification form in the Israeli daily *Davar* on May 16, 1993, caused a minor furor within the Israeli medical community. On June 21, 1993, the Israel Medical Association (IMA) president, Dr. Miriam Zangen, sent a letter to Prime Minister Yitzhak Rabin stating:

> If indeed such a form exists, it is the first time we are aware of it. Questions b, c and d on the form and the answers given to them by the doctors clearly constitute "participation in torture" as defined by the Tokyo Convention against Torture, which was endorsed by the World Medical Association and by the Israel Medical Association. This type of certification constitutes conduct unbecoming to a physician and is a clear violation of medical ethics.

---

[9] Affidavit submitted with a letter from Tamar Pelleg-Sryck requesting an official investigation, to Attorney General Yosef Harish, dated May 18, 1993.

The Complicity of Medical Personnel in Torture and Ill-treatment

Detention Center: **T** *[presumably an abbreviation for Tulkarm]*
Interrogation Section

Medical Qualification Form

9340404   *Ribhi A-Shukeir*   *23.3.93*
Detainee number   Name and family name   Date

1. On the date of *23.3.1993* I examined this patient and found that his medical findings are:
   a. _____
   b. _____
   c. _____
   d. _____
   e. _____

2. In light of this, the medical limitations on his condition of detention are:
   a. Are there any restrictions on a prolonged stay in an isolation cell? Yes/*No*
   b. Are there any limitations on tying the prisoner? Yes/*No*
   c. Are there any limitations on wearing a head/eye covering? Yes/*No*
   d. Are there any limitations on prolonged standing? Yes/*No*
   e. Does the prisoner have any physical injuries (prior to entering interrogation)? Yes/*No*
   f. His primary medical limitations are:
      1.
      2.
      3.
      4.

> Doctors are strictly forbidden to answer the questions appearing on the form, or to cooperate with the authorities, when these type of activities are in question. Doctors are permitted, and in fact are required, to treat detainees and to determine their physical condition and the medical treatment they require.

Shortly after this letter was sent, an IDF spokesman, Lieutenant Colonel Moshe Fogel, denied that doctors were involved in determining whether detainees were fit for interrogation.[10] Prime Minister Rabin replied to Dr. Zangen as follows:

> I was informed that the form was used as one of the documents that were distributed with the intention that medical examinations of inmates be conducted within the interrogation centers prior to interrogation. The forms were drawn up out of concern for their health.
>
> The form was accidentally distributed to the warden of Tulkarm Prison, who put it to use.
>
> After the accident was discovered, the IDF Military Police commanding officer ordered the warden of Tulkarm Prison and the Commanding Officer of the IDF Central Command [which has jurisdiction over the entire West Bank] to cease using the form.
>
> The form was intended to allow physicians to determine whether or not the interrogation could proceed in the case of inmates suffering from medical problems. The form's intent was to improve the medical treatment of inmates from the territories, and not as was reported in the article [the *Davar* story alleging that the form was aimed at

---

[10] Karin Laub, "Doctors Reject Forms That Would Approve Chaining, Hoods," Associated Press, June 30, 1993.

certifying detainees' fitness to withstand particular methods].[11]

The meaning of this letter is somewhat cryptic. The prime minister appears to deny that doctors are called upon to ascertain prior to interrogation whether detainees are fit to withstand the methods in question. The form, he seems to be saying, was to be used only in specific cases when an interrogation subject appeared to be suffering from medical problems, and has since been withdrawn from use. The prime minister did not deny that these methods were in fact being used during interrogations.

The methods, used in the manner that the GSS routinely employs them — long-term subjection to isolation cells that are closet-sized and often uncomfortably hot or cold, chaining in intentionally painful positions, prolonged hooding, and enforced standing in contorted positions — constitute impermissible ill-treatment if not torture. Doctors are not permitted, according to the above-cited norms of medical ethics, to participate in a process of certifying the fitness of detainees for methods constituting ill-treatment or torture. This prohibition applies whether the certification process is routine or, as Prime Minister Rabin's letter seems to imply, intended for selective use.

Physicians completing such a form could not credibly claim to have no idea they are certifying detainees to undergo some degree of abuse. Even if they argued that the first three methods listed — isolation, hooding and chaining — can in theory serve legitimate preventive purposes and be employed in a non-abusive way, the fourth item, "prolonged standing," serves no conceivable function other than to cause physical discomfort. IMA President Zangen took a tougher stand: "[Q]uestions b, c and d on the form and the answers given to them by the doctors clearly constitute participation in torture as defined by the Tokyo Convention Against Torture."

HRW does not know if such forms have been withdrawn from use, as claimed by Israeli authorities.

---

[11] As translated from the Hebrew for HRW by the Association of Israeli-Palestinian Physicians for Human Rights. The AIPPHR played a major role in drawing attention to these forms.

THE CASE OF NADER QUMSIYEH

A doctor's note obtained by lawyer Tamar Pelleg-Sryck from the Dhahiriya detention center suggests that IDF doctors in that facility, on occasion, also may have certified the fitness of detainees for abusive procedures. The note, dated May 6, 1993, was signed by Dr. Wizer Rahamim. It was sent by "The Clinic" (presumably Dhahiriya's medical clinic) and was addressed to the "Chief of Interrogators." It states that twenty-five-year-old detainee Nader Qumsiyeh of Beit Sahour has "no medical grounds preventing him from staying in *chadabim*," apparently an abbreviation for *chadrai bidud*, or isolation rooms.[12]

The term "isolation rooms" may be a euphemism for the "closets" that are commonly used in Dhahiriya. These stalls, approximately eighty centimeters wide, eighty centimeters deep and two meters tall, are used to wear down detainees between interrogation rounds (see Chapter Ten). According to Qumsiyeh's testimony to defense lawyers, he was placed in such a "closet" at least six times over the course of five days of interrogation, for periods sometimes exceeding four hours.

It is possible that the term *chadabim* does not refer to "closets," and that a doctor approving confinement in an "isolation room" may have had in mind an ordinary one-man cell rather than a "closet" expressly engineered to cause discomfort. But it is more plausible that a medical opinion would be sought for confining a detainee in a "closet" than for confining him in the far less stressful ordinary solitary cells. At least some

---

[12] The document reads as follows (HRW translation):

From: *The Clinic*   May 6, 1993
To: *Chief of Interrogators*

Re: Medical examination of a detainee being transferred to the interrogation wing.

1. The detainee — name: ***Nader Raji Mikhail Qumsiyyeh, detainee number 93/706.***
2. Results of the medical examination prior to beginning the interrogation: ...***There are no medical grounds preventing staying in chadabim*** [apparently an abbreviation for *chadrai bidud*, or isolation rooms].
3. This form should be filed in the detainee's registration file, and a copy should be given to the chief of interrogators.
4. The examination was carried out by a: paramedic/***doctor***.
5. Details of the examiner: ***Dr. Wizer Rahamim***
                                                                          M.D. 17568

members of the medical staff at Dhahiriya were aware of the existence of "closets" in the interrogation wing, as made clear by the testimony of paramedic Avshalom Benny (see Chapter Ten).

Unless the doctor was deliberately misled by the interrogators, his certification in Qumsiyeh's case indicates the following: if he knew that "isolation rooms" meant "closets," he was complicit in mistreatment; if he did not know, then he abdicated his ethical responsibility to know the conditions he was declaring a detainee medically fit to withstand.

In Qumsiyeh's case, the evidence of medical malfeasance goes well beyond the check-in examination. Qumsiyeh told his lawyers, Mary Rock and Tamar Pelleg-Sryck, that on several occasions interrogators beat him, including on the testicles. A paper trail raises strong suspicions that medical personnel were aware that Qumsiyeh had been beaten during interrogation but did nothing about it:[13]

> On May 11, 1993, Dhahiriya military officials transported Qumsiyeh to Soroka Hospital in Beer Sheva, inside Israel. He was brought to the emergency room, where, according to a hospital form, he was examined by a doctor. The form bears a hand-written name that appears to be "Dr. Mor," although it is not clear whether he or she was the examining physician. The form states that Qumsiyeh was examined for "swelling in his testicles," and continues, "The patient received a blow to his testicles two days ago."[14]
>
> On May 12, 1993, Qumsiyeh was brought to an extension-of-detention hearing in Dhahiriya. The protocol of the session noted that the detainee told the military judge, "Yesterday and two days ago they hit me in the testicles during interrogation." The judge

---

[13] For a detailed account of the case, see Amnesty International, *Israel and the Occupied Territories: Doctors and Interrogation Practices: The Case of Nader Qumsieh* (London: Amnesty International, August 1993). Qumsiyyeh was arrested on the night of May 3–4, placed under interrogation from May 7 to May 19, then given a four-month term of administrative detention (imprisonment without charge), later reduced on appeal. He was released on July 20, 1993.

[14] "Blow" is used here to translate the Hebrew word *maka*, which can mean any form of painful impact, whether or not intentionally delivered.

extended his detention, but noted that an IDF investigation of Qumsiyeh's complaint was under way and requested that its findings be reported to the judge who presided over the next extension-of-detention hearing.[15]

On May 19, 1993, Qumsiyeh was transferred from the interrogation wing to the general wing of Dhahiriya prison. He received a medical check-up from a Dr. Ali Tel-Or, who noted on a medical form that "as of two days ago the left testicle is swollen and painful."

An undated medical form entitled "Examination of Detainee Prior to Detention/Release" was completed for Qumsiyeh. The doctor, whose signature is not legible, may have examined Qumsiyeh on his departure from Dhahiriya or on arrival at Ketziot detention center. The form states, in a section entitled "Past Diseases/ Accidents/ Hospitalizations/ Operations," that Qumsiyeh had received "a blow to the testicles two weeks ago."[16]

The examinations conducted by these doctors suggest that they should have been suspicious about the cause of Qumsiyeh's injury. But at least one of them appears to have taken steps to cover up evidence of abuse. Dr. Mor addressed a handwritten note on Soroka Hospital stationery to an unnamed "Commander of the Unit" that was dated May 17, 1993 — six days after Qumsiyeh had been examined at the hospital. The note stated:

> Further to my letter releasing the above [Nader Qumsiyeh] on May 11, 1993.

---

[15] Military court form, "Request to Order Detention/ Extension of Detention," dated May 12, 1993. The form is reproduced (in Hebrew) in Amnesty International, *Israel and the Occupied Territories: Doctors and Interrogation Practices*, p. 15.

[16] In this case, the Hebrew word used for "blow" is *habala*, which is also neutral as to intentionality.

> The above reached the emergency room because of an injury in the area of the testicles.
>
> According to the patient, he fell down the stairs two days before being sent to the emergency room.
>
> Results of the medical examination: Superficial hematoma in the area of the testicles, which is consistent with the local injury being caused two to five days before the examination.
>
> Recommendation: Rest, ice applied to the area, and if the situation deteriorates, he is to be returned for a second examination.

There are good reasons to doubt Dr. Mor's suggestion that the injury to Qumsiyeh's scrotum had been caused by his falling down a flight of stairs. Such an accident would not seem likely to cause Qumsiyeh's particular injury, although it is perhaps easier to visualize if the detainee had been wearing handcuffs when he fell. But the tumble is not mentioned in any other document in Qumsiyeh's file, including the initial report bearing Dr. Mor's name that had been filed six days earlier, the day Qumsiyeh was examined at Soroka Hospital. Qumsiyeh himself denied to attorney Pelleg-Sryck that he had fallen down any stairs or that he had told any physician of such an incident. To the contrary, Qumsiyeh had testified at his May 12 extension hearing that his interrogators had beaten him on the testicles.

Within days of sustaining his injury, Qumsiyeh was checked by one if not more medical personnel. (It is likely that a doctor or a paramedic would have seen him prior to his referral to the hospital examination.) Yet, it appears that none of them took action on the basis of *prima facie* evidence that the injury had been caused by a criminal assault by those in charge of his custody. They did not exercise their authority to halt the interrogation pending the findings of an investigation into the injury. On the contrary, at least one of the doctors appears to have participated in a cover-up.

In June 1993, attorney Pelleg-Sryck submitted a complaint on behalf of Qumsiyeh about the injury he sustained, and requested an investigation. Later, Qumsiyeh was questioned about the incident by IDF investigators. On March 8, 1994, IDF chief prosecutor Lieutenant Colonel

Danny Be'eri responded to Pelleg-Sryck, stating in a letter that an investigation by the Military Police's Criminal Investigation Division had "found no basis for the allegations of the complainant, and as a result, the Central Command's chief prosecutor ordered that the file be closed." Lieutenant Colonel Be'eri's brief letter made no reference to the various medical reports on the injury, and gave no details about how the investigators had checked Qumsiyeh's allegations and determined them to be baseless. Pelleg-Sryck responded with a request to see the investigation file, and was informed she would need a power of attorney from Qumsiyeh. She told HRW on April 28, 1994 that she would seek it from her client.

HEBRON PRISON DOCTOR: "WE ARE NOT INTERESTED IN WHAT GOES ON IN THE GSS INTERROGATIONS"

In April 1993, Muhammad Adawi, a twenty-seven-year-old Palestinian charge with complicity in the laying of an explosive device, attempted to contest his June 1992 confession by arguing in court that it had been extracted by GSS torture. At Adawi's trial, the conflicting testimonies of a medic and a physician suggested that one of them was party to a cover-up.

Adawi stated that his confession had been obtained after he had been subjected to prolonged sleep deprivation, hooding, prolonged shackling on a "kindergarten chair," continuous loud music, and confinement in a "closet." (For more on the Adawi case, see Chapters Twelve and Eighteen.) He also said that on June 18, 1992, as he sat chained to the chair, an interrogator removed his hood and slammed his head against the wall, drawing blood.

During the April 20, 1993 court session, the GSS agent code-named "Billy" denied that he or any other interrogator had banged Adawi's head against the wall. He told the court that at 11:30 on the morning of Thursday, June 18, 1992, he discovered Adawi in distress:

> I found the accused in waiting after a soldier in the facility called me when he saw the accused acting strangely, laughing, being wild. He told me that the accused was banging his head against the wall. When I arrived there, I found the accused scratching his cheek against the wall. He

was bleeding and refused to calm down. I told them to bring a medic.[17]

"Billy" also testified that when summoned to see Adawi, he found him without his hood covering, although still handcuffed behind his back. "Billy" speculated in court that the scratches on Adawi's face may have been due to his having rubbed his face against the wall to force off the hood.[18]

The military prosecutor, Captain Oded Svurai, disclosed a classified GSS document that he characterized as a standard internal memorandum used by interrogators to report "exceptional incidents" (*mikrim harigim*, in Hebrew). The document is signed by "Billy" and provides an account that is consistent with his court testimony:

> A soldier in the facility reported to me that while he [Adawi] was in waiting, he pulled off his head covering and was acting strangely. When I arrived in the waiting cell I saw the interrogatee pounding his head and scraping his skin against the wall, causing bleeding. The interrogatee was released from waiting and was allowed to sit in the corridor until the medic arrived....The prison medic was summoned by myself to give treatment....After the examination, the medic returned the interrogatee to interrogation.[19]

The following day, Adawi was sent to be examined by the prison doctor, Eliezer Tupaylo, an employee of the IPS, the agency that runs Hebron prison. During the May 17, 1993 session of Adawi's trial, defense lawyer Shlomo Lecker cross-examined Dr. Tupaylo.

In court, Dr. Tupaylo displayed indifference toward what went on in the GSS wing of the facility where he was employed. He testified that the guards who led Adawi into his office informed him that Adawi had been

---

[17] Hebron Military Court, case 2332/92, April 20, 1993 session, p. 19 of the protocol.

[18] Ibid., p. 26 of the protocol.

[19] Hebron Military Court, case 2332/92, exhibit 2, internal GSS memorandum dated June 19, 1992.

refusing food and had banged his own head against the wall while waiting to be questioned.[20]

In his medical log, Dr. Tupaylo noted that Adawi's blood pressure and pulse rate were high (130/90 and 120 beats per minute), and that Adawi had "scrape marks on his right cheek (and a little on the left cheek) and on his nose." The doctor also noted that Adawi was "limping as he walked."[21] Dr. Tupaylo testified:

> I examined the patient, and found that he was in a state of mental pressure, but able and willing to cooperate, that is to say, he answered my questions and told me how he felt. I concluded that he was distraught because of being in the detention facility itself — since any detention is an upsetting event — and not specifically because he was under interrogation....
>
> His state lacked motoric quiet. He was agitated, near hysteria. So I gave him a pill to relax him, and sent him back. [Giving him the pill] worked, and I received no further complaints. I didn't see him again for four months.

When asked by the defense counsel whether Dr. Tupaylo had questioned the interrogators in an effort to determine what had led to Adawi's state of "near hysteria," the doctor replied, "No. At this stage, it was not necessary, because the suspect quickly quieted down." Dr. Tupaylo also acknowledged that he did not visit the place where Adawi was being held in an effort to determine whether the manner in which he was being held had contributed to his hysteria.

Dr. Tupaylo commented during the same session that he typically examines patients undergoing interrogation in one of two locations: his

---

[20] Ibid., May 17, 1993 court session. A Hebrew-speaking HRW representative observed the session, although he was ordered out of the courtroom during testimony by GSS agents. All of Dr. Tupaylo's statements quoted herein are as written down and translated by the HRW representative. They may differ slightly from the court protocols, which are not verbatim transcripts of the proceedings.

[21] Ibid. The doctor's log was submitted to the court as evidence. See p. 43 of the protocol.

main clinic, located in the general section of Hebron prison; or an office located inside the GSS interrogation wing. He told the court that he was unable to remember where he had examined Adawi, and had no written record of the location.

Tupaylo told the court that he had not requested to see the internal GSS "exceptional incident" memorandum about Adawi's injury (see above), explaining:

> We [prison physicians] are not interested in obtaining internal communications of the GSS. We are also not interested in what goes on during interrogation.

One month later, a paramedic took the witness stand and contradicted the version of the incident put forward by Dr. Tupaylo and "Billy." The paramedic, Moshe Turjeman, confirmed that he had been summoned on June 18, 1992 by the GSS to treat Adawi. But he testified that he had observed no signs of physical injury on Adawi's face or body, and that the interrogators had said nothing about an injury when he was first summoned. Turjeman said they had asked him to come because Adawi was in a disturbed emotional state:

> At 12:05 I was summoned by the GSS interrogator to examine the accused. The interrogator said the accused was not cooperating and had become shut off from reality. In my examination I found that the accused reacted to light (his pupils), that his reflexes were in working order, and that his vital signs were good.[22]

When asked about the scrape marks noted both by "Billy" and Dr. Tupaylo, and about his own failure to record any injuries in his medical log, Turjeman assured the court:

> Every visible thing has to be written down, even if I wasn't called because of it. If there had been any kind of external mark [on Adawi's face], it would have been documented

---

[22] Ibid., June 30, 1993 session, p. 86 of the protocol.

[by myself in my log]....If I had seen a thing like that [an injury] I would have written it down.[23]

Outside of court, defense attorney Lecker hypothesized about the contradictory accounts of Adawi's injury. He speculated that after interrogators had hit Adawi's head against the wall, "Billy" summoned Turjeman to check Adawi's condition. During the examination, Lecker hypothesized, Turjeman may have refrained from recording the injury in his log, either in order to conceal evidence of GSS violence or because he saw his function less as noting significant medical phenomena than as certifying the detainee's fitness for continued interrogation.

In court, Lecker confronted Turjeman with the GSS "exceptional incident" memo, which mentions that a medic had been called because of Adawi's facial injuries. Turjeman expressed bewilderment:

> I don't remember anything [like this]. If I had seen [an injury], I would have written it down. I don't have any explanation for Exhibit Two [the internal GSS memo].[24]

Turjeman also denied that the GSS had, as "Billy" claimed, informed him of Adawi's injuries when he was first summoned to treat him:

> When an interrogator has a problem, he calls me. I wrote down in this case what the interrogator told me, that the accused was not cooperating and was detached from reality. I wrote that down [in my log] because that was what the interrogators said. I am sure they did not call me because of an injury to the head of the accused. If that had been the case, I would have come specially prepared.[25]

The contradiction was clear: Interrogator "Billy" noted on June 18, and Dr. Tupaylo noted on June 19, that Adawi exhibited facial wounds. But

---

[23] Ibid., pp. 86-87 of the protocol.

[24] Ibid.

[25] Ibid., p. 88 of the protocol.

the paramedic told the court that when he examined Adawi between those two moments, he observed no facial injuries.

The interrogator and doctor would have no conceivable interest in claiming falsely that Adawi had been injured. A more plausible explanation for the discrepancy is that the medic omitted the injury from the medical log, and then, when testifying in court one year later, either lied or relied on his inadequate log when claiming that he had observed no physical injury.

Attorney Lecker suggested one explanation for the discrepancies between the two versions: Once documentary evidence existed of injuries, the GSS concocted the account of Adawi's "self-inflicted" wound, in anticipation of possible inquiries into the case. However, Lecker conjectured, the GSS failed, perhaps through neglect, to inform Turjeman of the new version of events.

The outcome of Adawi's trial is discussed in Chapter Eighteen.

PARAMEDICS ROUTINELY CHECK DETAINEES UNDER INTERROGATION

During Muhammad Adawi's trial, a GSS agent code-named "Gabi" rejected Adawi's charge that he had been denied medical treatment, and that interrogators had made access to care contingent on his signing a confession. "Gabi" assured the court that detainees receive care whenever needed:

> Medical treatment by a doctor is given to everyone routinely. The accused [Adawi] received medical treatment on the spot [after being injured in his head] with no preconditions.

"Gabi" also stated:

> According to Israel Prison Service regulations, the prison paramedic makes the rounds of all the cells in the GSS wing three times a day.[26]

---

[26] Ibid., April 20, 1993 session, p. 14 of the protocol.

Agent "Billy" also spoke of the routine presence of IPS paramedics during the interrogation process:

> He [Adawi] would not calm down, so I asked them [the guards] to call the medic. That's all there is in the facility. The moment there is a medical problem in the interrogation facility we request that someone from the clinic come, and they send whoever is there.[27]

Ex-detainees confirmed that paramedics routinely checked them while they were confined to position-abuse stations or in cells. Making routine tours of the interrogation wings, paramedics must be familiar with at least some of the interrogators' abusive tactics, and are made complicit in them when they monitor detainees to determine whether they remain physically able to continue to withstand the ill-treatment.

Many of the ex-detainees interviewed by HRW reported that when they were taken to prison clinics for injuries or ailments, they usually received nothing more than aspirin or another basic pain-reliever, and were then sent back to their interrogators.

Ali Radaydeh told HRW that in January 1993 he was badly beaten by Border Police in al-Bassa holding facility in Bethlehem prior to his interrogation by the GSS at Hebron. Radaydeh said that when he arrived at Hebron, the prison doctor dismissed his complaints:

> Before I went to the cell, I was taken to a doctor. He spoke in Arabic, was about forty-five years old, and was wearing a blue uniform. He told me to take off my clothes. There were marks on my body from the beating in al-Bassa. The doctor asked, "What's this?" I said, "This is from the soldiers." He said, "You are lying," and sent me away.

Occasionally, medical staff intervened to alleviate the pressure being placed on detainees. Some ex-detainees said they believed doctors had issued instructions that they be unhooded or taken off the "kindergarten chair." Ahmed al-Batsh said that in the tenth week of his interrogation at Ramallah:

---

[27] Ibid., p. 19 of the protocol.

> I told the medic that I couldn't breathe and that the pain was like needles over my right hip. I called to the soldier, and he pulled the hood off my face. He was a real human being. The medic came back and said that he would bring the doctor the following day.
>
> The doctor came and said, in Hebrew,[28] "Don't put the hood over this man's face, don't put him in a chair. Don't tie his hands." He also said, "The Shabak [GSS] have gone crazy. If this guy stays here another week, he will die."
>
> Then the interrogators had a problem. They couldn't put me in the main corridor with the others, because I didn't have a hood over my head. So they put me in a regular office, where I stayed for the next ten days.

Ah al-M., interrogated at Dhahiriya for fifty days during 1992, told of being sent to the doctor after a brutal beating by interrogator "Captain Amir":

> "Amir" went with me to the clinic. The doctor told him to leave the room. The doctor was very quiet and gentle. He was fat, had glasses, dark skin, and was about forty years old. He knew a little Arabic, but we spoke in Hebrew. He seemed nice, with compassion. He said, "Don't worry, don't be afraid." He gave me some liquid drops and three cups of water.
>
> He asked me, "Were you beaten?" I said, "Yes." The doctor called the chief of the administration[29] and spoke to him. I couldn't understand most of what he said, but I sensed that the doctor was telling him to stop it.

The beatings did not end, however. The officer whom Ah. al-M. called the "chief administrator" sat in on one interrogation round with

---

[28] Al-Batsh speaks and understands Hebrew fluently.

[29] Ah. al-M. was unclear about the exact title of the "chief of administration."

"Amir." During that round, "Amir" did not use violence. But, Ah. al-M. said, in subsequent rounds "Amir" beat him and kicked him in the testicles.

Reserve paramedic Avshalom Benny recounted several incidents in which he intervened on behalf of detainees suffering from ill-treatment. Benny recalled treating a detainee named Abd al-Ghani Hameida:

> He would sit in the waiting room for days with cuffs on his hands behind his back. I saw that they would tighten the cuffs very tightly. I asked and even ordered that they take the cuffs off several times. I took care of his wrists when they were swollen, with red marks because of the cuffs. He said to me that he had been beaten in the interrogation room, in the head, throat and legs. My own examination found no external marks on him other than swelling and redness on his leg. I dressed the leg.[30]

---

[30] Affidavit given to ACRI on September 14, 1992, section 23.

17
POLICE INTERROGATIONS

The Israeli police conducts far fewer interrogations of Palestinians than does the GSS or the IDF. In general, the Palestinians interrogated by the police are either suspected of criminal offenses that are not politically motivated, or are younger persons suspected of committing relatively low-level politically motivated offenses, such as throwing stones, writing nationalist graffiti, and throwing Molotov cocktails.

Police stations are scattered throughout the occupied territories. They are staffed mostly by Jewish and Druze officers, together with a few local Palestinians.[1] In some cases, police stations act as transit points for detainees on their way to IDF or GSS interrogation centers. During these transfers, police sometimes conduct a preliminary round of questioning.

HRW has no estimate of how many Palestinians are interrogated by the police, or of what proportion of these are subjected to torture or ill-treatment. However, we believe that the testimony presented in this chapter, together with reports published by other human rights groups, indicates that abuse during police interrogations is a problem that merits attention.

HRW interviewed four young Palestinians arrested the same evening in July 1992 and interrogated by police in Bethlehem. They said they had signed statements after having been subjected to severe abuse. All said they had been beaten and threatened: one said he was subjected to electric shocks and two others said they were threatened with electric shocks. (The four were later released without charge after other detainees confessed to the same offenses.)

In addition, an HRW representative attended a trial in Gaza Military Court of two youths who testified that they had been beaten, threatened with death, and subjected to electric shock during their February 1992 interrogation. During the trial, a Palestinian ex-policeman gave testimony that corroborated some of the youths' allegations.

---

[1] Prior to the beginning of the Palestinian uprising in late 1987, many Palestinians served in the police in the West Bank and Gaza Strip. Soon after the uprising began, activists called on the officers to quit their jobs. Most complied, out of conviction or fear of reprisal, or a combination of both.

Allegations of beatings, threats and electric shock in Israeli police interrogations are not new. In December 1991, the Palestine Human Rights Information Center, a Jerusalem-based independent group, published a report on the use of electric shock by interrogators at the Hebron police station. Two months later, Israeli reporter Doron Meiri wrote an exposé in *Hadashot* of a special mobile police interrogation unit that was operating in the West Bank. According to Meiri, the unit had gained a reputation for using brutal techniques to obtain confessions from Palestinian detainees. In 1990, B'Tselem issued a report charging abuse of minors by police interrogators at the Russian Compound.[2]

The details of the July 1992 incident investigated by HRW are as follows, as reconstructed from separate interviews with the four youths who were interrogated. On the night of July 7, two plainclothes agents, "Captain Nitzan" and "Captain Shai," accompanied by uniformed soldiers, entered the village of al-Khader, south of Bethlehem, and arrested Khaled Salah, who was sixteen at the time, Ibrahim 'Aser, sixteen, Mahmoud 'Issa, seventeen, and Marzouk Salah, age unknown. The four youths were taken for interrogation at the Bethlehem military headquarters, known locally as "al-Bassa." According to defense lawyers, police often interrogate Palestinians within the military compound.

Khaled Salah told HRW that upon arriving at al-Bassa:

> I went straight to the interrogation room. I was told to sit on a chair, and my hands were tied behind the chair. My legs were tied as well. They kept the blindfold on, and started asking me questions.
>
> After about an hour and-a-half, they put me on the ground and started hitting me. They used sticks and their legs. There were three persons beating me.[3]

---

[2] Palestine Human Rights Information Center, *Israel's Use of Electric Shock Torture in the Interrogation of Palestinian Detainees* (Jerusalem: PHRIC, December 1991); Doron Meiri, "Torture Unit," *Hadashot*, February 24, 1992; B'Tselem, *Violence against Minors in Detention* (Jerusalem: B'Tselem, June 1990).

[3] HRW interview in al-Khader village, Bethlehem district, March 5, 1993.

The second night, Salah said, he was subjected to a mock execution. His hands and legs were tied to the chair, and the interrogator known to him as "Captain Nitzan" sat in front of him, pressing his foot on his testicles. Then, Salah said:

> "Nitzan" took out his pistol, and put it to my head. He said, "I am going to kill you." I started to laugh, but my heart was beating very hard. I was looking down, I didn't look at him. Then I was quiet.
>
> It was a flat pistol, black. He put the barrel right up against my head. He held it for a few minutes. Then he started to pull the trigger. I heard clicks.

The pistol was unloaded. Immediately after the mock execution, Salah said, "Nitzan" told him that if he signed a confession, he could go home immediately:

> He said, "Sign, and you can go home. It is a normal procedure." So I wrote my name on about four pieces of paper.

Ibrahim 'Aser told HRW that on the night of his arrest, he was taken into an interrogation room with five interrogators. He said that as he lay on the floor with his hands cuffed behind his back with thick plastic bindings, one of the interrogators, whom the other policemen called "Husni," kicked him hard in the stomach. Then, he said, they used electric shock on him:

> It was the interrogator named "Nitzan" who did it. He is tall, blonde and thin with glasses. He is bald in front, but looks about twenty-five years old.
>
> The electricity machine is small, and has two wires leading from it. They put the wires on my body, on my chest. You begin to shake when they do that. They took off my shirt, and they put the wire on my stomach. They raised and lowered the level of current.

> I was shaking and screaming. He took it away and then put it back, maybe four or five times. Each time, he did it for about fifty seconds. The other interrogators laughed when he did it. One of them said, "It is much better for you to confess."[4]

Two of the other three youths said they had been threatened with, but not subjected to, electric shocks. Both said they were shown an "electric instrument" that emitted sparks, and were told that if they didn't confess, the instrument would be used against them.

All four of the youths told HRW they were repeatedly threatened, punched and kicked. Two said they had been choked with a metal bar by an interrogator standing behind them. Mahmoud 'Issa said that during his second round of questioning:

> I was sitting on a chair, hands tied behind my back. They had brought me to the room blindfolded, but in the room, they took it off. They asked, "Who throws stones in the village? Who writes graffiti?"
>
> Then one of the interrogators, whose name is "Caspi," stood behind me. He was holding a black metal bar. He put my head between his knees, put the bar on my throat, and pulled it back a little until it began to choke me. He asked, "Who is throwing stones?" Then he pulled again, harder, and said, "I'll kill you." He did this about five times.[5]

The four youths were held in cells during the day and questioned at night. All of them said they eventually signed their names to documents written in Hebrew, a language none of them can read. They said they had believed that they were confessing to relatively minor offenses, including throwing stones and writing graffiti. However, they learned later that they had signed confessions involving more serious offenses, including setting fire to the shops of suspected collaborators.

---

[4] HRW interview in al-Khader village, Bethlehem district, March 5, 1993.

[5] HRW interview in al-Khader village, Bethlehem district, March 1, 1993.

The four were jailed for six months while they awaited trial. On January 7, 1993, they were freed without charge after the police revealed they were holding another group of youths who had signed confessions to the same offenses.[6] According to Shlomo Lecker, the lawyer for one of the youths, the official explanation for their release was that the authorities had determined that the charges against them were unfounded.[7] A Justice Ministry investigation into possible wrongdoing by the police in its handling of the case found insufficient evidence to bring charges. The youths chose not to cooperate with the official investigation, according to Lecker.

HRW also heard allegations of abuse by police, including electric shock, at a trial in Gaza Military Court. At the March 10, 1993 session of their trial, two sixteen-year-old defendants from Nuseirat refugee camp, Ra'ed Jibali and Iyad Kafena, attempted to challenge the voluntariness of their confessions

According to the youths' lawyer, Ali Naouq, the two had been arrested and interrogated at a local police station, known as the "Mid-Camp station."[8] They signed confessions stating that they had thrown Molotov cocktails at Israeli troops. In challenging their confessions, the two said that they had been forced to sign after being beaten, threatened with execution, and subjected to electric shock. Naouq told HRW that he had decided to challenge the admissibility of their confessions after hearing similar accounts from other youths about the Mid-Camp police interrogators.

Iyad Kafena testified that on the night of February 1, 1992, he was arrested and brought to the police station. He described his interrogation:

> The policeman said, "Do you know why you are here?" I said that I didn't. So he said, "You know why," and began to hit me with a stick. I fainted. He threw water on me, and began to question me. He said that there were some people saying that I had thrown Molotov cocktails. I said

---

[6] See Muna Muhaisen, "Four Youths 'Confess' to Crimes They Did Not Commit," *Al-Fajr* English weekly, February 15, 1993.

[7] Phone interview with Shlomo Lecker in Jerusalem, November 21, 1993.

[8] Nuseirat is one of several refugee camps located in the central Gaza Strip, known to residents as the "middle camps."

I hadn't thrown Molotovs, and he began to hit me again with his fists and with a stick.[9]

In the second round of questioning, Kafena recalled:

> They asked me questions again. I said I didn't know anything, that I didn't know why I was here. Then one of them began to hit me in the legs, the head and the stomach. Then one of them said, "I will bring you an electric instrument." He brought the machine. Then he put the electricity on me. He put it on my face, on my testicles, and on my fingers. I was tied with my hands behind my back; he came up to me and put the wires on me.

Kafena eventually signed a statement that he had thrown Molotov cocktails, and was placed in detention pending his trial.

Summoned to testify during the mini-trial, the policemen denied the allegations, testifying that they had never beat, threatened or used electric shock against the two youths or in any other interrogation.

The defense also summoned Muhammad Mazra'awi, a Gazan former policeman who was working at the Mid-Camp Station at the time that the two defendants had been interrogated. Despite Mazra'awi's apparent discomfort at testifying in a military court against his former employers, his comments lent credence to some of the defendants' allegations. Mazra'awi said that his job was to man the desk in the hallway of the station, directly outside the interrogation room. He guarded prisoners as they waited in the hallway, and maintained the log that tracked when prisoners were brought in and out, and which interrogators and policemen were on duty.

Mazra'awi testified that he had seen detainees leave the interrogation with injuries. On occasion, he summoned a doctor to examine them. Mazra'awi also said detainees awaiting interrogation were forced to remain for hours in the hallway without access to toilets. At the end of his testimony, he told the court that he had heard detainees talking

---

[9] The quotes are as written down by an HRW observer, based on the translation from Arabic into Hebrew of the court interpreter.

Police Interrogations 239

among themselves about how electric shock had been used on them during interrogation.

The following exchange took place between defense attorney Naouq and Mazra'awi at the March 10, 1993 court session. It is presented as noted down by a Hebrew-speaking HRW observer.[10]

Naouq: Usually, if a detainee is brought in at midnight, what do you do with him?

Mazra'awi: He sits on a bench, blindfolded, until the interrogator comes at about 7:00 A.M.

Naouq: Until the morning, for seven hours?

Mazra'awi: Yes.

Naouq: Who takes care of him? How does he go to the bathroom?

Mazra'awi: It is difficult. You can't take him to the bathroom, because you have to guard them all.

Naouq: You mean that sometimes, the detainees go to the bathroom on themselves, in their clothes?

Mazra'awi: Yes.

Naouq: Do interrogations sometimes take place at night?

Mazra'awi: Yes. If there is someone from the intelligence section on duty at night.

Naouq: What is the distance between your station and the interrogation room?

Mazra'awi: Eight meters.

---

[10] Naouq and Mazra'awi spoke Hebrew to each other during the cross-examination.

Naouq: The interrogators told this court that they never touched any detainee. Did you ever see them hit someone?

Mazra'awi: Well...sometimes. There was a push, a shove, a slap, in the corridor. This was what I could see. I never went into the interrogation rooms.

Naouq: When the detainees come back from the interrogation room, where do they go?

Mazra'awi: To the bench next to me.

Naouq: What is their condition when they come out?

Mazra'awi: I don't check them too closely. Sometimes they have marks on them, sometimes they cry that they are hurt. Sometimes I call a doctor for them, and they get released from interrogation.

Naouq: Did you ever hear from detainees about electric shocks?

Mazra'awi: They don't complain to me. But they used to talk to each other. They were right next to me, so I could usually hear what they were saying. Sometimes they would say that they had been given electric shocks.

The testimony of the policeman failed to sway Military Judge Shaul Gordon. In the end, he ruled the defendants' confessions to be admissible, and Jibali and Kafena were convicted and sentenced. (See Chapter Eighteen for more details of their trial.)

18
THE ADMISSIBILITY
OF COERCED CONFESSIONS

> Members of the service swore before us, not without a touch of pride, that they never failed to check that a confession brought before the court was a true confession — no matter what means were employed to extract it. They explained that a confession was never submitted to court without it first being checked by other intelligence sources, even sources that cannot be cited in court....
>
> One interrogator told us that he didn't feel that he had ever condemned an innocent man....
>
> In so far as the interrogators were convinced that the confessions were entirely true, it made it easier for them to submit them to court, even at the price of giving false testimony.
>
> > — The Landau Commission report, explaining how it came to be routine that interrogators lied in military court when denying the use of coercive methods, and judges accepted their false testimony (paragraph 2.41)

Confessions signed by Palestinian security detainees following their interrogation by the GSS or IDF are the cornerstone of the military judicial system in the occupied territories. (See Chapter Eight for a brief overview of the military court system.) According to defense lawyers, the vast majority of convictions in all cases excepting those involving relatively minor "disturbances of the public order" are based on confessions. This was confirmed by a senior officer in the Judge Advocate-General's corps.[1]

Authorities explain the heavy reliance on confessions by noting that standard police methods of collecting evidence (testimony from witnesses, material clues, etc.) are rarely possible in the occupied territories, because most Palestinian witnesses are unwilling to help investigators or give evidence against their compatriots, due either to their political sympathies or fear of retribution.[2] Israeli defense attorney Shlomo Lecker put it this way: "It's much easier for [the GSS] to get a confession than it is to go out and try to find material evidence in the field."[3]

Adnan Abu Leila, a Nablus-based lawyer, told HRW that roughly ninety percent of his clients were convicted, sixty percent of them primarily on the basis of their own confessions. Of the remaining forty percent, he said, most were convicted mainly on the basis of third-party confessions (see below for a discussion of the admissibility of third-party confessions and the "Tamir Law"). Abu Leila told HRW, "On those rare occasions when the interrogators don't have a confession by the defendant himself or by others against him, they are in trouble. Then they have a hard time getting a conviction."[4]

As for Palestinians who serve as GSS informants, they play a crucial role in identifying activists for arrest and interrogation, but are less useful when it comes to prosecuting suspects in military court. If such informants

---

[1] HRW interview, Tel Aviv, November 18, 1993. The officer spoke on condition of anonymity, but in an official capacity. The Landau report also acknowledged the centrality of confessions in the prosecution of "terrorist" cases:

> [E]very time a truthful confession is obtained from a person under interrogation, then...the accused's confession...is almost always the main evidence against the accused....In trials of the type discussed here [rejection of the confession] is tantamount to an acquittal of the accused. (Paragraphs 2.19 and 2.26)

[2] See e.g., Landau report, paragraph 2.18.

[3] HRW interview, Hebron Military Court, May 17, 1993.

[4] Interview, Nablus Military Court, February 15, 1993.

were to identify themselves when testifying for the prosecution — as the rules of evidence would require — they would jeopardize their physical safety and/or their future usefulness to the security services.[5] The incriminating evidence they provide outside of court, however, is often the basis for administrative detention orders (internment without charge), in the absence of corroborating *admissible* evidence against the detainee.

Heavy reliance by the prosecution on confessions is not inherently improper. In many court systems — including the one inside Israel's borders — confessions are very often central to convictions. However, when other admissible evidence is relatively hard to collect and safeguards against the use of torture and ill-treatment are weak, the incentives are very strong for interrogators to resort to abusive means of coercion.

In both civil courts in Israel and military courts in the occupied territories, the rules of evidence require that a confession be freely given in order to be admissible. Section 12 of the Evidence Ordinance states that a confession of an accused will be admitted only if it is proved that it was made "freely and voluntarily." Section 477 of the Military Jurisdiction Law (1955) states, "A military court shall not admit the confession of an accused as evidence unless it is convinced that the accused made it of his own free will."

During their trial, defendants have the right to file a motion to discard their signed out-of-court confessions on the grounds that they were not given voluntarily. The voir-dire hearing on such a motion is called a "trial within a trial" or "mini-trial" (in Hebrew, *mishpat zota*), and takes place during the course of the trial itself. (Mini-trials may not be initiated by a detainee seeking to contest the validity of evidence provided against him by a third party; see below.)

In the mini-trial, the burden of proof lies with the prosecution to demonstrate that the confession was given voluntarily. However, both civil and military courts have found a considerable degree of coercion during interrogation to be consistent with a "free and voluntary" confession. The leading school of thought in the Supreme Court, which is currently divided on this issue, holds that even if the interrogation methods used are coercive

---

[5] For more on collaborators, see B'Tselem, *"Collaborators" in the Territories during the Intifada*.

or abusive, the confession may be admissible if it can be shown that when the defendant signed his confession, he did so of his own free will.[6]

On occasion, however, trial courts inside Israel have declared confessions obtained by GSS methods to be inadmissible. In a recent case, a Tel Aviv District Court threw out a confession taken shortly after the defendant had been subjected to prolonged interrogation and sleep deprivation of up to seventy-two hours, with no more than two to three hours of continuous sleep being allowed, while being held shackled in a tiny "waiting room," part of the time with a hood over his head.[7]

In military courts, successful attempts by Palestinian defendants to have their own confessions disqualified on the grounds of non-voluntariness are rare if nonexistent. It is not possible to establish how often mini-trials have succeeded, since there is no public repository of legal rulings in the occupied territories. None of the Israeli or Palestinian defense lawyers interviewed by HRW could cite a single successful attempt. HRW sought such information from the IDF in a letter sent on February 13, 1994, but received no answer.

In theory, the mini-trial procedure provides an important venue for scrutinizing the closed world of IDF and GSS interrogations. In practice,

---

[6] Israel's Supreme Court, according to the Landau report, has:

> rejected the view that a confession taken by use of excessive pressure must be disqualified without even investigating whether it is truthful....The court reaffirms the test of the credibility of the confession, and also adopts the earlier interpretation which equates the freedom of choice of the person interrogated with his free will. Nevertheless, the judges introduce a reservation by disqualifying confessions obtained by violating basic accepted values. (paragraph 3.19)

[7] Tel Aviv District Court, case 201/93, *State of Israel v. Abdul Hakim Gibali*, unpublished decision, March 9, 1994. See Yosef Algazy, "Vice President of Tel Aviv District Court Strikes Down a Defendant's Admission after Determining That Shabak [the GSS] Extracted It by Illegal Means," *Haaretz*, April 13, 1994. In another case before an Israeli civilian court, a Jerusalem District Court judge invalidated the confession of a teenage Palestinian girl because of the conditions under which she had been interrogated at the Russian Compound facility in Jerusalem. See Bill Hutman, "'Unacceptable' Police Interrogation Procedure Nullifies Girl's Confession," *Jerusalem Post*, March 9, 1993.

The Admissibility of Coerced Confessions 245

considerable pressures and obstacles, analyzed later in this chapter, deter defendants before military courts from initiating and pursuing to the end a challenge to their own confession. The vast majority of defendants agree to plea bargains, in which the prosecutor agrees to drop some charges or reduce the penalties demanded in exchange for a guilty plea on other charges. In agreeing to a plea bargain, defendants forfeit the option to contest their own confessions.

Nearly all military court proceedings end in convictions. According to official statistics, of the 83,321 Palestinians tried in military courts in the West Bank and Gaza Strip between 1988 and 1993, only 2,731, or 3.2 percent, were acquitted.[8] Seventy percent of convictions are based on plea bargains negotiated before the trial begins, according to an IDF statement issued in July 1992.[9] This estimate of the proportion of plea bargains was roughly consistent with estimates provided to HRW in 1993 by defense lawyers.

THE ROLE OF CORROBORATING EVIDENCE

According to the rules of evidence, the prosecution must have some piece of corroborating evidence (in Hebrew, *dvar ma nosaf*) in addition to the confession in order to obtain a conviction. This requirement is usually satisfied by an item of minor or debatable evidentiary value. Often, the corroborating evidence consists of the court protocol from the suspect's extension-of-detention hearing. During that hearing, the judge asks the detainee to respond to the accusations against him. If the protocol shows that the detainee pled guilty to any of the charges or that he did not clearly deny them, then this protocol might be accepted as sufficient corroborating evidence for the confession. This occurs despite all of the due-process

---

[8] Letter to HRW from Lieutenant Colonel Moshe Fogel, Head, Information Branch, IDF Spokesman's Unit, February 24, 1994. During 1993, the letter stated, 15,676 Palestinians were tried in military courts, of whom 320 were acquitted.

[9] IDF Judge Advocate-General's Corps, "Reply to Lawyer Committee Report," [sic] July 1992, p. 6, contained as an appendix in Lawyers Committee for Human Rights, *A Continuing Cause for Concern: The Military Justice System of the Israeli-Occupied Territories* (New York: Lawyers Committee for Human Rights, February 23, 1993).

shortcomings that seem commonplace in the extension-court hearings, including the absence of the detainee's lawyer (see Chapter Eight). Such a practice demeans the requirement of corroborating evidence.

CONTESTING CONFESSIONS

A defendant wishing to contest his out-of-court confession enters a plea of "not guilty" and requests a mini-trial. When this occurs, the military judge halts the trial of the charges facing the defendant and instructs the military prosecutor to prove that the defendant's confession was freely given. The prosecutor often sets about this task by bringing into court the policeman who recorded the defendant's confession after the interrogation had been completed by the IDF or GSS interrogator.

The value of this police agent's testimony to the prosecution derives from a neat division of labor that is maintained at the end of the interrogation process: once the interrogators obtain an oral statement from the suspect, a police agent who had nothing to do with the interrogation then prepares and accepts the written statement. The police agent is thus able to deny plausibly that has any reason to believe that the defendant who signed the statement before him had been coerced into signing it.

The standard police confession form contains a preamble to the effect that the detainee understands that the person recording his statement is a member of the police; that the detainee is providing the statement freely and may elect to say nothing; that the detainee fully understands the contents of his own statement, and that it may be used against him. The confession is usually written in Hebrew, even though most Palestinians cannot read Hebrew and have no lawyer or independent interpreter on hand when they sign the form. At this stage, many, if not most detainees have not seen a lawyer since their arrest.

Obviously, the defendant's signature is no guarantee that a confession was freely given. The defendant may prefer to sign a confession, even if wholly or partly untrue, rather than face the likely prospect of renewed interrogation.

When summoned to mini-trials, police confession-recorders have generally been able to testify without being discredited that the confession made in their presence appeared voluntary to them. But defense lawyers have occasionally succeeded in exposing how the compartmentalization of the confession process seems tailor-made to yield plausible deniability for the confession-recorder.

On February 15, 1993, an HRW observer in the Nablus Military Court watched a policeman testify with absurd implausibility that he was utterly ignorant of the events preceding the detainee's arrival in his office.

Attorney Lea Tsemel was representing Yusif Taher Faris, a Palestinian charged with murdering a suspected collaborator. The police witness, Master Sergeant Hussein Amar, who is attached to the police's "Samaria Investigations Unit," had recorded the defendant's confession in Hebrew after his 1992 interrogation in the GSS wing at Nablus prison. Tsemel sought to establish that the the GSS ran the confession-recording process behind the scenes, and that the policeman must have been aware that her client had been subjected to coercive GSS methods.

Under cross-examination, Master Sergeant Amar made a string of implausible statements to the court. He testified that when he came to work in the morning, he "found" interrogation logs — which include the information supplied by the detainee during questioning sessions — in a drawer of his desk. He said that after glancing at the log, he knew what the detainee had told the interrogators and what he had agreed to confess to. The policeman claimed to have no idea who drew up the forms or how they got into his drawer. He told the court:

> When I come into the office in the morning, if there are forms in the drawer, I know there is work. If not, there is no work. I do not consult with any interrogators about this.[10]

The gist of Master Sergeant Amar's testimony was as follows:

- He never saw or consulted with interrogators about detainees, and his only contact with the interrogators was through the anonymous forms dropped in his drawer;

---

[10] Nablus Military Court, case 6637/92, February 15, 1993 session. The testimony was written down and translated from Hebrew into English by the HRW observer.

- He did not know the names or code-names of any of the interrogators, or which agency the interrogators worked for, or which agency prepared the interrogation logs;

- He never entered the interrogation wing, and did not know which agency had jurisdiction over it or what methods of interrogation they used; and

- He could not recall any instance of seeing detainees hooded or handcuffed; of a detainee complaining to him of being beaten during interrogation; or of a detainee arriving in his office in a dirty or bad-smelling state.

The following excerpt conveys the flavor of the cross-examination of Master Sergeant Amar:

Tsemel: I submit to you that my client was in the Shabak [GSS] interrogation wing the entire time before you took down his confession.

Policeman: I know that he was in the interrogation wing, but I don't know who is responsible for that wing.

Tsemel: But you said earlier today, in a different context, "Yes, the Shabak is responsible for this facility." I can point to that statement in the court protocol, if necessary. So were you lying then or are you lying now?

Policeman: I don't lie.

At this point, the military prosecutor remarked, "Okay, Lea, so you caught him, why don't you keep on going with your cross-examination?" Tsemel turned to the judge, Major Dan Margaliot, who did not comment on the witness's contradictory statements and urged Tsemel to continue. A short time later, Tsemel again pressed the policeman on the nature and extent of his interaction with GSS interrogators.

Tsemel: What happens if, when the detainee arrives in your office, he doesn't want to confess?

Policeman: I write a note.

The Admissibility of Coerced Confessions

Tsemel: To whom do you write this note?

A short pause ensued, during which the policeman may have realized that his answer might contradict his earlier assertion that he knew nothing about the interrogating agency or the responsible interrogators. He evaded the question with a joke, replying, "I write the note to Ma'atz" (Israel's Division of Public Works, which builds and maintains the country's road system). The soldiers guarding the courtroom guffawed at the wisecrack; Judge Margaliot made no comment, and motioned Tsemel to continue her cross-examination.

Several moments later, Tsemel asked Master Sergeant Amar about the interrogation logs that he claimed to discover in his desk drawer in the morning, placed there by anonymous interrogators:

Tsemel: I submit to you that the GSS logs have the words "General Security Service" written on them, and that they include three options, "waiting," "cell" and "rest," one of which is always circled.[11]

Policeman: I do not look at the top of the form, nor do I look at the sides, nor at the bottom. I look only at the contents themselves, what is written, never at the top or the bottom of the form.

In the end, defendant Faris abandoned efforts to disqualify his confession, and was sentenced to twenty-five years in prison for homicide.

***

A defendant who persists with a mini-trial can summon the GSS interrogators themselves to testify. When interrogators are called to the stand, the judge typically orders that the courtroom be closed to all except the witness, defendant, defense counsel, prosecutor, and court staff.[12]

---

[11] According to two sets of GSS logs obtained by HRW in other trials, these three options are indeed listed on the forms, which seem to be standard issue. See Chapter Twelve.

[12] Military Order 378, in Article 11, states, "The military court shall hold cases brought before it in public. However, a military court may order that a case brought before it shall be conducted wholly or in part behind closed doors if it

GSS interrogators are not required to identify themselves by name to the court, and testify under assumed names.

There are limits to the questions that can be put to the interrogators. While the agency has in some cases furnished the courts with logs tracking the location of the detainee throughout interrogation, prosecutors frequently request that the judge disallow certain questions, on the grounds that the answers would reveal classified information. Interrogators often come to court bearing an order stipulating that certain details of interrogation methods cannot be disclosed. (This order, signed by a regional military commander, is called a "document of secrecy"; in Hebrew, *teudat hisayon*.) Thus, defense counsel is hampered in its efforts to document the methods to which their clients have been subjected.

In addition to cross-examining the prosecution witnesses, defense counsel also calls witnesses — usually only the defendant himself, who typically alleges that abusive interrogation methods constrained him to sign a statement against his will.

At the end of the mini-trial, the presiding judge decides whether the confession is admissible. If the judge declares it to be inadmissible, the prosecution can continue to seek conviction on the basis of other evidence. If the confession is held admissible, then it is generally treated as reliable, with no further inquiry into its truthfulness. The judge is supposed to explain his or her reasoning on the admissibility of the confession in the final written verdict for the case.

There is no special venue during the trial for appealing the judge's ruling on the admissibility of the defendant's confession. The defendant and/or the prosecution can only appeal the ruling as part of an appeal of the final verdict in the case, if the verdict is susceptible to an appeal (see Chapter Eight).

Since the odds are stacked against defendants in mini-trials, most lawyers told HRW that they discouraged clients from launching them. Instead, lawyers advised clients to plea-bargain with prosecutors and seek leniency in sentencing. When they are initiated, mini-trials are often chiefly defense maneuvers in the plea-bargain process, according to many prominent lawyers who have undertaken them, including Lea Tsemel and Abed Asali.

---

considers it appropriate to do so in the interests of the security of the Israel Defense Forces, justice, or for public safety."

Tsemel, Asali and other lawyers told HRW that military prosecutors often respond to the prospect of a mini-trial by stepping up the plea-bargain negotiations. The frequent preference of prosecutors for a plea-bargain over a mini-trial may be due to diverse factors: overloaded court dockets, a reluctance to pull interrogators from their work in order to testify, and an aversion to putting interrogation methods under court scrutiny.

Obstacles Facing Palestinians in Mini-Trials

In practice, few mini-trials in military courts continue to their resolution. Most end with a plea-bargain agreement and the defendant's abandonment of the challenge to his confession. The main reasons for this are the difficulties in proving improper coercion to the court's satisfaction; the delays in the trial that the mini-trial is likely to cause while the defendant remains in prison; and the likely prospect of a far longer sentence if the defendant spurns the prosecution's offer of a plea bargain and is convicted.

For defendants who persist in mini-trials, the obstacles are many. They include the five factors that are listed here and described in greater detail below:

Classified interrogation guidelines that permit certain methods of pressure: GSS interrogators work from a set of classified guidelines that permit some forms of psychological and physical pressure. In mini-trials, GSS agents have acknowledged some methods of pressure, such as prolonged sleep deprivation and position abuse, without prompting the military judges to discard the subsequent confessions;

Lack of witnesses for the defense: Defense counsels rarely have anyone to call as witnesses besides their own clients;

Judges' acceptance of interrogators' testimony over that of detainees: In situations where material evidence is slight and judges are required to choose between the conflicting accounts of a single Palestinian defendant and one or more members of the security forces, judges typically prefer the latter;

Palestinian lawyers ill-equipped before the military courts: Most Palestinian defendants are represented by lawyers from the occupied territories rather than from Israel and East Jerusalem. In the military courts, many of these lawyers are no match for the prosecutors and their witnesses from the security forces, because they are neither fluent in Hebrew nor well-trained in Israeli law; and

The use of out-of-court third-party confessions: Under interrogation, suspects frequently give statements incriminating third parties. Under Israeli law, such statements can later be introduced as evidence against the third party. The defendant cannot contest the third party's incriminating statement on the grounds that it was not provided voluntarily.

Classified Interrogation Guidelines that Permit Certain Methods of Pressure

The Landau report noted that confessions obtained with the aid of pressure or deception could still be admissible so long as "the interrogator did not use extreme means which contradict accepted basic values or are degrading."[13] The report's classified appendix authorized certain means of psychological and "moderate" physical pressure. These guidelines have since been reviewed and modified, but remain classified (see Chapter Three).

HRW's findings in this report suggest that the approved methods include, but are not necessarily limited to, prolonged hooding, position abuse, and sleep deprivation. Interrogators readily admit on the witness stand to using these methods.

By contrast, certain methods that HRW believes to be commonplace are routinely denied by interrogators. To our knowledge, no interrogator has ever testified in a mini-trial that he had beaten a detainee or threatened to kill or injure him.[14]

---

[13] Paragraph 3.19.

[14] We are aware of only one case in which a GSS interrogator admitted out of court that he had beaten a detainee. The admission was made to an independent pathologist investigating the 1992 death in detention of Mustafa Akawi, who did not die from the blows. See Chapter Nineteen.

The Admissibility of Coerced Confessions

Following court precedents, military judges do not require military prosecutors to prove that no pressure was exerted on the defendant. In general, prosecutors need only to persuade the judge that the methods applied were neither "degrading" nor contradictory to "accepted basic values" and that they did not deprive the defendant of a choice at the moment when he signed the statement provided to the police.

The Mini-trial of Muhammad Adawi

A 1993 mini-trial at Hebron military court illustrated the GSS practice of admitting to some forms of strong coercion while denying others. In particular, the GSS rejected allegations by the defendant, Muhammad Adawi, that he had been beaten during interrogation, despite the introduction of evidence that appeared to support the defendant's claim (see Chapter Sixteen).

While denying all allegations of beating, interrogators testifying at the mini-trial readily acknowledged placing Adawi in the "waiting" mode for periods ranging from forty-one to one hundred and nine hours. (The latter included two breaks, one for two hours and one for three hours, during which time Adawi was able to sleep. See Chapter Twelve and the related log in the Appendix.) The interrogators stated that, in general, detainees in the "waiting" mode sat on small chairs with a hood over their head and their hands shackled, either to the chair or to an immovable object fixed to the wall. During cross-examination, the GSS agents conceded that detainees might have difficulty sleeping during "waiting," but said that some detainees might be able to "doze."

One interrogator acknowledged that sleep deprivation was intentional. In the June 30, 1993 session of Adawi's mini-trial, an agent code-named "Thompson" testified:

> With respect to prevention of sleep, any detainee who wants to talk can immediately thereafter go to sleep. If I had wanted him [Adawi] to sleep, I would have sent him to sleep. That is our position.[15]

Presiding military judge Major Michal Rahav did not pursue with the interrogators the conditions of Adawi's sleep deprivation or

---

[15] Hebron Military Court, case 2332/92, June 30, 1993 session, p. 77 of the protocol.

confinement in a chair while hooded and shackled. In an informal discussion after the court session of May 17, an HRW representative observing the trial asked the judge whether such methods might cast doubt on the admissibility of the confession. Judge Rahav replied without elaborating, "Some methods are permitted, you know."

In the end, the mini-trial was aborted when the defendant agreed to a plea-bargain offer from the prosecution that included dropping all charges based on his second, more significant confession, and dropping the sentence demanded from seven years to two years.

The Mini-trial of 'Abd al-Qader al-Khatib

'Abd al-Qader Seif al-Din Mon'em al-Khatib was arrested on May 5, 1992, and interrogated by the GSS at Ramallah and the Russian Compound. He was charged with membership in an illegal organization, illegal possession of weapons, and recruiting others to carry out several unsuccessful shooting attacks on IDF and Israeli civilian vehicles in the West Bank.[16]

The only evidence offered by the prosecution against al-Khatib was his own confession, the statement of the policeman who took the confession, and a third-party confession by Ibrahim Mahmoud Hassan Helwe, who was arrested, interrogated and charged with carrying out some of the shooting attacks on al-Khatib's instructions.

The prosecution said that, on instructions from al-Khatib, others had planned to carry out five attacks, but had in fact fired their guns on two occasions only. The first alleged attack was carried out by Helwe at al-Khatib's instructions at night on a road leading to the Anatot settlement in the West Bank. Helwe allegedly fired three shots, missing the vehicle. The second alleged shooting was carried out by Helwe and a third person on the same road. They allegedly fired three shots and again missed.

Despite knowing the general area, time and nature of the alleged attacks, the prosecutor presented no witnesses or police reports on the incidents, or any other evidence beyond the statements that interrogators had obtained from the defendant and an alleged accomplice.

Al-Khatib contested the validity of his confession in a mini-trial, saying it had been extracted through torture. He said interrogators handcuffed him for many hours at a time, beat him, hooded him, deprived

---

[16] Ramallah Military Court, case 4614/92.

him of sleep, and threatened him with a variety of abuses against himself and his family, including the demolition of the family home.

During the mini-trial, according to al-Khatib's lawyer, Abed Asali, the GSS agents acknowledged placing al-Khatib in the "waiting" mode for very long periods, which they said included confinement in a chair while hooded and handcuffed to an immovable object. Asali said the GSS witnesses justified these measures as necessary to ensure that al-Khatib did not escape or identify other detainees while he awaited questioning.[17] The interrogators denied beating or threatening the defendant.

The GSS interrogation logs presented as evidence during the mini-trial reveal that al-Khatib was subjected to particularly long periods of "waiting" during his first ten days in detention, alternating with questioning sessions and brief rest periods. The logs strongly suggest that he spent at least five periods, each between nineteen and forty-eight hours long and some possibly far longer, in the "waiting" mode, prevented from sleeping (see Chapter Twelve).

In court, al-Khatib could produce no evidence to support his allegation that he had been beaten by the GSS. Attorney Asali told HRW that during the course of the mini-trial he sensed that neither the allegations of beating nor the better-documented claims of sleep deprivation and position abuse would persuade the military judge to discard al-Khatib's confession. His client elected to abort the mini-trial and accept a deal from the military prosecutor by which four charges would be dropped in exchange for a guilty plea on the remaining charges. Al-Khatib was given a ten-year sentence, half of what Asali said his client would have faced had there been no plea bargain.

Lack of Witnesses for the Defense

Detainees rarely have any witnesses to call upon to corroborate allegations of torture or ill-treatment. Prison personnel and interrogators rarely if ever identify themselves by name to detainees during interrogation, so they cannot easily be located and summoned to testify at trials several months later. Fellow detainees cannot testify as eyewitnesses because they were not present with the defendant inside the interrogation room, and otherwise spent most of their time either hooded or blindfolded or isolated in tiny cubicles.

---

[17] HRW interview, Jerusalem, July 18, 1993.

Occasionally, medical professionals can be summoned to testify at a mini-trial if the detainee sustained an injury and was examined shortly thereafter. But the medical personnel to whom detainees have access while under interrogation have sometimes been complicit in covering up abuse. For example, disturbing evidence of a cover-up emerged in the mini-trial of Muhammad Adawi when a prison medic and physician were summoned to testify (see Chapter Sixteen).

The prospect of obtaining other witnesses to testify about the sequelae of violent abuse is very slim. This is because beatings by IDF and GSS interrogators are usually carried out in a way that leave few marks that are still visible by the time the detainee exits the interrogation wing and is seen by his lawyer and family.

Some defense lawyers have sought to buttress their clients' credibility by introducing the testimony of other Palestinians who allege that they too were ill-treated or tortured at the same interrogation facility during the same period. But lawyers state that military judges are disinclined to allow such attempts to demonstrate patterns of abuse, arguing that it is not directly relevant to the case at hand.

An HRW representative witnessed one such effort in the Gaza Military Court on March 10, 1993, in the course of a mini-trial initiated by lawyer Ali Naouq. Naouq represented two Palestinian youths—Ra'ed Jibali, and Iyad Kafena, both aged fifteen when arrested—who were interrogated by police in February 1992. The two youths signed confessions stating they had thrown Molotov cocktails at Israeli troops, but later contested the statements, saying they confessed only after being hooded, beaten, threatened with death and subjected to electric shocks by their police interrogators (see Chapter 17).

During the March 10, 1993 court session, Naouq told military judge Shaul Gordon that he intended to call as witnesses twenty other Palestinians who would testify that they had been subjected to similar interrogation methods in the same station by the same interrogators during the same general period. Naouq contended that their detailed testimony would lend credibility to his clients' allegations of abuse. Military Judge Gordon ruled against accepting their testimony, saying, "We are not running a commission of inquiry here. These witnesses were not in the police station at the time of the specific interrogation under question, and

The Admissibility of Coerced Confessions 257

are therefore not relevant."[18] In the end, the judge ruled the confessions of Jibali and Kafena to be admissible and convicted them.

In a similar vein, judges have routinely rebuffed defense efforts to introduce into evidence studies by human rights groups documenting systematic patterns of abuse at Israeli interrogation centers. According to defense lawyers, judges have declared such documentation to be irrelevant to deciding the specific case before the court.

Judges' Acceptance of Interrogators' Testimony over That of Detainees

In military courts, the judges are appointed from the ranks of military prosecutors, and both judges and prosecutors appear in uniform wearing the insignia of the same IDF unit to which they belong, the Judge Advocate-General's corps. The appearance of partiality is especially pronounced during mini-trials, in which the judges must often weigh the word of a Palestinian suspect against Israeli security personnel involved in the interrogation.

The problem of bias was addressed by the Landau Commission. Its report noted that interrogators had routinely perjured themselves about the use of coercive methods when testifying in trials of Palestinians. But, rather than entertain the possibility that judges had been knowing parties to the cover-up (paragraph 2.45), the commission concluded that the judges had simply been more willing to believe interrogators than Palestinian defendants:

> The survivability shown by the method [of "constant and methodical lying" by GSS agents] for 16 years is...quite surprising. There is no doubt that for years the method drew encouragement and viability from the courts' trust in the interrogators who appeared before them as witnesses. From the testimonies we heard it turns out that the percentage of cases in which a confession was rejected due to the court's disbelief or doubt in the interrogators' statements on the witness stand was very small. In the vast majority of cases the courts preferred the interrogators'

---

[18] The judge's statement was written down and translated by an HRW observer present in the courtroom.

testimonies to the accuseds' allegations concerning the use of illegitimate methods against them.[19]

Today, the problem of partiality may be even tougher to uproot. Now that GSS interrogators have been authorized to use certain coercive methods, interrogators called to testify no longer need to deny categorically having used any form of coercion. Thus, they appear more credible when they deny some — but not all — of the allegations made by defendants who wish to challenge their confessions.

Faced with a situation that pits their word against that of one or more interrogators, defendants have few tools to make their allegations credible to the court. Defense lawyers told HRW that military judges often ask detainees to give highly detailed accounts of their experiences, complete with the times and dates of the abuse, and descriptions of the relevant interrogators and guards. The disorienting physical and psychological pressures of interrogation impair the ability of most detainees to recall their experiences in full detail. This makes their accounts vulnerable under aggressive cross-examination by prosecutors.

Palestinian Lawyers Ill-Equipped before the Military Courts

With the exception of a handful of lawyers from Israel and East Jerusalem, most lawyers defending Palestinian security detainees in military courts are themselves Palestinians from the West Bank and Gaza Strip. Many of them lack the Hebrew fluency and training in Israeli law necessary to cross-examine security force personnel effectively. As graduates of law schools in Lebanon, Egypt and other Arab countries, they are less steeped in Israeli law and practices. They often cannot even read the relevant legal documents, and must hire someone to translate them.

Efforts by Palestinian lawyers to contest confessions should be seen in light of the atmosphere of the military courts. The courts are, to many Palestinians, intimidating and hostile environments under the best of

---

[19] Paragraph 2.36. For a critique of the Landau Commission's credulousness toward assurances by GSS interrogators that they can tell true from false confessions even while using coercive means (e.g., the passage cited at the very beginning of this chapter), see Mordechai Kremnitzer, "The Landau Commission Report: Was the Security Service Subordinated to the Law, or the Law to the 'Needs' of the Security Service?" *Israel Law Review* 23 (1989), pp. 216-279, especially pp. 223-225.

The Admissibility of Coerced Confessions

circumstances. Many lawyers shrink from the task of aggressively cross-examining GSS interrogators, who are seen as agents of a secretive and all-powerful agency against whom legal redress is impossible. Those who do challenge the credibility of the GSS and of military prosecutors are in some cases treated by the judge as if they are wasting the court's time.

The Hebrew-Arabic translation services provided in the military courts constitute another obstacle to the defense. They often appeared grossly inadequate to the HRW observer who attended trials in the military courts in Nablus, Ramallah, Gaza, and Hebron. The translations are sequential, rather than simultaneous; that is, a speaker says something in Hebrew or Arabic, and then is supposed to pause to allow the court-appointed translator to provide the translation for the benefit of the others.

HRW's observer, a Hebrew-speaker, noted that the translators — most of whom are members of the Druze minority inside Israel — were frequently sullen and telegraphic in their translations of the Hebrew proceedings, and sometimes neglected to translate portions altogether. Judges sometimes had to order translators to resume translating in response to defense requests. At other times, prosecutors and judges did not pause in their deliveries, forcing the translators to speak over the voices of the Hebrew speakers. The result was confusion and cacophony.

The problem was exacerbated by the physical set-up of the court, in which lawyers stood close to the judge at one end of the room, their backs facing or at an angle to the rest of those present. On many occasions, the proceedings resembled a private conversation between the judge, prosecutor and defense counsel, leaving everyone else, including the defendant, unclear as to the course of events. Defendants' relatives, who were sitting in the audience, told HRW's observer that they had only a vague idea of what was going on. Even Hebrew speakers seated in the audience sometimes found the proceedings difficult to follow.

The Use of Out-of-Court Third-Party Confessions

Under the "Tamir law,"[20] an out-of-court statement made by a third party is in many situations admissible as evidence against a defendant without that party making the statement in court and submitting to cross-examination. This out-of-court testimony remains admissible as evidence

---

[20] Article 10A of the 1971 Evidence Ordinance, as amended in 1979. The law is named after Shmuel Tamir, the incumbent minister of justice when the amendment was enacted.

even if the witness is called to testify and attempts to retract his statement.[21]

Enacted inside Israel in response to the intimidation of witnesses by organized crime figures, the Tamir law is an effective tool in the hands of military prosecutors and interrogators in the occupied territories. According to ex-detainees interviewed for this report, GSS and IDF interrogators both attempt to extract incriminating statements from detainees about third parties, and pressure detainees to cooperate by announcing that incriminating evidence has already been collected against them (i.e., hinting that the punishment resulting from their impending conviction will be reduced if they provide information).

Israeli attorney Avigdor Feldman told HRW that he was forced to abandon a mini-trial at the Lod Military Court inside Israel when confronted with a number of third-party statements incriminating his client, even though the witnesses had later retracted their confessions on the grounds that they had been extracted through ill-treatment and torture.

Feldman's client, twenty-one-year-old Suheib Hassan Ahmed Hassuna of East Jerusalem, was charged with twenty-three offenses, including membership in an illegal organization (the mainstream Fatah faction of the PLO), recruiting others into the organization, and organizing "disturbances of order" during 1991 and 1992, including graffiti writing, throwing stones at Israeli troops, erecting road blocks, and torching and breaking the windshields of Israeli cars. He was also accused of organizing the interrogation of suspected Palestinian collaborators.[22]

Hassuna was arrested on April 15, 1992, and confessed to a number of the charges against him after a lengthy interrogation by the GSS at the Russian Compound police station. In addition to Hassuna's own confession, the prosecution offered as evidence the confessions of eight alleged accomplices who had also been interrogated by the GSS at the Russian Compound.

Feldman initiated a mini-trial, arguing that Hassuna's confession had been extracted after prolonged position abuse, hooding, beating, sleep deprivation, threats, and confinement in the "grave," a small, enclosed, and foul-smelling enclosure.

---

[21] However, if the witness were to successfully contest his confession in a mini-trial, it would become inadmissible.

[22] Lod Military Court, case 35/92.

Soon after Feldman began his presentation for the defense, the military prosecutor abandoned Hassuna's confession as a piece of evidence and relied on the eight third-party confessions. Feldman told HRW that each of the eight witnesses — all of whom were still detained and faced a variety of charges — said their confessions had been extracted using methods similar to those used against Hassuna. All said that they provided Hassuna's name in their confessions only under GSS coercion. These witnesses did not attempt to launch their own mini-trials, however, and the judge in the Hassuna case indicated that he would consider their initial statements admissible. This prompted Hassuna to abandon the mini-trial and accept a plea-bargain offer from the prosecution.

Attorney Dalal Eid Fares has represented hundreds of Gazan security detainees over the past decade. She estimated that third-party confessions play a major role in the conviction of one in three defendants who are found guilty, while self-confessions are central to the conviction of nearly all of the rest.[23] Fares' estimates were close to the sixty-forty ratio provided by Nablus attorney Adnan Abu Leila (see above), concerning his clients who are convicted.

PRESSURES TO PLEA-BARGAIN

Faced with obstacles to overturning a confession, most defendants accept a plea bargain before the end of the mini-trial. In many cases, they were offered deals by the prosecution once they notified the court that they intended to initiate a mini-trial, but were warned that the offer would be withdrawn if they persisted with their efforts. Several defense lawyers interviewed by HRW said they were convinced that if they persisted with the mini-trial and lost, their clients would face stiffer sentences.

For most defendants, the pressures to plea-bargain begin well before the opening of the trial. Most suspects who face moderate or serious security charges have been held in detention for months pending the start of their trial. Initiating a mini-trial would significantly prolong the judicial process, in some cases resulting in their spending longer in pre-trial detention than they would spend in prison if convicted.

Gaza attorney Ali Naouq told HRW that the prosecution offered to release his clients, Ra'ed Jibali and Iyad Kafena, who had already served a

---

[23] HRW interview, Khan Yunis, February 12, 1993.

year in pre-trial detention, if Naouq dropped his effort to overturn their confessions on the grounds of torture by police interrogators (see Chapter Sixteen).[24] The prosecutor warned that if the defendants persevered with the mini-trials, they would receive stiffer sentences if they were eventually convicted on the gasoline-bomb charges they were facing. The defense refused the offer, and the two youths were convicted and sentenced.

Israeli defense attorney Avigdor Feldman was offered a deal if his client Suheib Hassuna (see above) pleaded guilty. According to Feldman, prosecutor Cap. Ofer Shapira notified him that the deal would be offered only so long as Feldman did not call GSS agents to the stand in a mini-trial. The moment GSS interrogators were summoned, Shapira warned, he would cancel the offer and seek the maximum sentence. Concerned about incriminating confessions against him from third parties, Hassuna accepted the deal and received eight years in prison instead of the maximum of fourteen. Feldman said that a secret appendix to the plea-bargain agreement further reduced Hassuna's sentence by a significant number of years, provided that Hassuna upheld certain undisclosed promises to the authorities.[25]

The mini-trial procedure provides a rare and valuable opportunity to expose interrogation methods to scrutiny. Unfortunately, the interest that human rights activists might have in seeing mini-trials pursued to their completion usually conflicts with the best interests of the defendant, given the workings of the interrogation and military court system. According to defense attorney Lea Tsemel:

> You can never win a mini-trial outright on the merits of the case. To win, you need a doctor or a GSS agent acknowledging that beating took place, which will never happen. Mini-trials can, however, be used to improve your position in a trial. The GSS are uneasy with mini-trials, since it wastes their time and manpower, which is limited anyway, and exposes parts of the interrogation system to the public.

---

[24] HRW interview, Gaza Military Court, March 10, 1993.

[25] HRW interview, Tel Aviv, July 8, 1993.

Therefore, when you begin a mini-trial, the prosecutor almost always offers you a deal. With the threat of a mini-trial in the air, you can get better terms. Never, never, try to win a mini-trial. You will always lose. Always plea-bargain toward the end.[26]

---

[26] Remarks delivered at a conference entitled "The International Struggle against Torture and the Case of Israel," sponsored by the Association of Israeli-Palestinian Physicians for Human Rights and the Public Committee against Torture in Israel, Tel Aviv, June 14, 1993.

19
DEATHS UNDER INTERROGATION

Since 1992, at least three Palestinians have died under interrogation in circumstances that indicate that interrogation methods and/or medical negligence directly or indirectly caused their death. A fourth died in what authorities ruled a suicide.[1] The issues raised in these cases relate closely to the patterns of severe abuse during interrogation, and medical complicity in the abuse, which are the subjects of this report.

The four cases since 1992 are summarized in this chapter, based on investigations by Palestinian and Israeli human rights organizations and on reports prepared by independent pathologists investigating the deaths.

Israeli authorities have, with increasing regularity, permitted the families of Palestinians who died in detention to appoint an independent pathologist to join the Ministry of Health pathologist in conducting the autopsy. In at least two remarkable instances since 1989, the independent pathologist was permitted to tour parts of the GSS facilities in which the detainee died, and question GSS agents there. Such access to interrogation facilities has been steadfastly refused to other independent monitors, such as lawyers, journalists and human rights organizations.

In all four cases since 1992, independent doctors participated in the autopsies. Since there are no Palestinian forensic pathologists residing in the West Bank or Gaza Strip, Palestinian families have brought in pathologists from abroad. These visits were coordinated by local human rights organizations working with the Physicians for Human Rights organizations based in the United States and Denmark.

In three cases, the independent pathologists pointed to medical negligence or the conditions of interrogation as contributing factors in the deaths. At least two, and possibly all three of these cases involved detainees who had been put under interrogation with preexisting ailments that either went untreated or did not prompt a halt to the rigors of interrogation. There is no available evidence to suggest that their treatment was harsher

---

[1] For profiles of the cases of deaths under interrogation that occurred prior to 1992, see B'Tselem, *The Interrogation of Palestinians During the Intifada*, pp.39-44, and Joost R. Hiltermann, "Deaths in Israeli Prisons," *Journal of Palestine Studies* 19, no. 3 (Spring 1990), pp. 101-110.

than the norm; rather, it seems that they received the usual treatment, but in their fragile health they did not survive it.

Israeli authorities state that a criminal investigation is conducted each time a prisoner dies while under interrogation. For cases in Israel Prison Service or GSS facilities, the Israeli police is officially charged with conducting the investigation. When the person dies in IDF custody, responsibility for investigating lies with the Criminal Investigation Division of the Military Police.

All four of the cases described here were supposedly the subjects of official investigations. As far as we know, in none of these cases did an official finding of wrongdoing lead to criminal charges against interrogators or medical personnel. In one case, however, disciplinary measures were reportedly ordered by the State Attorney.

Thus, there is a gap in some of these cases between the findings of the independent physicians and the official conclusions about the culpability of those involved. The granting of access to independent physicians, however commendable, does not go far enough in promoting accountability. Much of the material essential to conducting a proper inquiry into the cause of death continues to be withheld from the public and from the independent physician who participates in the autopsy. This information includes the interrogating agencies' records of what interrogation methods the detainee experienced and for how long, and what medical attention he received throughout the interrogation phase. The release of such records, along with access for the independent pathologist in each case to the place of interrogation, would provide a sounder basis for judging the factors contributing to a death in detention.

MUSTAFA AKAWI

On February 4, 1992, Mustafa Akawi, thirty-five, died under interrogation in the GSS interrogation wing of Hebron prison.[2] The immediate cause of Akawi's death was heart failure brought on by severe arteriosclerosis. Israeli officials used this autopsy finding to claim that Akawi had died of natural causes, and to deny any causal link between his

---

[2] For a fuller discussion of this case, see Middle East Watch, *Israeli Interrogation Methods Under Fire After Death of Detained Palestinian* (New York: Human Rights Watch, March 1992).

treatment during interrogation and his death. A police investigation recommended clearing Akawi's interrogators of criminal wrongdoing, and then-Police Minister Ronnie Milo stated that the GSS had "acted as it should, and there were no grounds for the complaints and accusations against it."[3]

Dr. Michael Baden, director of forensic sciences for the New York State Police, attended the autopsy on behalf of the Akawi family, and was then permitted to visit the GSS wing at Hebron and interview interrogators and prison medical personnel. In his final autopsy report, Dr. Baden reached very different conclusions from the police about the causes of Akawi's heart failure. He charged that it had been precipitated by:

> the very cold conditions that he was exposed to, by the bag over his head, by the way he was seated on an uncomfortable stool with hands cuffed behind his back for a considerable period of time, and by the emotional stresses that he was under.

In addition, Dr. Baden accused the medical staff of negligence:

> If this possible cardiac episode had been recognized by the paramedic because of the typical symptoms and signs — an EKG [electrocardiogram] may have been very helpful — strict bed rest and removal to a hospital might have permitted a non-fatal outcome.[4]

Dr. Robert Kirchner, a board member of the Physicians for Human Rights and Chicago's Chief Medical Examiner, concluded, "If we had a similar case in the U.S., this kind of death should be classified as a homicide."[5]

---

[3] "Israeli Interrogators Cleared in Arab's Death," *The New York Times*, February 14, 1992.

[4] Autopsy report, available from the Physicians for Human Rights (U.S.).

[5] *New York Times*, February 14, 1992. Commenting on the case, Hebrew University Law Professor Mordechai Kremnitzer stated, "If you didn't check at the start to make sure that Akawi wasn't ill, then you take responsibility, even if the violence was 'light.' For some prisoners, 'light' violence may suffice to kill."

In speaking with Dr. Baden, the GSS interrogators at Hebron revealed a surprising amount about their methods, even going so far as to admit to beating and shaking Akawi. Dr. Baden recalled:

> The interrogators acknowledged...that on the second or third day that [Akawi] was in custody the interrogator took him by the lapels and pushed him back and forth, both punching the chest and wiggling the head back and forth....I was advised by [Palestinians] that the technique of whiplashing the head back and forth is one technique of getting the person to be uncomfortable, to be more willing to talk, and doesn't leave marks upon him.

Dr. Baden found small bruises on the neck and larger bruises on the chest that he attributed to blows, commenting, "They had to be pretty strong punches to get diffuse hemorrhages about four or five inches in diameter each on the chest." He added, however, that they did not contribute to the death or cause internal injury.[6]

Dr. Baden learned from the interrogators that during most of the twelve hours before Akawi's death at dawn on February 4, the prisoner had been kept seated on a tiny chair in a bitterly cold, exterior hallway, with his hands cuffed behind his back and a hood over his head. Dr. Baden said that on the night of Akawi's death, the temperature was "at most 0º centigrade. There was snow outside." He also said that the corridor had broken window panes, so that the cold winter air flowed freely into the corridor where Akawi was kept. Dr. Baden was not sure what Akawi was wearing during the various phases of the night, but pointed out that he was told that after Akawi complained of pain, a prison paramedic gave him a jacket and blankets. This suggests that Akawi did not have warm clothing prior to that time. Dr. Baden said that he himself felt cold when he visited the same

---

Quoted in Moshe Reinfeld, "Investigate the Death of Akawi for Possible Manslaughter, Causing Death by Negligence, or Beating," *Haaretz*, February 14, 1992.

[6] Comments made at a Physicians for Human Rights press conference, New York, February 12, 1992. Transcript available from the Physicians for Human Rights (U.S.).

hallway four days after Akawi's death, even though he was wearing street clothing and a long raincoat.

It is not known whether Akawi was able to sleep during the night before his death, but, Dr. Baden said, "if he were going to sleep, he'd have to sleep in this little chair with the handcuffs behind his back and the hood over his face."[7]

Akawi was apparently subjected to standard GSS interrogation techniques. The ex-detainees interviewed for this report described being hooded and shackled to "kindergarten chairs" for prolonged periods. The physical force that the GSS interrogators acknowledged using is consistent with accounts by ex-detainees of having their heads whiplashed back and forth and being punched in their upper bodies. HRW interviewed ex-detainees held at Hebron who, like Dr. Baden, noted the broken or open windows at the facility. The guards patrolling the corridor in February must have realized that the detainees, confined and unable to move about to keep warm, would suffer from the cold.

It is possible that Akawi might have survived the heart attack if his interrogators and prison paramedics had displayed greater responsibility. On the evening before his death, Akawi was examined by a paramedic, who later told Dr. Baden that he had recommended that Akawi see a physician the next day.

Despite the paramedic's suspicion that Akawi was in poor health, the detainee was ordered into the cold exterior hallway for the night. This paramedic failed to insist that Akawi see a doctor immediately. Nor did he order the interrogation team to ensure that Akawi spend the night in a warm room, unhooded, uncuffed, and on a mattress instead of a tiny chair.

Later in the night, Akawi told a guard that he needed to see a doctor. An interrogator brought Akawi down two flights of stairs to the paramedic, who told Dr. Baden that he had checked Akawi's blood pressure and pulse, found them to be normal, and then sent Akawi back upstairs, advising only that Akawi's interrogators give him hot tea. The interrogator said he placed Akawi in a closet-sized space, unhooded and unhandcuffed, and went off to prepare tea. When he returned, he found Akawi unconscious. Akawi was pronounced dead some two hours later.

The surprising openness of the Israeli interrogators, who admitted to keeping Akawi for long hours on a small chair, handcuffing and hooding him throughout, and to using physical force in at least one instance, is

---

[7] Ibid.

indicative of the increasing willingness of the GSS to acknowledge using a number of abusive interrogation methods. It is likely that this willingness stems from their knowledge that these measures are authorized by the official but secret interrogation guidelines.

When B'Tselem sought to determine which authority was responsible for investigating the death, they encountered a remarkable chain of buck-passing. The Israeli Prison Service told B'Tselem to contact the IDF spokesperson, who referred them to the police spokesperson. The police spokesperson sent them to the agency's spokesperson for the "Judea region" (Israel's official term for the southern West Bank area), who informed them that the agency was responsible neither for the prisoner nor for his interrogation, and told them to contact the IDF spokesperson of the local command. That person then said that since the case was a GSS rather than an IDF affair, they should contact the police spokesperson.[8]

The State Attorney closed the police file on the death, confirming the finding of no criminal wrongdoing in the case. However, on February 17, 1993, the Israeli daily *Davar* reported that the Attorney General had recommended that unspecified interrogators and medical personnel be disciplined in connection with his death.

AYMAN SA'ID NASSAR

Ayman Sa'id Nassar, twenty-two, died of lung failure in an Israeli hospital, reportedly on April 2, 1993. He had been arrested on March 20, 1993, in the Deir al-Balah refugee camp in the Gaza Strip. According to human rights organizations, local residents stated that the IDF had forced Nassar and three other suspected activists out of a hideout using tear gas or smoke bombs of unknown composition.[9]

According to Israeli lawyer Lea Tsemel, the other three men reported being taken to interrogation in the GSS wing in Ashkelon prison, where they were subjected to beatings, prolonged position abuse, hooding,

---

[8] B'Tselem, *The Interrogation of Palestinians during the Intifada: Follow-up*, pp. 57-58.

[9] Joint press release, Gaza Centre for Rights and Law, Palestine Human Rights Information Center, and the Public Committee against Torture in Israel, April 8, 1993.

and sleep deprivation. It is not known whether Nassar was subjected to similar treatment.

On March 23, according to the accounts of local residents, authorities escorted Nassar back to Deir al-Balah, reportedly to show his captors a weapons cache. Later that day, Nassar was brought to Barzilai hospital in Israel, suffering from acute breathing difficulties. The authorities reported that Nassar died on April 2, at the hospital.

An autopsy was carried out on April 7, 1993. Danish pathologist Jorgen Dalgaard participated on behalf of Nassar's family. Dr. Dalgaard concluded that Nassar died from "lung failure due to the accumulation of liquid from ruptured lung blisters." He stated that the rupture of the lung blisters could have been caused by irritating smoke. Dr. Dalgaard stated that this condition, "[if] adequately treated, has a good prognosis, but if untreated or maltreated, complications ensue, as in this case." Speaking to the press after the autopsy, Dr. Dalgaard said, "[Nassar] did not get appropriate treatment at the proper time. He received appropriate treatment but too late." Dr. Dalgaard said he did not know what caused the blisters, but that once they ruptured, Nassar's condition would have been obvious. "No such bursting can occur in any normal situation without being noticed."[10]

Israeli authorities have not, to our knowledge, released any records concerning Nassar's treatment or health while under interrogation in Ashkelon prison. However, the case is apparently not closed. The office of the State Attorney informed the Association of Israeli-Palestinian Physicians for Human Rights in a letter of January 1, 1994 that "the procedure for investigating the reasons for the cause of [Nasser's] death is taking place in the Magistrate Court in Ashkelon, before Justice Nachmias (file 7/93: investigation of cause of death). The hearing is scheduled for February 17, 1994." The AIPPHR requested information regarding the results of the hearing, but as of early May had received no reply.

---

[10] "Israelis Could Have Saved Prisoner — Pathologist," Reuter, April 8, 1993. See also the joint press release by the Palestine Human Rights Information Center, the Gaza Centre for Rights and Law, and the Public Committee Against Torture in Israel, April 8, 1993.

Mustafa Barakat

On August 4, 1992, Mustafa Barakat, a twenty-three-year-old from the West Bank town of Anabta, died while under interrogation at the GSS wing of Tulkarm Prison. The immediate cause of death was a bronchial asthma attack.[11]

Barakat had been taken into custody the day before his death, after responding voluntarily to a military summons. Little is known about his treatment during his two days in the GSS interrogation wing. The GSS has not divulged any documentation charting his treatment, although logs and medical records are evidently kept for each detainee under interrogation, at least at some of the agency's facilities.

When attorney Tamar Pelleg-Sryck of the Association for Civil Rights in Israel investigated the case, Lieutenant Shawan, the military commander of Tulkarm prison, would say only that Barakat had been examined upon arrival by a prison paramedic, who permitted him to keep his inhaler. When she asked about Barakat's conditions of detention, he reportedly told her, "The GSS has interrogation rooms. I don't set foot inside them — let them tell you."[12]

Barakat reportedly suffered from an asthma attack during a round of questioning on the evening of August 3. The next morning, prison doctor Eli Waldner examined him. Dr. Waldner instructed that Barakat be allowed to use an inhaler as necessary. There is no record that he ordered a halt to the interrogation.

In investigating the case, B'Tselem consulted an Israeli respiratory specialist, who gave a written opinion stating that asthmatic prisoners should not have their heads covered or their hands tied. If they suffer an attack, the specialist wrote, they should be examined by a physician and should not be interrogated pending a follow-up examination.[13]

Following his visit to the doctor, Barakat's hands were tied in front of him but he was not hooded, according to an anonymous "military source"

---

[11] This account is based largely on B'Tselem, *The Death in Detention of Mustafa Barakat in the Interrogation Wing of the Tulkarm Prison* (Jerusalem: B'Tselem, September 1992).

[12] Ibid., pp. 10 and 6.

[13] Ibid., p. 7.

cited by B'Tselem.[14] He was interrogated again for two hours in the afternoon, and then placed in the cell, where he lost consciousness one hour later. Attempts to revive him were unsuccessful.

Dr. Waldner examined Barakat outside the interrogation wing. There is no evidence that the physician made it his business to insure that the patient whom he was returning to interrogation be spared treatment that could jeopardize his fragile health. As far as is known, he did not order that Barakat be brought back for a follow-up examination later the same day.

Whatever triggered the fatal attack, it appears that Barakat did not get the close attention that was warranted after he was diagnosed as asthmatic. Dr. Waldner evidently did not order a halt to the interrogation, even though, according to the authorities, physicians are empowered to do so. If Dr. Waldner did order any kind of special treatment for his patient beyond the provision of an inhaler (e.g., no tying of his hands), his orders were ignored.

The Ministry of Health autopsy was attended by a forensic pathologist appointed by Barakat's family. The pathologist, Connecticut Deputy Chief Medical Examiner Edward T. McDonough, found no signs of physical violence. Nevertheless, he concluded, Barakat's fatal asthma attack was "brought about by conditions in detention." He speculated further, "The fact that Mustafa was previously healthy and that he experienced this attack or attacks after less than thirty-six hours of detention and interrogation, leads to the conclusion that he could have been subjected to severe mistreatment."[15]

The police concluded its investigation of the death by recommending that the criminal file be closed, according to the September 4, 1992 edition of the Israeli daily *Davar*. HRW knows of no further official action in the case.

It is possible that the fatal attack was triggered wholly or partly by factors other than severe mistreatment, such as anxiety or an irritant ambient in the prison air to which he had not been exposed outside the prison. However, against the background of abuses to which GSS detainees

---

[14] Ibid., pp. 6 and 11.

[15] Press release, Physicians for Human Rights (U.S.), August 11, 1992. See also Dr. McDonough's autopsy report, August 31, 1992, available from the Physicians for Human Rights (U.S.).

at Tulkarm are routinely subjected, the suspicions of mistreatment and medical negligence in Barakat's case cannot be dispelled in the absence of a public accounting by medical staff and the GSS of the health precautions that were ordered, and of the conditions of Barakat's detention: where and for how long he was detained, and whether and for how long he was questioned or subjected to hooding, handcuffing or other methods.

HAZEM EID

On July 8, 1992, Hazem Eid, a twenty-three-year-old student at Birzeit University, died at Hebron prison. Eid was arrested on June 22, and was first taken to the GSS interrogation wing at Ramallah prison. Eid was seen by his lawyers on two occasions prior to his death, at a bail hearing in Ramallah Military Court on July 1, and at an extension-of-detention hearing in the same place four days later. On July 5, the judge extended Eid's detention by a further twenty days. At some point prior to his death, Eid was transferred to Hebron prison, for unknown reasons. His family and lawyers said later that they had not been informed of his transfer.

The official pathology report, which noted multiple bruises on Eid's body, described his death as "suicide by hanging." Officials accepted the finding and closed the file, according to B'Tselem. The Prime Minister' office stated, "apparently the detainee had emotional-internal reasons for suicide for reasons it is not appropriate to specify here."[16]

A Palestinian doctor from al-Muqassid hospital in Jerusalem who was not a forensic pathologist attended the autopsy. Although he prepared no written report of his own, he criticized the forensic examination as inadequate. The doctor stated that the Health Ministry's forensic pathologist, Yehuda Hiss, did not visit the cell where Eid was allegedly found, where he could have examined his alleged body position in order to try to determine whether he indeed could have hung himself as described by his interrogators. Nor, the doctor charged, did Dr. Hiss closely probe Eid's treatment during his interrogation in order to determine whether his

---

[16] Cited in B'Tselem, *The Death in Detention of Mustafa Barakat*, p. 12.

death had been preceded by ill-treatment or torture.[17] For their part, the authorities have released no information, as far as we are aware, concerning the day-to-day conditions of Eid's interrogation.

---

[17] Public Committee against Torture in Israel, *Report on Third Year's Activity* January 1992-December 1992 (Jerusalem: PCATI, 1993), p. 7. See also "Birzeit Student Dies in Detention," *Birzeit Human Rights Record*, October 1992.

Dr. Hiss was similarly criticized by some independent pathologists in 1988 for preparing the autopsy report on detainee Ibrahim al-Umtur without visiting the scene of his purported self-hanging. See Felicia Langer, "The Death of Ibrahim al-Mator, or: The Closed File That Remains Open," September 1989, unpublished paper; and Eric Rosenthal, "Medicolegal Death Investigations in Israel and the Occupied Territories," September 1991, unpublished paper.

Emerging international standards on the conduct of autopsies recommend that pathologists visit the scene of a suspicious death if it might shed light on the cause of death. The Principles on the Effective Prevention and Investigation of Extra-Legal, Arbitrary and Summary Executions states, in Article 13, that a proper autopsy in cases of suspected unnatural deaths shall attempt to establish "the cause and manner of death." The distinction between cause and manner is important here: "manner" is broader and includes an examination into the circumstances leading to a killing. The Model Autopsy Protocol emphasizes that, optimally, medical personnel should themselves document evidence at the death site and should collect the physical evidence and obtain information from witnesses.

The Principles on Investigation were approved by the U.N. General Assembly in 1989. The Model Autopsy Protocol was published together with the Principles by the U.N. in the 1991 *Manual on Effective Prevention and Investigation of Extra-Legal, Arbitrary and Summary Executions*. These standards are not legally binding, but are put forward to "thwart the speculation and innuendo that are fueled by unanswered, partially answered or poorly answered questions in the investigation of an apparently suspicious death." (Introduction to the Model Autopsy Protocol)

20
ISRAEL'S RECORD IN PUNISHING ABUSERS

There is minimal accountability for acts of torture and ill-treatment by Israeli interrogators. Despite the high volume of credible complaints by Palestinians who have undergone interrogation, the criminal prosecution or court-martial of interrogators for Penal Code offenses such as assault, or striking or threatening a person in custody, are extremely rare.

The government claims that abuses are taken very seriously. In a submission to the U.N. Committee against Torture, it stated:

> The GSS Comptroller was instructed to check every claim of torture or maltreatment during interrogation. Since 1987, the Comptroller has carried out this responsibility, initiating disciplinary or legal action against interrogators in cases where they have been found to have deviated from the legal guidelines....
>
> The Israel Defense Forces, like the GSS, has a strict policy of investigating every claim of maltreatment of detainees by IDF investigators. Soldiers who are found to have deviated from the strict IDF orders against violence or the threat of violence in interrogation are either court-martialled or have disciplinary charges brought against them, depending on the severity of the charges.[1]

The government's claim that abusers are held accountable has never been substantiated by the disclosure of sufficient information about the trials or disciplinary actions that have occurred. Official statements usually allude to such measures in general terms only. Details of the nature of the offense and of the punishment — which could be anything from imprisonment down to a verbal reprimand — are rarely provided and cannot be verified. Typical of the official information made public is what

---

[1] Initial Report of Israel to the U.N. Committee against Torture, CAT/C/16/Add.4, February 4, 1994, paragraphs 38 and 45.

was provided to the U.S. Department of State and published in its 1993 *Country Reports on Human Rights Practices*:

> As of late November, sixty-one complaints of maltreatment during interrogation had been filed against GSS interrogators during 1993. Investigations into most of those complaints had not yet been completed. The Government claims that during 1993 unspecified legal or disciplinary measures had been taken in thirteen cases, approximately half of which had been initiated prior to 1993.[2]

As for the IDF, the data released about the disciplining of soldiers rarely if ever isolate cases involving interrogators. Again, the information furnished to and published by the U.S. State Department is indicative:

> According to the IDF, from January 1 to September 1 there were eleven indictments against twenty-four soldiers and officers for "intifada-related offenses." Twelve soldiers were convicted while none were acquitted. Five indictments are still pending. No information was provided as to the sentences in these cases.[3]

One statistic is known: Since at least the beginning of the intifada, if not well before that, there has been only one case in which GSS interrogators have gone to prison for abusing a detainee (see below).[4]

---

[2] U.S. Department of State, *Country Reports on Human Rights Practices for 1993* (Washington: U.S. Government Printing Office, 1994), p. 1205.

[3] Ibid.

[4] In a letter dated October 10, 1993, the GSS reported to the Knesset Law and Justice Committee that during the period 1988–1993, GSS investigators were put on trial on criminal charges in two cases: the 1989 death in Gaza prison of Khaled Sheikh Ali (see below), and the 1987 death in Jenin prison of Awad Hamdan. In the latter case, the defendant was acquitted in 1989 of causing death through negligence. Trials of GSS agents ordinarily are held *in camera*, and reporting on cases is subject to prior censorship.

Recently, the State Attorney referred also to eleven GSS agents being dismissed since 1989, presumably in connection with findings of mistreatment or negligence.[5]

Police interrogators have also been prosecuted on occasion. As this report went to press, the verdict was being awaited in the trial of ten members of the Minorities Division of the Jerusalem police, a division against whom there had been a long series of allegations concerning mistreatment. The defendants are accused of taking part in violently extracting a confession in 1989 that turned out to be false. (Only some are charged with acts of violence; others are accused of giving false testimony or fabricating evidence.) The Palestinian suspect in their custody was beaten on the soles of his feet, put in an isolation cell, made to stand for hours with his hands tied behind his back to a pipe, prevented from sleeping for days, and blackmailed. In the end, he confessed to and reconstructed a murder he did not commit.[6]

Although these cases show that abusers do occasionally stand trial, a large gap exists between the frequency of such cases and the rampant incidence of abuse. The causes of this gap are complex, but certainly include a lack of will on the part of the political establishment to deter excesses by aggressively investigating complaints and prosecuting abuses.

A second cause, the extent of which cannot be gauged so long as the GSS interrogation guidelines remain classified, is that some forms of ill-treatment are permitted to interrogators and are therefore not officially recognized as abuses. This problem is best illustrated by comparing the aftermath of two deaths in detention at GSS interrogation facilities. In both cases, human rights organizations charged that serious abuses had taken place, on the basis of uncontested information concerning what the two men endured. Yet in one case, the interrogators were charged, convicted and jailed, and in the other case, the interrogators were cleared of any criminal wrongdoing.

In the first case, which occurred in December 1989, an autopsy determined that Khaled Kamel al-Sheikh Ali, a twenty-seven-year-old

---

[5] State Attorney Dorit Beinish, in presentation to the U.N. Committee against Torture, April 25, 1994, as summarized in U.N. press release HR/CAT/94/11, of the same date.

[6] The charge sheet against the defendants is reprinted as an appendix to B'Tselem, *The Interrogation of Palestinians during the Intifada: Follow-up*, pp. 83-85.

Gazan, had been killed by blows to his abdomen inflicted while at the interrogation wing of Gaza prison. In the second case, Mustafa Akawi (see Chapter Nineteen) died of chronic arteriosclerosis after being subjected to prolonged hooding, painful shackling to a small chair in an extremely cold corridor, and at least one beating.

When an independent pathologist visited Hebron prison to investigate Akawi's death, the interrogators apparently felt no compulsion to deny committing these abuses. Their frankness, and the State Attorney's finding that no one involved should be charged with criminal wrongdoing, suggests that, in contrast to the treatment of Khaled Kamel al-Sheikh Ali, the methods used on Akawi, including the physical violence, were consistent with the classified GSS guidelines.[7]

Apparently, more IDF interrogators have been prosecuted than have their GSS counterparts. But little information is ever made available. For example, after publication of B'Tselem's report on torture and ill-treatment in 1991, the IDF appointed a reserve general to investigate IDF interrogations (see Chapter Three). Following completion of his classified report, the IDF stated that criminal investigations had been opened in eight cases of possible abuse by interrogators, but no details were furnished. HRW's written requests to the IDF for information about these cases went unanswered.[8]

---

[7] Although those involved were cleared of criminal wrongdoing, a report in the Israeli daily *Davar* in February 1993 said that the Attorney General had recommended that unspecified interrogators and medical personnel be subjected to disciplinary measures in connection with Akawi's death.

The same month, Israel Radio reported that the government was drawing up a provision for the GSS interrogation guidelines that would immunize agents from criminal liability in cases where a person died under interrogation, provided that the interrogator did not deviate from the guidelines. It is not known whether such a provision was subsequently incorporated into the regulations. Reacting to the report, human rights lawyer Avigdor Feldman asked, "If the regulations are within the law, why does immunity have to be given?" (Israel Radio, as reported in *MidEast Mirror*, February 5, 1993.)

[8] The government stated recently that "As a result of [this] inquiry, a number of interrogators found to have violated the norms were punished." Again, no details were provided. Initial Report of Israel to the U.N. Committee against Torture, CAT/C/16/Add.4, February 4, 1994, paragraph 45.

"The number of complaints about IDF interrogations has been reduced to a minimum," a senior officer in the Judge Advocate-General's corps told HRW on November 18, 1993.[9] Occasionally, the IDF chooses to publicize a particular case. In responding to a 1993 report by B'Tselem, the IDF spokesman referred to an unidentified case before the Military Court of Appeals:

> The court sentenced the soldiers to serve a prison sentence lasting several months [for striking a detainee], stating the following: "Behavior of this kind is completely unacceptable in a proper military framework. It tarnishes the image of the IDF among the local population and among anyone to whom morals and norms of conduct are not an alien concept."[10]

No further information was provided about the case, making it impossible to assess whether the reported punishment fit the offense.

In a similar vein, few details have been released thus far concerning an *in camera* court-martial in late 1993 that resulted in prison sentences ranging from thirty to forty-five days for six soldiers who mistreated Palestinians under interrogation at Dhahiriya.

According to the information made public after the court-martial, the indictment charged that three of the defendants had, on one occasion, kicked a prisoner in his stomach and groin, slapped him on the ears, kicked him in the face and back, and slammed his head against the floor. The other three defendants were accused of clubbing a prisoner on the head, back, shoulders, chest and feet while he was handcuffed.[11]

On January 4, 1994 Member of Parliament Tamar Gojanski, responding to the press account of the verdict, requested details from the Ministry of Defense. On March 16 Deputy Minister Mordechai Gur replied. Among the factors influencing the sentences, Gur stated, was the court's

---

[9] The official spoke on condition that his name not be used, even though he was speaking in an official capacity.

[10] B'Tselem, *The Interrogation of Palestinians during the Intifada: Follow-up*, p. 22.

[11] Eitan Mor, "Convicted for Abusing Prisoners: And Sentenced to Only 45 Days in Prison," *Yediot Achronot*, December 21, 1993.

conclusion that the defendants subjectively believed that exercising violence served an important security purpose, and that the defendants' superiors were aware of their methods. Gur stated that as a result of this case, changes were being implemented to strengthen military-command oversight of interrogations.

The prosecution of abusive interrogators is a welcome step toward deterring mistreatment. However, the short sentences raise troubling questions. The penal code provides for multi-year sentences for various forms of assaults; the military justice law provides a three-year sentence for maltreating a person in custody. Only by divulging information about the nature of the beatings and other evidentiary material can the IDF allay suspicions that the thirty- and forty-five-day sentences in this case represent slaps on the wrist rather than exemplary deterrence.

The circumstances, the sentences and the court's reasoning in this case raise another suspicion about the IDF: that an unstated policy exists whereby a certain measure of force during interrogations will be tolerated, but interrogators who overstep the line may risk punishment. This impression is reinforced by the gap between the infrequency of prosecutions and the systematic practice of beatings during IDF interrogations.

The lone case in which GSS interrogators reportedly were sentenced to prison[12] was also an *in camera* trial resulting in a seemingly short sentence. The deterrent value of a GSS interrogator being put behind bars should not be minimized, however.

The case involved the only instance during the intifada during which physical violence was determined to be the direct cause of death of a Palestinian under interrogation. The victim, Khaled al-Sheikh Ali, died in the GSS interrogation wing at Gaza prison on December 19, 1989. After an autopsy, both the state pathologist and an independent pathologist confirmed that al-Sheikh Ali's death had been caused by internal hemorrhaging caused by blows to the abdomen that could not have been accidental or self-inflicted.

Two GSS agents were eventually charged in the case, and were convicted for causing death by negligence, after a plea bargain reduced the charge from manslaughter. In her ruling, the district court judge stated that "the two did not cause the death on purpose, but rather out of negligence,

---

[12] It is impossible to confirm that the convicted defendants actually served time in prison, since their names were never disclosed.

disregard, carelessness and lack of responsibility that did not reach the level of criminal negligence."[13] In September 1991 the Supreme Court rejected an appeal by the defendants of their six-month prison sentence.

The case highlights the way that the secrecy of GSS interrogation guidelines hinders accountability. Does the short sentence in this case reflect a leniency toward severe transgressions of the guidelines, or a more understandable punishment for deviations from guidelines that are themselves lenient toward the use of force? In either case, a six-month sentence for the fatal beating of a person in custody indicates that the state's response to incidents of violent abuse is deficient.

INVESTIGATIVE BODIES

Accountability is diminished by the opacity of official investigations into GSS and IDF abuses.

The body responsible for investigating reports of deviations by IDF interrogations is the Criminal Investigation Division of the Military Police. The CID submits its investigation report to the office of the chief military prosecutor, who then decides what action is warranted. In contrast to the GSS, the absence of secret guidelines for IDF interrogators makes it easier, in theory, to hold them accountable for deviations from the Penal Code and Military Justice Law.

When the CID investigates the killing of a Palestinian by soldier gunfire in a street confrontation, it is often possible to obtain summaries of the investigation finding by requesting it from the IDF. But when the soldier under investigation is an interrogator, little information is disclosed about the information that was collected, who was interviewed, and the reasoning behind the conclusions. When the investigation leads to a court-martial or disciplinary hearing, closed-door proceedings are the rule.

Complaints against the GSS have, since 1991, been handled by a special ad hoc committee composed of members of the GSS and the Justice Ministry. An internal inquiry is supposedly also conducted by the GSS comptroller. In addition, the Knesset in 1994 voted to authorize the special unit within the Justice Ministry that handles complaints against the police to probe complaints against the GSS as well.

---

[13] See B'Tselem, *The Interrogation of Palestinians during the Intifada*, p. 43.

The ad hoc GSS-Justice Ministry committee is supposedly the main address for public complaints against the GSS. But this committee has failed to establish any credibility as an agent of external oversight. It is, first of all, nearly as secretive as the GSS itself. The Justice Ministry refuses to disclose the names of its members, and, when B'Tselem offered to bring complainants to testify before the committee, the offer was turned down.[14]

It is hoped that the newly empowered unit for investigating police abuse will develop into a credible overseer of the GSS by probing complaints against it with transparency and vigor.

Each year, scores of specific and detailed complaints are submitted to the IDF military prosecutor's office and the Justice Ministry by lawyers and human rights organizations on behalf of Palestinians who allege mistreatment under interrogation. In general, these lawyers and groups say, the replies take several months if they come at all, and rarely exceed a few sentences in length. They usually contain some variant of the following information: an investigation was conducted and found that the interrogation had been conducted according to the regulations; or, a deviation from the regulations was found to have taken place, and "disciplinary measures were taken against those involved as necessary"; or the investigation turned up insufficient evidence to support the complaint, and the file was closed.

For example, in April 1994 the office of the military prosecutor responded to the complaint filed ten months earlier by an Israeli lawyer representing Nader Qumsiyeh. Qumsiyeh claimed that he had been beaten in the testicles at the interrogation wing of Dhahiriya prison (see Chapter Sixteen). The official reply stated simply that an investigation had been conducted, and the CID had "found no basis for the allegations of the complainant, and as a result, the Central Command's chief prosecutor ordered that the file be closed." No reference was made to the various medical reports on the injury, and no details were provided as to how the investigators had checked Qumsiyeh's allegations and determined them to be baseless. (At least in this case, the investigators had contacted and interviewed the complainant.)

Sometimes, the official replies to complaints contain curious tidbits of information. For example, in August 1993 the State Attorney's office replied to a complaint from an Israeli lawyer representing a detainee

---

[14] B'Tselem, *The Interrogation of Palestinians during the Intifada: Follow-up*, p. 21.

Na'im Ibrahim abu Seif, who complained about various abuses during a GSS interrogation, including being bombarded by loud music. In denying the allegations, the letter noted, "With respect to the music, it was found that music was indeed played, but that it was not excessively loud."[15]

Authorities frequently explain that investigation files are closed for insufficient evidence because the Palestinians who had made allegations to lawyers and human rights organizations had then failed to cooperate with the official investigations.

Instances of non-cooperation do occur, for a variety of reasons, and certainly complicate the task of determining what really transpired. But it also frequently happens that willing complainants are not contacted by the investigating bodies unless those bodies are prodded persistently to do so by lawyers or human rights organizations.

The reluctance of some Palestinians to cooperate with official investigations cannot explain the failure to clean up an interrogation system in which hundreds of Palestinians have been subjected on a monthly basis to a regime of sleep deprivation, hooding, prolonged position and noise abuse, prolonged toilet and hygiene deprivation, and in many cases, deliberate exposure to heat or cold, confinement in small spaces, and beatings. The failure to end these practices means ultimately that they are condoned by the government of Israel.

---

[15] Letter from Rachel Sukar, deputy to the State Attorney, to lawyer Tamar Pelleg-Sryck, dated August 18, 1993.

APPENDIX A
THE INTERROGATORS

The ex-detainees interviewed for this report provided the code-names of some of their interrogators. Both GSS and IDF interrogators use assumed names, prefixed by the English words "Captain" or "Major." They go by the code-names even when they testify in court. Their real names are kept secret.

The list of code-names given below is by no means a complete or up-to-date roster of interrogators.

GSS FACILITIES

Ramallah prison
Head of interrogation team: Maj. Chaim
Interrogators: Capt. Maher, Capt. Naka, Capt. Rami, Capt. Carmel, Capt. Cohen, Capt. Benny, and Capt. Abu Ghazal

Hebron prison
Head of interrogation team: Maj. Mousa
Interrogators: Capt. Timson (or Thompson), Capt. Billy, Capt. Abu al-Yamin, Capt. Shuki, Capt. Sammy, Capt. Munir, Capt. Horni, and Capt. Itzik

Tulkarm prison
Head of interrogation team: Maj. Abu Shalom
Interrogation team: Capt. Tzadok, Capt. Boaz, Capt. Jimmy, Capt. Ofer, Capt. Abu Cohen, Capt. Louis

IDF FACILITIES

Al-Far'a
Head of interrogation team: Maj. Abu Ali-Micha.
Interrogation team: Capt. James, Capt. Baruch, Capt. Ofer

Appendices

Dhahiriya
Head of interrogation team: Maj. Karim
Interrogation team: Capt. Ofer, Capt. Rami, Capt. Jerry, Capt. Yunis, Capt. Yossi, Capt. Maradonna, Capt. George, Capt. Mike, Capt. Yoni, Capt. Dani, Capt. Sammy, Capt. Amir, Capt. Ali

Beach
Interrogation team: Capt. Abu Rami, Capt. Dani, Capt. Abu Saher, and Capt. Abu Jalal.

APPENDIX B
SOLDIERS INTERVIEWED FOR THIS REPORT

- Reserve first sergeant A.M., a Jewish-Israeli, completed his regular military service prior to the outbreak of the intifada. In 1989, he served as a military policeman with the IDF interrogation unit at al-Far'a.

- Shimon M., a twenty-eight-year-old Jewish-Israeli, served as a military guard at the Beach facility during 1990. He works as a physical education instructor in an elementary school in Ramat Gan.

- Reserve first sergeant Tal Raviv, a twenty-five-year-old Jewish Israeli, served as a regular soldier in the Givati infantry brigade from August 1987 to August 1990. His reserve posting is now with a reconnaissance platoon attached to the armored corps. He served as a military guard at al-Far'a detention center in December 1992–January 1993. He currently works as a computer programmer and studies economics at Tel Aviv University.

- Avshalom Benny, a resident of Kibbutz Givat Chaim Ihud, spent his April–May 1992 reserve duty as a paramedic at the Dhahiriya detention center, and continues to serve as a reserve paramedic. Benny was interviewed by the Association for Civil Rights in Israel on September 14, 1992, and by HRW on July 29, 1993. Most of the quotes cited in this report are taken from the ACRI affidavit.

APPENDIX C
TESTIMONY OF AHMED AL-BATSH
INTERROGATED FOR SEVENTY-FIVE DAYS
AT RAMALLAH PRISON

Ahmed Husni al-Batsh, forty-seven, was interviewed by HRW on February 19 and 26, 1993 in his home just north of Jerusalem. The interview was conducted in Hebrew, which he speaks fluently.

Al-Batsh is a former teacher in a technical trades school. He now works for the Arab Studies Society, directed by Palestinian political figure Faisal -Husseini.

Al-Batsh was arrested on September 9, 1992 and was interrogated until November 24 at the Ramallah GSS wing. He was released without charge.

The following interview was edited for clarity and organization.

The arrest

I was arrested at about one in the morning. There were about eighteen soldiers altogether. They climbed over the walls of the garden and the gate, and my daughter woke up, screaming *Jaysh, aj-Jaysh!* (Army!).

I woke up. They knocked at the door and said, "Army!" I opened the door, and they were standing there, guns pointing at the door. They pushed their way inside and began searching everywhere. One, in plainclothes, came up to me and said, "I am Captain Abu Seif." He is well-known in our area as the local GSS agent. He said to me, "Get dressed and say good-bye to your family." I said to him, "Tell me at least if I am being arrested." He wouldn't answer, and did not say what I was accused of or where they were taking me.

There were four jeeps waiting outside. They tied my hands with plastic cuffs behind my back and blindfolded me. They said, "Shut up and don't say a word!" I sat quietly on the bench of the jeep. They did not hit me.

Arrival at GSS interrogation wing of Ramallah prison

Then they said that we were at Ramallah jail. They took my name, details and valuables. Then the jailer cuffed my hands behind my back and put a hood over my head. I tried to ask something, but the soldier[1] said, "Shut up!" He pulled me along by the throat of the hood. They took me into a place, which I later knew to be a small corridor. They sat me down on a very small chair.

The chairs are lined up in the corridor; they are like kindergarten chairs. There are four, seven, even sometimes ten chairs there.

You sit in the chair, knees to your chin, your hands tied behind the chair's backrest, so that when you get up, you get up with the chair.

They left me on the chair until nine in the morning. You can't sleep. You keep thinking, "What did I do? Why am I here?" At about nine, Captain Carmel came and lifted my hood. I saw I was in a room, three and-a-half by four meters, with tables arranged in a T-formation.

Captain Carmel said, "Hello Ahmed, how are you doing?" I asked, "Could I please know why I am here?"

"We are the *mukhabarat*[2]," he said. "We know your whole story. When I am speaking, don't you dare speak. We know everything, your connections, your organization."

I was sitting all this time in the small chair, without the hood on my head, my hands still tied behind the chair. He sat in his own chair, in front of me, with his foot between my legs. He would press down on my balls.

He would say, "We know your story, we want names. Why do you continue to deny? It's hard on your kids for you to be here."

When I was in the interrogation room, Major Chaim, the chief interrogator, would call my home right in front of me and speak to my family. It was very frightening. It was if he was saying he knew exactly where they were. My daughter answered the phone the first time, but other times, my wife or son answered.

During the first, second and third days, we sat in the room for four or five hours at a time, talking. He would then call a soldier, who would put the hood on my head, and pull me out into the corridor.

On the third day, four interrogators came into the room, and said, "We are going to kill you. You will not come out of here alive. The only way you can leave is to confess, or to die or go insane. Trust us."

---

[1] Batsh referred throughout his interview to the presence of "soldiers" in the interrogation wing. It is not clear whether he used the term to refer specifically to IDF personnel or to guards more generally.

[2] Arabic for intelligence agents.

On the fifth or sixth day, someone came into the interrogation room and said, "What's with this son of a bitch?" The other interrogators said, "He is stubborn." So he said, "You son of a whore, I am going to kill you. You will see. I killed Mustafa Akawi, I killed Hazem Eid.[3] What street do you want them to name after you in Ramallah?" I said, "I want a street in the Old City."

He told me to get up. I did. I was without the hood, but my hands were tied. He lifted my chin, grabbed my collar, rolled it up until it was thin like twine, and then pulled it tight around my throat. He began to shake my neck from the collar. He shook me very hard twenty, thirty times, for three or four minutes, until I lost consciousness.

There were four interrogators plus the boss. They did the good cop-bad cop routine. When I woke up, they said to the boss, "It's OK, now he will talk, he's all right." I said, "I have nothing to say." Major Chaim, the one who shook me, picked up a chair as if he was going to hit me with it. The others told him, "Don't do it, he will talk, don't do it."

Major Chaim rolled up my collar again and began to choke me. My voice disappeared. I was yelling and only a thin groan came out, more like a squeak. I didn't think I was going to come out of it alive. There were marks on my neck, blood was coming from the gashes.

Then they said, "Rest up. Think. We will be back." Then they put me back in the corridor.

The next day, Major Chaim returned and did the same thing again. He screamed at me, hysterically, "You will go insane, no one leaves from here without speaking, either from the mouth or from the ass. You will see, in the end, you will talk."

I didn't sleep for ten days straight. They want to destroy you in those first two weeks.

Refrigerators
The refrigerators are small cells in which cold air is blown in. I was put in the refrigerator at the beginning and at the end. When I was released from the interrogation section to go home it was straight from the refrigerator.

After the first eight days, they put me for two to three hours inside the refrigerator, with my hands tied, but no hood. In one of the

---

[3] Akawi and Eid are security detainees who died during GSS interrogation. See Chapter Nineteen.

refrigerators is a stone ledge. In the others, there are none. Refrigerator number one has no chair. You can only stand in there. You cannot hear anything except the two fans going, blowing cold air in. The sound of the fans makes you crazy. In the second and third refrigerators there is a stone ledge. It is very cold, but there is no noise from fans.

The air is blown in on your head. In winter, they blow cold air. In summer, they send in hot air.

I was wearing a short-sleeved shirt. In the refrigerator it was especially cold because of the shirt.

Once a soldier took me to eat and saw me shivering. He gave me a blanket. Major Chaim came after an hour and asked, "Who is the bastard who gave him this?" and took it away.

Shabeh (position abuse)

During the first two weeks, my legs were shackled to the chair. I had a constant gash on the back of my legs from the seat of the chair. You are so filthy, the salt from your sweat gets into your wounds. It hurts so much that you think you will never be able to keep sitting.

The *shabeh* is the worst part. You sit alone, you talk with the floor, you laugh to yourself. They would say to me, "You can only dream about us hitting you, we won't hit you. It's more difficult this way." You get hysterical. I could hear others in the corridor laughing, crying, reciting verses from the Quran.

Once I was laughing and laughing. A soldier came up to me, pulled up the hood, and said, "What's with you?" Only then did I remember that I was in *shabeh*.

Sometimes I would fall off the chair. It was if I collapsed into sleep. If soldiers saw me falling asleep on the chair, they would come up to me and shake me awake.

All of your body hurts you in *shabeh*: your legs, your bottom, your back, everything.

Shabeh while shackled to the wall

In the courtyard, there are iron rings fixed to the wall. The courtyard is at the end of the corridor where the chairs are. They shackled me to the iron rings. When they do that you can't stand, you can't sit. You are bent over, with your arms behind you, up near the height of your shoulders. Your legs are shackled together. I was once on this wall for three straight days, with only a few breaks for the toilet and eating. This

Appendices

happened during the first period. It happened again towards the end of the interrogation, I don't remember exactly when.

When you are in the wall *shabeh*, the pain is in the arms and shoulders. For each person, there is a different pain.

Exposure to loud noise

In the corridor, outside the interrogation rooms, there is very loud classical music and screaming, on tape, so that you can never rest, never sleep. The music goes on twenty-four hours a day, while you are sitting on the chair.

The soldiers would sometimes be changed, and the new ones didn't know what the music was for. Some of these guys would change the tape and put their own music on. The interrogator would yell at them, "This is not a disco!"

I think that if the soldiers were to hear the music twenty-four hours a day as well, they would also go crazy.

Access to the toilet/meals in the toilet

The soldiers also are supposed to bring you to the bathroom when you are on the chair. Sometimes you call and call for them, twenty times or more, and then the soldier comes up to you and yells, "Shut up!" Others are nicer, they come and take you.

When you go to the bathroom they unlock your cuffs, make you stand up, and then relock your cuffs. They take you to the bathroom, undo your hands, and push you into the bathroom while pulling the hood off with the other hand, so that you don't see anything outside of the bathroom.

The bathroom is small and filthy. It is about 2 by 1.7 meters. There is no running water, no soap, no toilet paper.

They take you to the toilet with your hands tied and the hood over your head. At the entrance they untie your hands and pull off the hood while they push you inside.

The hood has a special smell. When they take off the hood for the toilet, they throw it on the ground, into the excrement and urine that's all over the floor. Then you put the same hood back on.

You eat your food in the toilet. You are given a tray, which is placed on the floor, and that is where you eat. In the morning, you eat a hard-boiled egg, a little margarine, a little jam. It was disgusting food.

Threat to demolish his family's home

During the last week, Major Chaim came and showed me an order, which he said was signed by the regional Civil Administration chief. He said, "This is an emergency order allowing us to demolish your house." He showed me about twenty pictures which had been taken all around my house, and said, "Look, this is the last time you will ever see it standing."

It was just a forgery, the order. It is psychological warfare. He said, "We will plant some guns in your house." This really scared me. My wife is a teacher, my son is at the university. I was sure that they would do that.

Major Chaim said, "Think about this until tomorrow." He took me out of the refrigerator and said, "Tomorrow we will demolish your home."

He said they were going to do it, and sent me back to the refrigerator. That night he came back and said, "Batsh, you are lucky, we delayed the demolition a few days."

Extension-of-detention hearings/access to lawyer

On the eighth day of my interrogation, they said, "Your lawyer is here, but you can't see her." After an hour he came back and said, "You are going to see her, but don't you dare say a word to her."

They brought me into the judge's room, and I saw Lea Tsemel, my lawyer, and my sister Majda. The prosecutor said, "I have an emergency military order here forbidding you to speak near the judge."

I said to the judge, "I want to talk." He said, "You can talk at the end." I tried to show him my neck, but the prosecutor told me to shut up. I said, "I am only showing him, I am not saying a word." The prosecutor said, "I will throw you out of here if you don't stop."

Before I began to talk to the judge, he ordered Lea out of the room. I told the judge, "They say that I have a story. I don't have anything. I am not in an organization, and have no connections. I have been sitting for eight days on a small chair with my hands tied and a hood over my head." I showed the judge my neck, and told him about the way that Major Chaim had shaken me. I said, "I can't move my head, it hurts so much." I showed him the marks, and said, "You are my witness, you can't say you didn't see. You are responsible for whatever happens to me. They want to kill me in here, and you are responsible for me."

I showed him my back, I took off my shirt, and showed him what the chair had done to me. I said, "Smell me, I stink." I took off my pants, and I showed him what the boards of the little chair had done to the back of my legs. My legs were cut as if by a saw.

Then Lea, my lawyer, came back into the room. I tried to talk to her and they ordered me out. The judge extended my detention for four more days, and said, "Bring him a doctor, and after the examination, I want to see the medical report."

So they took me to a doctor, who was from Russia and didn't speak a word of Arabic or English. There was a medic there, about thirty years old, in uniform and a white shirt, he didn't even put antiseptic on the cuts on my neck.

I was taken back to the interrogation wing. Captain Carmel said, "You see, you can't get out of here, the judge won't help you. Now he gave you four days, but tomorrow he will give you thirty. You won't get out of here."

After four days I did go to the court again. Lea was there, and she asked the court, "There are no witnesses against him. Why is he being held?" The prosecutor replied, "We have secret incriminating material, and only the judge can see it." The prosecutor asked for thirty more days, and the judge gave it to him.

When I returned to the interrogation wing, all the interrogators came over to greet me. Major Chaim said, "I promised you thirty days, and you got it. You won't come out alive. You will get another thirty and then another thirty. You will keep getting extensions, even if you have to stay here for six years."

During those thirty days I was interrogated only about four or five times. The rest of the time I stayed on the chair.

Finally, after seventy-two days, the judge gave the interrogators another seven days, and told them, "This is the last week I will give you." This was the same judge who had extended my interrogation for thirty days on two previous occasions.

Weekends

On Friday, they put you in the cells. There were four or five persons in a very small cell. There are two mattresses for everyone. The length of the cell was about two meters. There was a hole for the toilet, and no soap, toilet paper, or water.

The soldiers responsible for the cells were the worst. The cells are absolutely filthy, the situation there is terrible. They would say, "You are in a five-star cell. Some cells don't have a hole, they only have a bucket. You are lucky."

They didn't put me inside the cell every Friday. Sometimes they didn't. One time I was on the chair from Sunday to Sunday straight. There are always two interrogators on weekend duty.

The final period of interrogation

On the sixtieth day, I told the medic that I couldn't breathe and that the pain was like needles in my right hip. I called to the soldier, he pulled the hood off my face. He was a real human being. The medic came back and said that he would bring a doctor the following day.

The doctor came and said, in Hebrew, "Don't put the hood over this man's face, don't put him in a chair, don't tie his hands." He also said, "The *Shabak* [GSS] have gone crazy. If this guy stays here another week, he will die."

Then the interrogators had a problem. They couldn't put me in the main corridor with the others, because I didn't have a hood over my head. So they put me in a regular office, where I stayed for the next ten days. It was very hard in that room. I became hysterical, I was talking to myself.

So until the sixty-fourth day, I was in *shabeh* on the small chair. Between day sixty-four and day seventy-six I was in the small office.

On the seventy-sixth day, they brought in a lot of people from Islamic Jihad. They had no place to put them. They couldn't put me into the corridor without a hood, and the office was busy all the time. So they put me in the closet for two weeks.

I had been in the closet during the first two weeks as well. They are not really closets. They are refrigerators. They have a big fan and they are freezing.

The medic came and said, "Who put this guy in here?" and took me out. Then they put me back in later on. I was shaking from the cold.

On the last day, they sent me to a lie detector test at the Russian Compound police station in Jerusalem. They put me in the closet there. When I returned to Ramallah they said, "Batsh, you are back?" and hooded me, put me in the refrigerator. Water was coming in and it was freezing.

Release without charge

They released me from the refrigerator at three in the afternoon. They told me I could leave, and took me to the main gate. When I came out of the building I couldn't even tell which way was east or west.

My son was waiting for me, but I couldn't see him, because it was pouring rain. I was wearing the same short-sleeve shirt I had been arrested in.

The first few days after the interrogation, when I was at home, it was like coming back from the grave. In the beginning, it was difficult to return to life, simple life. You don't believe you are sleeping by your wife, your son. During the first week, whenever I hear anything making noise outside, it's as if I'm back in jail.

APPENDIX D
TESTIMONY OF MUHAMMAD ANIS ABU HIKMEH, INTERROGATED FOR TWENTY-TWO DAYS AT DHAHIRIYA

Muhammad Anis abu Hikmeh, twenty-one, was interviewed by HRW in his home in al-Bireh in the West Bank, on March 25, 1993. He was arrested on November 29, 1992, and was interrogated by the IDF until December 20 at Dhahiriya.

After his interrogation, he was ordered held in administrative detention without charge for three months, reduced to two on appeal. He was released from prison on February 28, 1993.

Abu Hikmeh studies history at Birzeit University in the West Bank.

After I was arrested, I was first taken to a small space, a cell. It is two meters high, one meter wide, and two meters long, about the size of a mattress. You can stretch your legs out all the way, but that's it, there is no more room.

It's a policy not to allow you to sleep for the first eighteen hours. The soldier would come and bang on the door very often, and would order me to call out my prisoner number. When he does that, you have to stand up, stand next to the door, and answer.

In the cell, there is a can which you are supposed to use for a toilet. Every day they let you empty the bucket. It stands right next to your feet. Because of the bucket, the cell smells very bad all the time, like sewage.

There is a light bulb attached to the ceiling. It is very strong, and you can't sleep because it shines twenty-four hours a day.

During the first forty-eight hours, the soldier comes every five minutes. You can't sleep. He allowed me to empty the bucket only on the second day. It was very cold; it was snowing outside. The Hebron area is cold, freezing at that time of year. They only gave me three blankets, and no extra clothes. I was wearing sweatpants and a wool sweater, plus a leather jacket. They wouldn't let me take heavier clothes when they arrested me. They took my scarf from me when I arrived at Dhahiriya.

Appendices

Initial stages of interrogation

On the third day they took me to interrogation with Major Karim. He said, "I know you study political science and history at Birzeit." With Major Karim, the discussions are always friendly. You are allowed to sit with your hands untied. A short session with Major Karim is five hours. This room is always friendly. He asks you how much you smoke, he suggests topics, and you talk, about studies, everything.

That day, the talk with Karim went on until 10 A.M. Then he said it was over, and called for a soldier to come. This soldier knows where to put you. He took me to the closet.

The closet

The closet is made out of very cold cement. It looks like a closet, but it is not really. It has a concrete seat about four centimeters wide, so you can't sit on it. You have to stand. You can't sit on the floor, it is so filthy, people go to the bathroom in there all the time. Even if you want to sleep, there is no way, there is no space. The entire closet is just a little taller than me.

Even when I put something down on the floor to sit on, to cover the filth, I couldn't sleep, because I was forced to contort my body. I had to put my legs high above my head, with my back bent double. It's so dark you don't know what you are eating.

I stayed for a maximum of twenty hours at a time in the closet. At other times I stayed for about four hours. You can't know the time really, since you don't see light, and don't know when the hours pass. You wait all the time in the closet until you are taken to the interrogation room, where you can see the watch on his [the interrogator's] hand. You don't know what day it is unless you keep close track, all the time, according to the times they take you back to the cell at night. You can tell when it's Saturday, because you are not taken anywhere.

In general, the first round of questioning would begin at 4:30 or 5:00 in the morning, when you hear the *muezzin* calling the people to prayer from the mosque in the village, which is near the interrogation center. Before that, the guards come around, banging on all the doors, waking everyone. You are taken to the interrogation room.

Questioning sessions

They change interrogators every two days or so. They write reports and send them to Major Karim. They give updates on your situation. They report if you have collapsed during the interrogation or if you are still holding strong.

The interrogation depends on the interrogator. Major Karim's policy is to be nice, to convince you to confess through words. If he fails, he hands you over to the others. Major Karim is the boss.

Even the other interrogators are very nice at the beginning. When they see you are stubborn, however, they start using violence. Captain Yunis, during the first hour, only talks, trying to convince you to confess. It's like a discussion. He gives you examples of people who have confessed, sometimes mentioning people you know. On the fourth day of my interrogation, at about 9 P.M. Yunis got very angry. He pulled me by my hair over to a metal closet and began banging my head against the door. He did that six or seven times. He then hit me with his knee in the groin, four or five times. I fell to the floor, and I felt that I was losing consciousness. When he saw me on the ground, he called soldiers, who took me to the cell.

Usually, it takes Captain Yunis about an hour of talking to get mad. Then he would order me to stand up and would cuff my hands behind me. He would say things like, "You don't know what interrogation is. You had better confess"; "If you now weigh sixty kilograms, you will leave here weighing forty, believe me." He also told me that I would lose the semester at university, and would miss my exams.

Once, Captain Yunis threatened my sister. He said, "I will bring your sister here and rape her." My sister is twenty-two years old, and lives with us at home.

Sometimes, Captain Yunis would bring a young female soldier into the interrogation room, and while I was kneeling, he kissed and fondled her, and laughed with her. She was not in uniform.

Captain Yunis would make me kneel in front of his chair, very close, and then would put his legs between my knees. This lasts for two or three hours, and is very difficult. You can't stand it, you must move around. When Yunis senses that you are getting exhausted, he puts some more pressure on you. He doesn't let you go to the toilet. He would say, "If you confess, you can go to the toilet."

There is another interrogator I remember, his nickname is Captain George. He is a Druze. He is a very big man, it looks like he lifts weights.

For the first hour with him, he just talks. He began by asking questions about my sister and father. I was sitting on the chair, hands tied behind me. Captain George ordered me to come close. I kneeled on my knees, next to his chair, at his side. Then he swivelled his chair around, grabbed my hair, pushed my head back, and punched me in the throat and chest. He hit me many times in the throat. I felt that I was choking.

All in all, I had about eight sessions with George during a four-day period. Every time he hit me. He put his foot between my legs, and then he would kick me several times lightly, and then very hard. He hit me in the throat one more time. All together, he kicked me in the testicles on six occasions.

Captain George's turn with me was over on the tenth day. Then, I was transferred to Captain Mike. Mike is the biggest man I have ever seen. He started talking, and then began to punch me in the stomach, while I was kneeling in front of him. Then he stood me up and pushed me against the wall and tripped me. I was lying on my face, and my hands were cuffed behind my back. He began to walk over my back and hands.

Then he put me back on the chair. He sat on the table facing me, and he put his foot between my legs and started pressing like he was on a gas pedal. I tried to push my knees close together. When he saw me trying to do that he forced my knees apart again and kept on pressing. The pressing hurt me more than when they kicked me, because when they kicked me, they would often miss my testicles. When they press, however, the pressure is direct. He did this for about ten minutes.

On about the seventeenth day, Captain George came back and hit me in the left side with his fist, many times. It was difficult for me to breathe, I was panting. My hands were not tied, and I made as if I was going to hit back. He tied my hands, grabbed my neck and began to choke me. It looked like he was going to choke me to death. Then he slammed me against the wall, grabbed my windpipe between his fingers, and threatened that he would disfigure my face. He held me against the wall with one hand and traced a design on my face with the other, saying, "I will cut here, here and here."

Pipe *Shabeh* (position abuse)

Behind the closets there is an area with pipes in the wall. Sometimes you are in *shabeh*, standing tied to the pipes.

There are two types of pipes: The first is at waist level. They tied my hands behind my back to the pipe. In that position, I was bent over, and couldn't move, because the cuffs were fixed to the pipe. The maximum amount of time which I spent in this position was for about twelve hours.

The other type of pipe is one that runs over your head. They tied my hands to the pipe, above my head. My toes were on the ground, but my heels were in the air.

During the first twelve days, they would put me in the closet between interrogations. After that, I was tied to one of the two pipes between interrogations. After the twelfth day, it was a continual rotation between interrogations, the pipe and, at night, the cell. After day twelve, they tied me to one of the pipes every day except Saturday.

When they first tie you to the pipe, you are in real pain. One minute is like a year. Eventually, you get used to it. You may even prefer pipe shabeh to questioning. They cover your head with a piece of cloth or with your jacket, and you can even fall asleep sometimes.

Nights in the cell

At night, in the cell, I couldn't really sleep, because the guard would come pretty regularly, and would yell out questions to me. When he does that, you are supposed to get up and stand near the door to reply. They also move you around at night. If you stay in one cell you become accustomed to it, your body becomes relaxed. So they move you around.

The cells face an open yard. The guards put the radio on through loudspeakers all night.

During the interrogation, they said I was a member of an illegal organization, and was a leader in my neighborhood. They asked about names, about people who were in prison for carrying out military activities.

I never saw my lawyer, and didn't even go to an extension-of-detention hearing with a military judge, even after the eighteenth day.

APPENDIX E
TESTIMONY OF SGT. TAL RAVIV

Reserve first sergeant Tal Raviv, aged 24, served as a regular soldier in the Givati infantry brigade from August 1987 to August 1990. His reserve posting is now with a reconnaissance platoon attached to the armored corps. He currently works as a computer programmer while studying economics at Tel Aviv University. He was interviewed in his Tel Aviv home on June 16, 1993.

I was at Far'a [detention center] for reserve service from December 29, 1992 until January 18, 1993. We were there to guard the facility. Most of the guards at Far'a are reserve military policemen. There are very few regular-service soldiers there.

What were your duties at al-Far'a?

My job was to assign the guard duty roster. I was responsible for assigning different people to the different posts every day.

Our general job there as reservists was to provide security. We stood on guard in posts all around the detention center, and we accompanied the military policemen when they took detainees to different places.

Describe the interrogation section.

There is something there we call the "*Shabak* wing,"[4] which is where they do interrogations. Some of the interrogators are Druze, others are Jews. There is one Jewish woman who works there as well. We would see them as they drove in every morning into the base for work. There were over twenty interrogators. The *Shabak* wing is a closed square area. You can see into it only from one [guard] position.

The regular army soldiers called the detainees' stint in the yard *yibush* [Hebrew for "drying out."]....The way they tie them is in itself torture. Their hands are tied very tightly behind their backs.

---

[4] Raviv's reference to the *Shabak*, the Hebrew acronym for the GSS, is probably not accurate. According to HRW's information, interrogations at al-Far'a are conducted by IDF personnel. Rank-and-file soldiers commonly use *Shabak* to refer to military intelligence as well as the GSS.

What were they wearing?

The clothes they were wearing were very thin, and it was very cold then, it was winter. At night, it was about 5o or 6o centigrade (41o or 43o fahrenheit). Some of the people are left there in the yard throughout the night. In fact, I think that there is more activity there during the night.

When were you exposed to the "*Shabak* wing"?

I did guard duty four or five times at what we called the "*Shabak* roof" post. That is on the roof of the interrogation rooms. Each time I spent about four hours there. It was always at night.

What did you see or hear from that position?

While I was on guard duty on the roof of the "*Shabak* wing," I heard beating. I heard them beating people. You hear people being hit, and you hear them screaming and crying. It's right under your feet, in the interrogation rooms.

During those times, I heard the hitting, and the crying, each time. It was intermittent. The interrogators yell and then you hear slaps and punches.

In the yard, I also saw violence against detainees. Some of them want to go to the toilet, and they aren't allowed. When they ask they get hit. It is usually the interrogators who do the hitting. They stink from going in their pants. Sometimes, they were taken to the bathroom. It all depends on what stage of the interrogation they were in.

Most of the torture is not the interrogation rooms, it is being tied, blindfolded. It's frightening, and they are helpless, all tied up, and then they are hit in the yard by the guards. Their arms are pulled back and you can see that it hurts.

Some detainees asked for their cuffs to be removed, and the guards did it. Others didn't. The cuffs are very tight, and are placed high up on the arms so that the elbows are joined together behind their backs. It goes on for a long time, that's the whole point, that's the torture.

They often ask for things. The interrogators come over and hit them, slap them. When you are tied and blindfolded, this must be very frightening.

Once, I went up there during the day to talk with the guard about something. I saw about twenty people standing there in the yard, with their hands tied behind their backs. Usually, when I was there during the night, they would sit with their hands tied. I was amazed to see them all standing there, all together like that, so many. At night, there are only two or three standing at a time, sometimes five.

I saw people in the yard staying there for at least the four hours that I was there. I saw one guy there one day after another. I went up for one guard duty, and then when I came for guard duty a day later, he was still there.

Describe the cells in the "*Shabak* wing."
There are about ten cells. Others are kept in cells in the general section, which are linked to the "*Shabak* section" by a corridor.

How about medical checkups?
Everybody gets checked by a doctor when they arrive. They stand without their clothes, only in underpants, in the yard outside the doctor's office. I saw this once when it was freezing, it was night. There were ten to fifteen people standing there. It was very humiliating for them, standing there naked. It's regular, routine. There were even older people there.

The doctor was a reservist, a psychiatrist, he didn't know anything about treating diseases. He sent all the soldiers to the clinic, but the detainees, he just didn't do much for them.

He used to check the detainees through the mesh of the fence. The check-ups were all very cursory. I used to accompany the doctor on his checkups.

***

What really bothered me was that everyone there in the interrogation section had only been detained, none of them had been charged. Everyone always said "the bastards," "the criminals," but not one of them had actually been convicted of anything.

There were about five hundred prisoners there in all, in the general section and in the interrogation section.

The prison commander told us not to talk, touch or look at the prisoners. All direct contact was supposed to be through the military policemen, most of whom were reservists.

What contact did you have with the military judges?
One day I brought sixty of the detainees to the extension-of-detention court. It's not really a court, it's just a booth in the prison. They

went in, three by three, and after three minutes they came out. Within one hour we had finished with everyone. That can't be a real court, because how can they deliberate about whether to extend in one minute?

The whole thing, the court and the interrogations, it has the feeling of a factory, as if it's an industry. Lots of people are put through the routine. There is a sense as if it's a regularized system, and everyone gets the same treatment, no matter what they actually did.

APPENDIX F
TESTIMONY OF SGT. A.M.

Reserve first sergeant A.M. was interviewed by HRW on June 15, 1993. He spoke about his reserve duty in 1989 working with the IDF interrogation unit at al-Far'a detention center. He gave his full name and address to HRW but asked that only his initials be used in print.

What was your job in the army?

I was a military policeman, first in the regular army, and then in the reserves.

In 1989 I was sent to al-Far'a. The first day I got there, we were collecting our equipment and they came up to me and said, "Hey, how long are you here for?" I said, "Thirty days." So they said, "You want to do something interesting during your time here?" I said sure.

So they took me over to the interrogation section. It has a big yard out in front, and behind a wall, the interrogation rooms. They are regular rooms, in a line, maybe six or seven of them. Behind the rooms are the cells, lots of cells.

Anyway, they took me inside a room, and there was an interrogator there, he was in army uniform, but he was a Druze. They were all Druze in uniforms. There was a detainee there, and they told me to hit him. I did.

Afterwards, I didn't like it, I said, "Look, this is not for me, thanks a lot, I don't want to do this." So they showed me the detainee's file, and said, "This guy is a terrorist, now you see, we need to do this."

That's how they work, they get you all mad at the Arabs, at the terrorists, and then you are willing to keep doing it. So I kept on going, until the end of my reserve duty.

What was your job?

My job was to guard the interrogator. I stood inside the room with the interrogator and the detainee. The interrogator sat facing me, the detainee with his back to me. And they would talk, in Arabic. I don't understand Arabic. And then, when the interrogator didn't get the answer he wanted, he made a sign, and I hit the detainee.

What did you hit him with?
With a club, my hand, foot, anything. Just hit him, we "blew him up" (*potzatznu auto*), beating like I can't describe. Just beating and beating.

Were there any orders about how to beat?
No, nothing. They would just say, "Try not to kill him." That's all. We hit them everywhere — head, face, mouth, arms, balls. Interrogations were a combination of beating and questions. I didn't understand the questions.

Were the detainees blindfolded when you beat them?
Yes, unless they were beginning to talk, so you would take their blindfolds off. If not, you hit them while they were still blindfolded.

Describe an interrogation for me.
Well, the detainee comes in, he is handcuffed behind his back, and blindfolded. The interrogator sits in front of him, at the beginning behind a desk. The detainee sits on a chair, for as long as he is able. Then the questions start. I didn't understand, you see, it was in Arabic. But if the answer was not good, he gave me a sign.

How did he give you a sign?
He...I don't know. You just knew what he wanted. It was clear. He didn't need to say anything, he just looked at me. And then I would hit. Wherever I wanted. There were no rules.

Describe the beating.
The beating? What, are you kidding? Have you ever seen a broken arm before? The arm is all straight, up until a certain point, and then just collapses, goes down, at an angle, just hanging there.

Did you break many bones?
More than I can remember. Lots of people had broken arms, legs, teeth. The dentists in the territories must have had tons of work, even now, they still have work from then.

We kept on beating, and if he fell down on the ground, the interrogator would tell him to get back up. If he couldn't, we hit him on the floor. Just hit him everywhere.

If the beating didn't help anymore, because he was about to die, and you just couldn't keep hitting him, they would pour something on the open wounds. It was like acid or something, I don't know. They kept it in a bottle, and poured it. And when that happened, well, it's hard to describe. They just screamed and screamed. Screams like I have never heard.

Did you pour the liquid?

No, I never did that. It was the interrogator's job.

Did the detainees make any noise while this was going on? Was there any crying or screaming?

Screaming? Everybody screamed, all the time. From almost the first minute they came into the room, they were crying, screaming. You could hear the screams in the cells and in the yards, that was part of the whole idea. They wanted them to see and to hear. I think everyone could hear the screams, in the prison, everywhere, even down in the village of Far'a they could hear, I'm sure.

What was their situation after they left the rooms?

In 99.9 percent of the cases, they couldn't leave on their own. They had to call for a couple of detainees from the yard, who came and carried them back to the cells, or to the yard. They simply couldn't walk on their own.

The interrogator would say to me, "Take him out, and bring me in so and so."

Did they go to see the doctor?

I never saw the doctor. I guess they went, you know, after a couple of days. Not straight away.

How many detainees did you beat?

I don't know, maybe eight or ten a day.

For thirty straight days?

Yes.

So that meant between 250 or 300 in your entire period?
Yes, that's about right.

Was anyone not hit during interrogation?
Well, some didn't go through the whole story, you know. Some talked right away or whatever. Everyone was beaten up, however. Without beatings — that's impossible. At one point they all got it, somehow. They were like footballs. If it was during the arrest, or when they arrived. Every military policeman who passed hit them, kicked him, whatever. Everyone got it.

What were most of the detainees suspected of?
Well, nothing serious, really, mostly throwing stones, intifada stuff, demonstrations.

Were there any people who were suspected of using weapons?
Maybe one or two, not many, really. Those types went to the *Shabak* [the GSS], not to us. The hard cases went there, not to us.

What other types of things happened to detainees?
Sometimes, they would tie people up. You know, tie their hands and legs, and leave them somewhere for a few days. They did this to the tough ones, to the ones who wouldn't talk.

Where did they do that?
They usually left them tied up in one of the interrogation rooms. When that happened, the room was out of commission for a few days.

Were they sitting or standing?
If they were in one of the interrogation rooms, they were sitting. We would also tie them up to the posts outside, and there they would stand.

Were their special posts for this?
No, they were regular posts, you know, just posts, pillars, for the building.

How many were tied up during the day, at any given moment?
We had maybe one or two tied up each day.

Appendices

What were the conditions for detainees before they are interrogated?

When the detainees are brought to Far'a they are put in the yard. Their hands are tied, their eyes are blindfolded. They sit there until they go into interrogation. The ones who are lucky, go in after one day. Some stayed there for a week, just sitting there, or standing, all tied. We kept them sitting apart, so that they couldn't talk.

They got food once a day, that's all. When they wanted to go to the bathroom they had to ask. And if they were lucky, and you wanted to be nice to them, you would take them. If not, and usually not, and you wanted to screw them, they stayed there, asking to go, and in the end, they went in their pants.

Did that happen often?

Sure, they went in their pants a lot....

They told us not to beat them while they were in the yard. The reason was that there were *shtinkers* [collaborators] there among them, and we didn't know who they were. Nobody knew except the interrogators, so they were afraid we might beat one of them, the wrong guy, you know.

The military policemen could not come into the interrogation area. We would call out, "Bring me so and so!" and they would bring the detainee to the door of the wall surrounding the interrogation rooms, and then I brought them in.

At one stage or another, all of the guys in the yard would go into interrogation.

How many people were there in the yard?

There could be anything from fifty to four hundred in the yard, depending on how many the paratroopers brought in that day. There was no rule; if they had gone on a big sweep, they brought in a lot. If not, there were fewer there.

How many were there, would you say, on average in the yard?

There were about two hundred or more, on average, during my time there.

And in the cells, persons undergoing interrogation, how many of those were there at any given time?
It's difficult to say, it varied. There were also about two hundred, more than in the yard.

How many were in the interrogation rooms?
Just a few, at any one time, one each in a room, maybe seven total.

So all together, there were, on average, between four and five hundred persons involved in the interrogation process at any one time?
Yes, that's about right.

What was the purpose of the interrogation?
As I understood it, the goal was to get a confession. There were a lot of people there who were simply picked up to get information about the leaders in the neighborhood, who was organizing the stone-throwing, the bottle-throwing. Lots of time we had people who did nothing themselves, the interrogators just wanted names. Lots of times, there were kids, aged fourteen, fifteen, sixteen, and seventeen.

The interrogators wouldn't stop until the detainee talked.

Did everyone talk?
Everyone talked in the end. Some, it took ten minutes. Others, it took three days, of going in and out of interrogation. In the end, everyone talked.

We worked ten-to-twelve-hour shifts. There was no time limit for detainees. Some were in for a few minutes only, others were in for days.

Did they all sign confessions?
Almost everyone signed something. If they were so badly beaten they couldn't sign right away, we sent them to the cells, and after four days or so, they were able to sign.

Did people sign false confessions there, do you think?
I can't really know, I don't speak Arabic. But believe me, they would sign anything towards the end, no matter whether they did it or not. Anything.

Describe the cells.

The cells are about, from here to there [six meters by two meters.] There are five double beds in there. They would put them in there and leave them, until interrogation, and afterwards bring them back to the cells. They never left there unless to go to interrogation, or to the showers, every four days or so.

Where did they relieve themselves in the cells?

They have these black boxes, you know, made of plastic, with seats. I don't know how anyone can sit on it. Anyway, they relieve themselves on that, all of them.

How many were in the cells at one time?

It depends on how many there were in the prison. Usually, six or so, sometimes ten people. It was pretty crowded in there.

They had lots of *shtinkers*, they got better treatment there. We would order them to get up out of the yard, as if they were going in to interrogation, and they would go into an interrogation room. Then the interrogators would give them food, drink, let them go to the bathroom, and would ask them what was new, what was going on. You couldn't let the others find out, because they would kill them, so you had to be careful. And then they would go back to the yard, or cell, crying, pretending they were hurt. Also, they would scream a lot in the room.

If they really wanted to screw someone, they would take him out into the yard, the interrogator would stand next to him, telling him what to say. And he would yell out, "I am a *shtinker*, my brothers, I told on you, I said you threw stones, I am sorry, I had no choice." And everybody would know who it was. And then the interrogators would bring him back and put him in the cells, and wait to see what happened. We could look through the windows of the cells. They beat the hell out of him like you have never seen.

APPENDIX G
DECLASSIFIED GSS INTERROGATION LOG
(SEE CHAPTERS TWELVE AND EIGHTEEN)

		Muhammad Adawi's June 1992 Interrogation in Hebron Prison Adawi's Movements between His Position-Abuse Station ("Waiting"), Rest Station ("Rest"), Cell and Questioning Sessions[1]			
Day	Date	Where Held	From	Until	Hours in Position
Wednesday	6/10	First interrogation period begins.			
Wed.[2]	6/10	"Waiting"	19:00	21:45	2h15
Wed.	6/10	Questioning	21:45	24:00	2h15
Thursday	6/11	"Waiting"	24:00	03:10	3h10
Thursday	6/11	Questioning	03:10	04:25	1h15
Thursday	6/11	"Waiting"	04:25	06:50	2h25
Thursday	6/11	Questioning	06:50	08:10	1h20
Thursday	6/11	"Waiting"	08:10	10:30	2h20
Thursday	6/11	Questioning	10:30	10:50	0h20

[1] Based on GSS interrogation logs released to Adawi's Israeli attorney, Shlomo Lecker, during the course of Muhammad Adawi's 1992-1993 attempt to have his confession disqualified on the grounds that it was extracted through torture.

[2] According to Adawi's attorney, Adawi said that he had been awakened on Wednesday at 5 A.M. in the Bethlehem holding facility, where he was imprisoned before being sent to Hebron for interrogation. Thus, Adawi had been awake for fourteen hours prior to beginning his interrogation on Wednesday evening.

Appendices

Day	Date	Where Held	From	Until	Hours in Position
Thursday	6/11	"Waiting"	10:50	—>	—
Friday	6/12	"	—>	10:45	23h55
Friday	6/12	Questioning	10:45	13:00	2h15
First period without proper sleep: 55 hours[3]					
Friday	6/12	Cell	13:00	—>	—
Saturday	6/13	"	—>	—>	—
Sunday	6/14	"	—>	09:30	44h30
Sunday	6/14	Second interrogation period begins.			
Sunday	6/14	"Waiting"	09:30[4]	14:45	5h15
Sunday	6/14	Questioning	14:45	17:10	2h25
Sunday	6/14	"Waiting"	17:10	—>	—
Monday	6/15	"	—>	23:20	30h10
Monday	6/15	Questioning	23:20	—>	—
Tuesday	6/16	"	—>	01:00	1h40

[3] This figure includes the fourteen hours Adawi had been awake prior to his arrival at Hebron prison.

[4] Adawi said he was awakened in his cell on Sunday morning at 5:45 A.M. Thus, when he was returned to his weekday "waiting" position after the weekend break, he had already been awake for three hours and forty-five minutes.

Day	Date	Where Held	From	Until	Hours in Position
Tuesday	6/16	"Waiting"	01:00	07:00	6h
Tuesday	6/16	"Rest"[5]	07:00	09:50	2h50
Tuesday	6/16	Questioning	09:50	11:30	1h40
Tuesday	6/16	"Waiting"	11:30	23:30	12h
Wednesday	6/17	"Rest"[6]	00:30	03:30	3h
Wednesday	6/17	"Waiting"	03:30	10:00	6h30

---

[5] According to Adawi, he was not given a real opportunity to sleep during the "rest" period. He was allowed to eat, go to the toilet, get off the "kindergarten chair," and have his hands unshackled.

[6] Again, this "rest" period does not appear to have given Adawi a real opportunity to sleep.

Appendices

Day	Date	Where Held	From	Until	Hours in Position
Wednesday	6/17	Questioning	10:00	13:00	3h
Wednesday	6/17	"Waiting"	13:00	15:00	2h
Wednesday	6/17	Questioning	15:00	18:00	3h
Wednesday	6/17	"Waiting"	18:00	——>	—
Thursday	6/18	"	——>	00:30	6h30
Thursday	6/18	"Waiting"[7]	01:30	17:30	16h00
Second period without proper sleep: 104 hours[8]					
Friday	6/19	Adawi sees the prison doctor after suffering a head injury.		
Saturday	6/20	During this time, Adawi remains in his cell, recovering from the head injury.		
Sunday	6/21			
Monday	6/22			
Tuesday	6/23	Third and final interrogation period begins.		

---

[7] According to the internal GSS document presented as evidence during the trial, Adawi sustained a head injury at about 11:30 in the morning, during the "waiting" session. Several hours later, Adawi was taken out of "waiting" and was returned to his cell.

[8] This figure includes the two "rest" periods Adawi received, each three hours or less, since, according to Adawi, neither were genuine opportunities for restful sleep. It also includes the over three hours that Adawi was awake in his cell prior to being sent to "waiting" on Sunday, June 14, at 9:30 in the morning.

Day	Date	Where Held	From	Until	Hours in Position
Tuesday	6/23	"Waiting"	20:15	—>	—
Wednesday	6/24	"	—>	—>	—
Thursday	6/25	"	—>	10:45	34h30
Thursday	6/25	Questioning	10:45	11:15	0h30
Thursday	6/25	"Waiting"	11:15	14:15	5h
Thursday	6/25	Questioning	14:15	15:50	1h35
Thursday	6/25	"Waiting"	15:50	17:25	1h35
Third period without proper sleep: 42 hours					
Thursday	6/25	Cell	17:25	Interrogation ends.	